THE
ORVIS
GUIDE TO FINDING TROUT

THE
ORVIS
GUIDE TO FINDING TROUT

Learn to discover trout
in streams and moving water

TOM ROSENBAUER

LYONS
PRESS

Essex, CT

An imprint of Globe Pequot, the trade division of
The Rowman & Littlefield Publishing Group, Inc.
4501 Forbes Blvd., Ste. 200
Lanham, MD 20706
www.rowman.com

Distributed by NATIONAL BOOK NETWORK

All photos by the author
Illustrations by Tim Johnson

British Library Cataloguing in Publication Information available

Library of Congress Cataloging-in-Publication Data
Names: Rosenbauer, Tom, author.
Title: The Orvis guide to finding trout : learn to discover trout in
    streams and other moving waters / Tom Rosenbauer.
Description: Essex, Connecticut : Lyons Press, [2023] | Includes index. |
    Summary: "A completely new, full-color book from Tom Rosenbauer and the
    Orvis Company on how to find trout in all types of water"— Provided by
    publisher.
Identifiers: LCCN 2022042935 (print) | LCCN 2022042936 (ebook) | ISBN
    9781493061013 (paperback) | ISBN 9781493061020 (epub)
Subjects: LCSH: Trout fishing.
Classification: LCC SH687 .R676 2023 (print) | LCC SH687 (ebook) | DDC
    639.2/757--dc23/eng/20221118
LC record available at https://lccn.loc.gov/2022042935
LC ebook record available at https://lccn.loc.gov/2022042936

♾️™ The paper used in this publication meets the minimum requirements of
American National Standard for Information Sciences—Permanence of Paper
for Printed Library Materials, ANSI/NISO Z39.48-1992.

CONTENTS

INTRODUCTION

In 1988 I wrote a book called *Reading Trout Streams*. Somebody must have liked it, because it's still in print. Since then, I've fished hard, have met lots of guides and other anglers who have taught me what they've observed on the water, and have kept up with the scientific literature on trout habitat and behavior. I've learned so much more. I'm not saying I understand everything in academic studies, especially when they spout formulas with square roots and superscripts, but I studied fisheries in college and still remember enough to parse the good stuff that's useful to us as anglers in search of trout. And I talk to fish biologists whenever I can. But there are still days when I wonder "Where the heck are the fish, and what are they doing?"

There is much I've learned about trout in the years since that book, and honestly I still learn something new about finding trout every time I walk down to a river. You'll gain new knowledge as well, and you will observe things I haven't mentioned in here or see behavior that contradicts what I've said. Don't rule out your own observations. If you meet someone who tells you they know everything about finding trout and can always predict where to find them, I'd hesitate before lending them a fly rod. Trout can be unpredictable and even individuals in the same population—or even the same pool—can exhibit different behavior depending on their experience and where they happen to lie in a current.

Experienced trout anglers can look at a piece of water and, without deep thought, figure out the most likely places to find trout. They often don't even know what they see, but thousands of hours of casting over trout water successfully and unsuccessfully burns recognizable patterns into their brains. I fished that way for a long time, but then thought that if I spent more time thinking about the "why" rather than the "where," I might be able to get even better at finding fish. Maybe my mind just works that way, but I'm constantly curious about why a trout prefers one spot over another. They're endlessly fascinating creatures.

If you're fishing a river and aren't catching anything, as I see it there are four possibilities and probably more, but these seem to be the most common:

The water is cold, below 45 degrees Fahrenheit, and the trout are just not feeding actively.

The fish have been frightened by boats or other anglers and are hiding.

There are no trout where you are fishing.

You have the wrong fly or are not presenting it properly.

Most anglers blame number 4 when not catching anything, but I can tell you from experience that this is the least important issue. Even if you have the wrong fly, or you aren't presenting it properly, you'll often get at least a bump or a swirl from a fish that sees your fly and chases it but changes its mind at the last moment. In many cases number 3 is the culprit. Don't assume that, even in the best trout streams, you're always

The fly pattern you pick does help to fool a nice brown trout, but it's one of the least important parts of the equation. Presenting your fly in the precise spot that will bring it to the trout in a natural manner is the most critical aspect of fly fishing for trout, and without knowing where trout feed, much of your effort can be in vain. Of course, no time on a trout stream is really wasted, as you are in a spectacular environment— but it's also nice to catch a fish now and then.

Experienced anglers know where to wade or where to park their boats in anticipation of finding feeding trout. They sometimes can't even articulate why they pick a specific place, and they often get it wrong. But their odds are better than those of someone who doesn't understand what a trout needs and how the environment affects its feeding.

dropping your fly on top of a trout. They have specific requirements that often restrict them to a narrow range within the wetted area of a river. And they sometimes move around if conditions don't suit them.

Trout only live in a limited part of a stream channel. Fishing for them is not horseshoes and it's not hand grenades. *Almost* doesn't cut it, because you risk dumping your fly line on top of a fish and spooking it by casting blindly or trying to cover all the water without any thought. Trout fishing is more like throwing darts— placing a soft hackle so that it rises to the surface right in front of a trout or casting a nymph or dry fly so you get that short dead drift over precisely the right spot requires precision casting, but it also entails having a good estimation of where a trout might be lying. If you watch videos or read books about Euro nymphing, you'll be exposed to a methodical grid system they use to cover all the likely water in front of them. To me, that's boring. I'd rather look at the water, estimate where the very best spots might be, and then make fewer casts but over more likely water. It's more like painting a watercolor than painting a bathroom ceiling.

In this book I wanted to add what I've learned since the 1980s, but I also want to explain much more than reading surface currents. I want to help you find trout in any kind of water condition, from a raging flood to the bony low water of summer. I also want to help you find a stream by looking at a map or driving around, giving you the tools to estimate if a river might hold trout, and then look at an entire river system to figure out which section, and what type of water, might hold the most fish. So, I've divided the book into two parts. The first is a general education on trout and their physical and chemical environment, and the second is where I try to tell you where to expect trout in various types of water. I'm not going to tell you how to swing a wet fly or fish a Euro nymph rig. You can find those in other books or videos, or from a good guide. I will suggest methods that usually work best in various types of water, though.

I'm going to give you a lot more than you need to just "read the water." I hope to give you an understanding of what makes a trout stream tick so that you can draw your own conclusions when you are out on the water or exploring new places, because exploration is so much of the enjoyment of finding trout. If we found them everywhere without difficulty, it would not be much fun. It's using the knowledge you've discovered to find trout that makes it so satisfying.

PART 1

A TROUT'S WORLD

I know you want to jump right into the diagrams where I show you exactly where trout will be in your favorite riffle. After all, your time on the water is limited and you want some shortcuts, right? You just want to have a day catching trout. But I'd be doing you a disservice by telling you exactly where to find the fish, and in fact I'd be lying to you if I told you I knew exactly where trout feed, even in a riffle that I fish three or four days a week. Those diagrams I'll show you are only as reliable as the advice you get from a financial advisor about where a stock might be a year from now. Scratch that. They are even less reliable. But it's the best I can do.

Finding trout, for you, might be about finding the right river in an expansive watershed full of moving water that could hold trout. Or it might be finding the right place to fish in a new river. It could even be finding trout in a river you've fished for years, under changing conditions that might not peg them in their usual haunts. You are not going to get that from a static diagram. You'll have to use what you learn in Part 1, and from your own observations, to predict where trout might be feeding in a small riffle in the middle of the day around the first of June. And that requires understanding how trout feed, how water chemistry affects their feeding habits, how the landscape helps you predict where to find them, where they might feed in relation to the protection of a rock, log, or deep water, and the all-important effect of water temperature on where they feed.

Currents are mystifying and complex, and even physicists don't understand exactly why water moves the way it does in certain cases. But currents call the shots. They are the buffet table. Being able to read currents, regardless of whether they occur in a riffle or run or pool, will help you read any kind of water, because the water you encounter will always be slightly different from what I show you in a diagram. In fact, even if you fish a pool that I've used as an example in this book, telling you where I would expect to find trout, a change in water level or the shifting of a gravel bar after a spring flood can scramble all the chess pieces on the board. This is why I devote an entire chapter to currents, trying to make them comprehensible to us as anglers, not hydrologists.

Enjoy this process. Trout as an animal to be observed are as endlessly fascinating as watching a Labrador retriever puppy explore every corner of your room on the first day you bring it home. You can predict some of the antics and mischief it will get into—then, suddenly, it will pick up a shoe bigger than its head and you realize, despite the many puppies you've welcomed into your home, that every one is a bit different. Trout surprise you in similar ways. They are not genetically identical clones, and finding one in a spot you predicted it would be feeding, even though you had never caught one in that spot, is one of the most gratifying experiences in fishing.

CHAPTER 1

How Trout Feed

Understanding *how*
trout feed will go
a long way toward
determining *where*
you'll find them feeding.

One of the most inane platitudes ever uttered by outdoor writers is the expression "Think like a fish." Trout aren't very smart. Otherwise they wouldn't eat flies that only look remotely like insects and minnows, with a hook sticking out of one end and a piece of string on the other. They also eat bits of stone and sticks that they mistake for food. Think like a human. We're the most efficient predator that has ever lived, and by accident or design we've removed hundreds, perhaps thousands, of species from the planet.

To be fair, trout are superb predators and are perfectly adapted to feeding in moving water. They've had about 700,000 years to develop the skills they need to survive in an environment where food choices must be quick and efficient. You can't truly appreciate how quick these decisions must be until you go underwater in a trout stream, or leave an underwater camera in a river, as I have done many times, and watch how quickly food drifts in the current. Even in a slow pool, insects drift past so quickly that our superior human brain has trouble distinguishing food from debris. It's like trying to identify fall warblers in flight. I can only assume that a trout's brain works differently from ours and must be able to process visual stimuli at a pace we're unable to match.

The poor survival of hatchery fish in many streams is blamed on their inability to effectively forage for food. Observations of hatchery brown trout, when they have been released in a stream with wild trout, show that the wild trout spend much more time feeding with few wasted motions. The hatchery fish, however, dither around and swim back and forth for no apparent reason, like we would if they moved all the items in our local grocery store without warning. These fish are also easy pickings for predators like otters and ospreys, but in the absence of predators they waste away and starve before the end of the season.

Besides visual aptitude, trout are also capable of finding the exact micro-currents where they can capture food without expending more energy than they gain from the effort of feeding. They possess an array of sensors along their bodies, including the lateral line, which senses pressure in the water and seems to be integrated with the inputs from their fins and other surfaces to feel their way through the invisible eddies of turbulence to find just the right spot. We can only estimate where these places might occur, but the whole idea of fly fishing is to stick a hook in a trout's mouth because it thinks what we're offering is food. So understanding how they feed is the best way to find and catch them.

In addition to feeding, trout have other physiological needs for current. They can't stay put in totally stagnant water. They need at least four parts per million of oxygen flowing by their gills in order to breathe, and if a trout lies in water without current flowing over its gills, it will soon use up the available oxygen in its vicinity. The other reason is removal of waste products. Besides carbon dioxide waste coming from their gills, trout excrete copious amounts of dilute urine through a tube that leads into a vent on the underside of their bodies. This is why trout in lakes and ponds are always swimming. If they stop, they risk being awash in their own waste products.

THEY FEED IN DIFFERENT WAYS

Like all wild animals I'm aware of, trout must obtain more energy for growth than they expend getting those calories. Otherwise, they don't live to reproduce. Those fish that burn more energy than they take in are fated to lose their genetic material to the ether. Evolution has produced trout that are efficient in their predation, and somehow they instinctively feed in ways that allow them to survive. At least the successful ones do. Trout use a variety of methods for capturing their prey, and what they do depends on the physical environment, the food available, and sometimes just the personality of a fish. Trout are individuals, not robots, and there's always

some variation from one fish to the next, even in the same pool, on how they feed.

I'm lucky enough to have a trout stream with a population of wild fish in my backyard: mostly rainbows and browns with a few brook trout mixed in. Aside from some seasonal shuffling, I can go down to the river every evening, when they often feed on the surface, and observe them, sometimes fishing for them, often just watching. I can distinguish each fish by the way it rises. The 8-inch rainbow that feeds alongside the riffle is always flashy, with a funny flip of its tail. The 9-incher on the other side of the riffle in about the same current speed is more sedate, just poking its head into the surface film. There's the brown trout in the middle of the pool that usually rises backward, turning and following an insect downstream a few inches before taking it. I can always spot that fish from downstream because I can see the white flash of its mouth facing me when it rises. So, each fish is different, which is why both for fly selection purposes and for finding fish in a stream, there are no absolutes because as soon as you think you have everything figured out, you'll find one that didn't get the memo.

Trout are opportunistic feeders and their position in a river is determined by the procession of food coming

Wild, undisturbed trout drift feeding in a Wyoming river. The brook trout in the foreground and cutthroat in the background are waiting for the right food to drift to them in the current. The brook trout in the middle has spotted something interesting and has risen off the bottom to intercept it.

This brook trout and the cutthroat behind it have just fed on the surface and are sliding back to the bottom where the current is more comfortable. You can tell they fed on the surface by the remains of the splash they made above them.

down in the current, called drift feeding. They don't really position themselves to favor one kind of food over another but take what the current serves up. In a study of the stomach contents of 171 rainbow and 120 brown trout in southern Appalachian streams, biologists found 97 different organisms in their food, ranging from worms to crayfish to insects to fish eggs.

Drift Feeding

The most energetically efficient way for a trout to feed, and the method most of them employ, is to place themselves where they can maintain their position without wasting much energy, but also a spot where they can see what is drifting in the current ahead of them so they can move to intercept the insect. This applies whether a fish is moving to surface or subsurface food. The spot is usually on or close to the bottom, or on top of the trailing edge of a rock because the current is less there, and the way a trout's eyes are situated it is much easier for it to spot prey above its position than below.

When a trout spots a morsel that looks like food, it merely tips its fins up like elevators on the tail of a plane, rides the slipstream up with almost no energy expended, and intercepts the food. In the process it gets pushed slightly downstream by the current, and it then swims back upstream, usually close to the bottom where the current is calmer, until it is back into its observation position. It takes twice as much energy to swim back upstream into position than it does to intercept its prey, which is why trout avoid fast current. High velocities push them farther downstream and more effort is required to get back into position.

Although the current at the base of this waterfall is swirling and turbulent, it soon settles down to that uniform current that trout like. David Coggins is fishing the uniform flow, which is more likely to hold feeding trout than the area at the base of the waterfall because they can see their food and predict its trajectory.

When drift feeding, trout may move from side to side or up into the water column, but they seldom move down to take something off the bottom. A trout may move 2 feet for a piece of food, if it is big enough and desirable enough for a trout to notice it at that distance. Or when food is abundant or the water is cold and a trout's metabolism is low, they may not move more than a few inches side to side or up to grab something. A trout may also chase something downstream and take it on the run, although that requires more effort and isn't the most efficient way to feed. I think that sometimes a trout doesn't notice a piece of food until it is too late to intercept it efficiently and has to chase it downstream. My rainbow in the example above from my backyard often fed in quite foamy water and I don't think that fish could see the insects until they were almost past its position, so it had to feed in a downstream direction.

The most exhaustive study of the behavior of drift-feeding trout was done by Dr. Robert Bachman for his PhD thesis at Penn State, "Foraging Behavior of Free-Ranging Wild Brown Trout (*Salmo trutta*) in a Stream." He spent three full seasons in the years 1979 to 1981 on Spruce Creek in Pennsylvania, observing wild brown trout from an observation tower. Bob has become a close

My daughter Brooke is fishing the 2- to 4-foot-deep slot along the far bank. You can gauge this because you can see every rock on the bottom in the shin-deep water at her feet, but the bottom details get hazy as the water reaches the prime depth.

friend over the years, and I often bounce my crazy theories off him and still refer to his studies often because they are so telling about the behavior and habitat preference of trout.

During his study, Bachman observed over 15,000 feeding events and quantified each one. Most of the feeding was drift feeding in the current, either in midwater or on the surface. The trout spent 86 percent of total daytime hours lying in a search-and-wait mode. Returning to their lies after feeding accounted for 8.4 percent of their time, while only 3 percent was spent pursuing food. This left only 3 percent for moving around or chasing other trout out of their locations.

In nearly every study that has been done of feeding trout, an amazing consistency has been observed: They prefer to feed in water that is moving at between 1 and 2 feet per second, and 2 to 4 feet deep. I say amazing because often scientific studies come up with conflicting

These three trout are feeding in that optimum 1- to 2-foot-per-second current that is the optimum balance between obtaining food without extra effort but getting enough food so they don't need to move. You can see the faster water at the top of the photo—these fish are right on the edge, in the seam.

conclusions and theories, so it's important to take each one with a grain of salt seasoned with a pinch of your own observations. The optimal current speed where the difference between growth benefit and cost has shown to be about 1 foot per second. The benefit is how much food a trout can take in at a given velocity, and the cost is how much energy a trout burns to maintain swimming speed in that current. That's optimal. Trout continue to obtain an energy benefit until the current speed gets above 2 feet per second, at which point the energy cost of holding in the current is higher than the benefit obtained. You'll often see recently released hatchery fish holding in much stronger current for hours at a time—which is why you often don't see many survivors after a month.

Trout are adaptable and opportunistic creatures, and what a biologist sees in one river may not apply to others with different conditions. But this current speed rule we can almost take as gospel, as it also agrees with most of my observations of trout in over fifty years of chasing them, as well as the observations of the best anglers and fishing guides I know. And, of course, you'll find exceptions. But if you want to play the percentages, keep this in mind.

I wanted to see this for myself, though, so I bought a current meter and one season I tried to measure each spot where I regularly caught trout. In places where

trout rose, the surface current was always in this velocity range. And even in places where the water on the surface looked much faster, where I would catch fish subsurface on nymphs, I'd take the current meter and measure the velocity below the surface, where it was much slower— right in the Goldilocks range.

How do you begin to recognize this current speed? If trout are feeding on the surface, pay attention to the exact current thread they're rising in and burn that image into your brain. Or throw a stick in the water, count out 10 seconds, estimate how far the stick has drifted, and divide by 10. Throw the stick in fast and slow water until you get an idea of what 1 to 2 feet per second looks like. If you're not good at math or don't like throwing sticks, it's about the speed of a slow walk.

When trout choose a place for resting, they'll be in this water velocity, and they'll also try to feed in that same current range, although they will occasionally dart out into faster or slower water if a choice piece of food drifts by. Sometimes you can find the right velocity, especially in smaller streams, by just looking at surface currents. But you can't always tell what is going on below the surface, and it's not as intuitive to find 1 to 2 feet per second when surface velocities are different from currents close to the bottom. That's why I have included a later chapter on stream hydraulics and some basic physics behind it.

A small brown trout at the instant before it inhales a tiny mayfly. You can even see the surface of the water bulge right before its snout breaks the surface.

If the current is not too fast, sometimes trout will hover farther from the bottom, especially when food is abundant. These cutthroats are actively feeding on a hatch of large mayflies and are holding above the bottom in slower water, where it is easier for them to capture food drifting on and near the surface.

With this knowledge you can begin to make accurate predictions about hidden currents.

Besides those depth and current velocity parameters, I have also noticed a few other aspects that make feeding sites desirable for trout. (And believe it or not, I'm not even including cover here. We'll discuss that in another chapter, but in order to find feeding trout, cover is not as important as many anglers believe.) First, they like uniform current as opposed to big swirls of turbulence (more on that in the "Currents" chapter). They also prefer to be in a spot where they can see their food coming. They must be able to see it in time to calculate an intercept in the current, and if they can't see their prey until too late, they'll miss it. And, finally, their feeding place must be adjacent to some part of a main current thread. Perhaps not right under it except in very slow water, but if a trout is way off in a corner, not close to drifting food, it won't have access to most of the drifting insects in the current.

Trout will turn around and chase food downstream, especially if they don't spot it right away and don't have time to intercept it. This brook trout turned downstream to capture its food, and you can tell it has turned around because the cutthroats in the background are holding near the bottom, facing into the current.

These rocks are covered with caddis larvae, which trout will graze on if the water is dirty and they can't see drifting food. But it's a lot more work for a trout to grub on the bottom, and they prefer to pluck food from the current if they can.

Hovering

Hovering or sipping trout is really a subset of drift feeding, but their behavior and habitat selection is a bit different. Hovering occurs when a heavy hatch covers the surface of the water with a large mass of insects, and trout can feed multiple times in the same pass as opposed to returning to the bottom or near the bottom each time. Current velocity also must be slow, less than 2 feet per second at the surface, or trout are reluctant to sip because they waste too much energy swimming against the current to stay in place. If the water above a trout's resting location is slow enough, it will simply rise higher in the water column and stay there until the food supply diminishes. But trout will often move to slower water, especially shallower water along the banks, to take advantage of a brief feeding spree, as insect hatches this heavy don't occur regularly, except in very rich watersheds.

Epibenthic Feeding

Epibenthic feeding is a fancy biologist's term for feeding directly off the bottom. One of the most telling statistics of Bachman's study is that only 12 percent of the feeding events recorded were trout taking prey directly off the bottom, despite the fact that the bottom

of Spruce Creek is carpeted with mayfly, caddisfly, and stonefly nymphs. And although I think the trout in Bachman's study are typical of most trout streams, it's not always the case.

In a study of the McCloud River in California by Tippets and Moyle in 1978, they tried to determine the reason for the slow growth rate of the river's native rainbow trout. They noticed that adult trout did most of their feeding off the bottom and attributed this to the high turbidity of the stream, preventing trout from drift feeding on a regular basis because they had difficulties spotting drifting food. One of their hypotheses was that the trout grew slowly because of the indigestible material the fish took in when feeding off the bottom, such as algae and stones that made up larval caddis cases. But they felt the most important reason was that epibenthic feeding requires more energy. Instead of lying in wait for food to come to them, these trout needed to move around constantly, looking for new places to graze off the bottom, which requires more swimming activity and thus burns more energy.

We see all those insect larvae on the bottom and have trouble figuring out why a trout doesn't take advantage of it more often. But don't forget that a trout is stationary and any food on the bottom right in front of it would be eaten quickly and not easily replenished. Imagine playing a game of catch. Do you think you would burn more energy if the ball was tossed right to you every time, or if your partner only rolled the ball on the ground halfway to you and you had to run after it each time? Then imagine picking up those ground balls with a 40 mph headwind. That's why trout, if they can, spend most of their time drift feeding.

Thus, unless the water in the stream you're fishing has low visibility, trout will bias toward drift feeding, lying in wait for prey at a selected spot. In cases like this, it's easier to predict where they might be. If the water is dirty from a rainstorm or a release from a dam, or is normally turbid from lots of sediment, all bets are off and the fish could be moving around, grazing off the bottom. And you will need to fish your nymphs right on the bottom, as opposed to drifting a foot or so off the bottom. Luckily, this scenario is less common

Hunting

As a trout grows, its energy demands are higher because it has more body mass to support. In many streams with drift-feeding trout, even with abundant food the maximum length of a drift-feeding trout is somewhere shy of 20 inches. In Spruce Creek, even with its abundant insect supply, Bachman figured the maximum size for drift-feeders was 14 inches, no matter how old the fish was. Because a larger trout must expend more energy to intercept food items than a small trout, it gradually reduces the smaller food items in its diet, and as a result larger trout don't feed as often as smaller trout, which is one reason they're more difficult to catch—we just don't get as many chances.

If there is an adequate population of baitfish, young trout, crayfish, or even mice, a certain portion of a trout population makes a jump from drift feeding to hunting for bigger morsels of food, enough to increase growth beyond the limits of drift feeding. Bachman calls them "sharks," which is an appropriate term. Instead of lying passively waiting for food to come to them, these fish actively hunt for prey, more like a smallmouth bass than a trout. They spend most of their days hiding in deep water or in logjams, resting and not wasting energy. When light levels are low—at dawn and dusk, and sometimes after dark—these fish go on the prowl. They may move quite a bit in their search for prey, sometimes as

Large trout, especially large browns, often switch to hunting for larger prey like smaller fish, crayfish, frogs, and mice. They might pick an ambush point and lie in wait for prey, but they may also range long distances when hunting for bigger meals.

If insect food is abundant enough and easy to capture, even large brown trout will feed on smaller prey. You sometimes have to be lucky to catch them at exactly the right time—this mayfly-eating brown trout took an emerger at the height of a spring mayfly hatch.

much as a mile every night according to a study of radio-tagged brown trout in Michigan.

We don't know what induces a trout to reach a certain size and decide to focus on a hunting strategy, but it appears to be a small percentage of each population and probably depends on the availability of suitable large prey. I remember talking to lodge owner Alan Kelly on the Bighorn River in Montana about the development of that fishery. The Bighorn tailwater trout fishery was created with the construction of Yellowtail Dam in 1965, which turned a warmwater fishery into a near-perfect environment for trout because of the constant cold-water releases. Kelly was the fish biologist for the Crow reservation, who own the land surrounding this stretch of the Bighorn, so he got to see the fishery in its infancy. At first, the wild browns and rainbows were small and grew slowly, but Kelly watched and waited for mountain whitefish to begin exploiting the coldwater environment, because he knew as these fish moved up the river the resident trout would be able to exploit young whitefish as prey. And when the whitefish arrived after a few years, trout growth suddenly exploded. Drift-feeders were able to transform into hunters.

Some streams, especially smaller streams where baitfish populations are low, will have few or none of these hunters. Bigger rivers, especially those down lower in valleys where warmer waters support different varieties of baitfish, may support more of these "sharks," but it's still typically a small percentage of the population. I have some friends who regularly float the Battenkill when the water is high and catch very large brown trout with streamers. But it can be a mile or so between strikes, and as the season progresses my friend Shawn Combs often stops fishing for them because, he says, "I get tired of catching the same half-dozen fish and it loses its magic."

Brown trout are the trout species most likely to turn into sharks. Rainbow trout seem to remain drift-feeders longer into their life cycle, which is why very large rainbow trout are not as common as large brown trout. An honest 20-inch rainbow is uncommon in most trout streams, and places where you catch rainbows beyond that size invariably are connected to large lakes, where it's easier to grow large because there is no current to fight. A baitfish-eating cutthroat in moving water is even more rare, but you do hear of the occasional huge cutthroat caught on a streamer.

Brook trout also stick to drift feeding in most streams, although where insects are not abundant they can turn into hunters. The giant brook trout in northern Canada develop very sharp teeth and during the summer seem to feed primarily on mice and baitfish. I once fished for brook trout in the 3- to 6-pound range in Labrador and most of the trout we caught were on mouse patterns or big streamers. Fishing for these trout seems more like fishing for large brown trout than the way I fish for tiny brookies close to home.

It's likely a trout that eats a large crayfish or baitfish or mouse may not feed for a day or more afterward. These critters take much longer to digest than a stomach full of insects, thus our chances of catching one of these extra-large fish in a feeding mood is greatly reduced. Plus there aren't as many large trout in most streams as smaller trout, so expecting to catch one every time you go out is a matter of both luck and timing. Low light and dirty, high water even the odds for a large trout hunting prey. Just because a 24-inch brown trout lives in the same pool as a couple hundred blacknose dace doesn't mean that fish is constantly on the prowl. Something must disorient those baitfish, like a rise in water that pushes them out of their normal hiding places. These little fish are nimbler than a battleship of a trout, and in bright sunlight and clear water they can evade a big trout with ease. But as soon as they show a bit of distress, a big trout senses their vulnerability.

I once had a big logjam in the stream in my backyard and small rainbow trout rose beside it every day. I spent many hours fishing that logjam and never saw a fish bigger than about 8 inches. There were also hundreds of small dace in the same pool. I also walked my dogs a couple of times a day along the riverbank and never even spooked a big trout. Yet one morning I hooked a 6-inch rainbow on a dry fly and the minute it flipped in the current a huge brown trout bolted out from under the logjam and grabbed the fish. It soon got off, and as always happens in these situations, I put on a streamer and cast over and over and never saw the fish again.

I threw a streamer past that logjam numerous other days during the summer and nothing ever took a pass at it. I even tried a mouse pattern after dark. But in late summer, when the state came in to electroshock the section of stream in my backyard to do a fish count, up he came when stunned by the direct current. He was there all the time but was just waiting for one of those small fish in the pool to show a moment of weakness. Either my streamer was just not good enough or the times I cast it around the logjam just didn't fit into his schedule.

Fish that turn into hunters will still drift feed and eat bugs on occasion. The largest brook trout caught all season in the camp in Labrador I visited a few years ago

Biologists weighing an oversize brown trout after electroshocking it from my backyard stream. It's not a huge fish but it was fully twice the size of the average fish in the river, and it lived under a logjam, probably hunting for sculpins, crayfish, and smaller trout in high water or after dark. Despite being under my nose, I never once saw this fish rise or spook. I now fish streamers in high water more than I used to.

was caught on a size 14 Parachute Adams. And all but the largest brown trout will occasionally feed on insects, even on the surface, if an insect hatch is dense enough and the fish can feed efficiently on a large number of insects (typically larger ones) in a short time period. Green Drake mayfly hatches in both eastern and western trout streams, the giant Hex mayfly, and big stoneflies like the Salmonfly and Golden Stone can tempt bigger fish to eat insects. You often have a narrow window to catch a trout over 20 inches on something other than a streamer. This is why people leave their jobs and spouses to catch these hatches at just the right moment.

HOW MUCH DO DRIFT-FEEDING TROUT MOVE WHEN FEEDING?

Trout make seasonal adjustments in their locations, due to changing water levels, spawning migrations, and changes in water temperatures. We'll examine those large-scale movements later. But trout also change positions during any given day. They don't wander from one place to another randomly, though. In Robert Bachman's three-year study, he recorded from one to thirty-two discrete spots for each individual fish. Most of them had three or four favored places, and these were discrete spots that fish would move to quickly before they began feeding again. The spots were not very far from each other; most of the fish occupied a home range of roughly 100 square feet. And note that I use the term *home range*, which is different from a territory. Trout don't have a true "territory" (defined as a location an animal defends against others) because several trout feeding in one general area would trade places, like marbles in a Chinese checkers game (Bachman's term). And the most telling part of this is when one trout vacated a feeding spot and another moved in, the second fish would use the spot in exactly the same position as the first fish, indicating a precise ability to lean into exactly the right micro-currents for efficient observation and feeding.

Because Bachman could identify individual fish by their spot patterns, he also noticed that the same fish would often return to the same feeding position in the spring, year after year, unless floods changed the bottom structure or nudged a rock into a location where it was not as energetically desirable as before. So if you caught a trout from one spot last year, that same fish, or another fish, will likely be in the same place this year because the current flow is just right. However, remembering that the fish might be next door borrowing a cup of caddisflies at another feeding location, precisely the same spot might be empty right now. And in five minutes it could host a fish again.

In my experience, trout have primary feeding spots where they are a bit more secure—in deeper water, close to logs, in pockets between weed beds. They'll stay here, feeding occasionally if something tempting drifts by but not moving too far. These are the trout that are often caught by Euro nymphing, which places a nymph right in their faces, or by fishing nymphs deep on an indicator, close to the bottom. These fish may also respond to a streamer if conditions are right, like a rise in water or low light levels.

When food becomes more abundant, for instance when water temperatures begin to rise and more insects are in the drift, or in late morning when terrestrial insects get more active and fall into the water, trout may move farther for food or slide into places easier to feed—typically less protected, shallower, and closer to a main thread of current. I've seen this behavior on nearly every trout stream I have fished for more than a day, where all of a sudden fish seem to be "on." It's partially a matter of them feeding more actively, but I believe it's also that they move into shallower water, where they are easier to catch because they are more likely to notice your dry fly or nymph, or to chase a swung soft hackle, when they are in these spots.

I regularly fish a local river where I can almost predict where trout will be just by paying attention to the weather. The stream is clear enough that I can move up to a pool and see fish spook from where they've been feeding into refuges under cover. In fact, many times I'll just walk the bank without a rod, sneaking up on a pool and then suddenly standing up so that I can spot the fish as they spook. On cold days, I'll spook the fish from deeper water, about 4 feet deep, where they'll just make a quick dart into crevices under rocks and logs. On sunny days, when insects are starting to hatch, I'll spook the trout from much shallower spots, and they'll often be grouped together in choice feeding areas. When I spook these fish they'll often dart back and forth in the pool, pushing each other out of refuges like a game of musical chairs, and may not settle down into secure refuges for a few minutes.

On days when I do have a rod, if the weather predicts they'll be in their deeper haunts, I know I'll need to fish deeper, a dry fly won't be as effective, and the fish will be more alert and easier to spook. If I see a few insects in the air and the weather is stable, I know the fish will be shallower, typically grouped together in feeding spots, and, preoccupied with food, they'll be easier to approach and less likely to be spooked by my casting.

During heavy hatches of insects, trout may also abandon their normal lies for temporary feeding stations to take advantage of a feeding orgy that may only last for

15 minutes. The places they move to are usually even shallower and slower than their normal haunts, where the current is slow enough to enable them to hover just under the surface without wasting energy. Trout seldom leave a pool or general area to do this but may move sideways into shallow water along the bank or drop down to the tail of a pool. If you know an area holds trout and you see abundant insects, make sure you check the shallows carefully before wading in and plunking your flies in the usual likely haunts. The fish may be in much slower and shallower water than you usually find them.

Some trout don't need to move and occupy what anglers call "prime lies": where they remain protected from predators and feel secure but still have access to food and the right current speed for feeding. If you spot a place where the water is 2 to 4 feet deep and runs about 2 feet per second, right next to a big rock or log or undercut bank with some brush, you may have found a prime lie. Whether a *trout* thinks it's a prime lie, of course, depends on some things we can't see or don't understand. But these are always places worth trying.

DIFFERENCES BETWEEN THE SPECIES

Trout (and char because a brook trout is technically a char) aren't that much different in the way they behave or where they live. I've often seen and caught two or even three species of trout in the same water, side by side. But the different species do have idiosyncrasies that sometimes come into play, and knowing about them may help you pinpoint where they feed when you know what species is in the river you're fishing.

Rainbow Trout

Rainbow trout are said to love fast water, and they do. But they also love slow water. In fact, rainbow trout love any kind of water. We do often find more of them in fast water, though, because of their metabolism and feeding methods.

Rainbows appear to feed more often than other species, and often where you find them they'll always be on the alert, whereas other species sometimes hang back and loaf. Biologist Bob Bachman told me it's because rainbow trout are the most efficient species when it comes to converting insect parts into calories, which is why you see rainbows hovering in riffles eating tiny midges. You would think they would burn more energy in just holding their position than they get in return by eating small insects, but they seem to be successful at just that. It's not that rainbows love to feed in faster water, it's that they *can*. You'll also find rainbows in very slow water, the same places you would expect a brown trout to prefer. Whatever feature of their metabolism that helps them feed in fast water works just as well

Rainbow trout love fast water—but they also love slow water. It's true that they seem to prefer the protected pockets in the middle of faster current over other trout species, but you can also find them cruising the slower parts of a river and everything in between.

Although you'll catch brown trout in fast water, chances are they will be in a slower pocket within the raging current. Browns seem to be more efficient than other trout when feeding, and will seek out slower pockets where they can feed without burning a lot of energy.

in slow water. So when fishing a river that has a rainbow population, I'm afraid you have to look everywhere, not just in the fast water.

Another behavioral aspect of rainbows is that, when frightened, they're more likely to use deep or fast water as a refuge than a logjam or a pile of rocks. I live on a small stream with a population of both wild rainbows and browns. I can always tell which pool the rainbows prefer because when I spook them when fishing or walking my dog, if the river is clear every fish in a pool or run will bolt for the deepest part of the pool and hover there, jockeying for position like kindergarten kids lining up for the afternoon bus. The browns? Most of the pools have brown trout as well, but I never see them when I spook a pool. The browns head for some dark hole in the bank or under a log well before I get a look at them.

So when looking for rainbows, don't rule out a piece of water that has no traditional "cover" like overhanging trees or large rocks. As long as there is some water over a couple of feet deep close at hand, you could find rainbows there.

Brown Trout

Brown trout appear to be much moodier, binge feeders than any other species. You can fish a river full of browns, but if they're not feeding due to circumstances that only brown trout understand, the river can seem completely dead. Browns seem to be, or perhaps need to be, more efficient feeders than other species. They often appear to wait until food is plentiful before feeding, especially in rivers with abundant insect life where they apparently sense that they don't need to feed right now while the pickings are slim. They wait for more abundant food, when they can be more efficient. Don't give up on your stream-reading skills in a brown trout river if you don't have any success. They might not be willing to play.

Brown trout, efficient feeders that they are, prefer to feed in a place where they can be lazy and efficient, which usually means the slower pockets. I've caught plenty of browns in tumbling liquid that looks like "rainbow water," but odds do favor slow water along the banks, in front of large rocks, and in the tails of pools. Where they occur together with rainbows, a common occurrence in many rivers, you'll find the browns in the slower margins and the rainbows closer to fast water. And brown trout seem to prefer cover more than any other species, so they will often be close to logs, overhanging trees, and large rocks. Browns may move out into the open when feeding heavily, but you'll seldom find them too far from protective structure.

Cutthroat Trout

Cutthroat trout behave more like brown trout in that they'll often seek out the slower pockets in a stretch of

It's often difficult to distinguish a hybrid cutthroat/rainbow from a pure variety of either species. This trout looks just like a pure rainbow, except when you peak under its lower jaw and notice that telltale red slash.

Cutthroat trout prefer to feed in slower water, and they're primarily insect-feeders even when they grow quite large. They are also fond of moving into very shallow water when food is abundant, like during a hatch. This one is from the Yellowstone River within Yellowstone National Park, so it's likely this is a pure-strain cutthroat.

water. They do, however, freely hybridize with rainbow trout because they are closely related, and depending on the mingling of genes in an individual, they can behave more like pure cutthroats or pure rainbows. Often you'll find different permutations in the same piece of water, so it's difficult to predict exactly how they'll behave.

Where you have pure cutthroats, however, or at least hybrids with mostly cutthroat genes, you will see them prefer certain currents and feeding spots. They like to feed along slow banks, in the tails of pools, and in more moderate current. You won't see cutthroats as often in the fastest water in a riffle or run and are more likely to find them feeding where riffles and pocket water slow down and moderate. They also have a tendency to feed on the surface whenever they can, which means they will slide into shallow riffles or along the banks, with barely 6 inches of water above their heads, because it's much easier to pluck bugs from the surface when you have only a short round-trip when moving from a resting place close to the bottom. Wherever you find cutthroats, make sure you always check the shallows. Never wade into a river before checking to make sure you don't have feeding fish just off the tip of your rod.

Brook Trout

Brook trout evolved in very infertile waters with little food. They get their reputation for being stupid and easy because in the places they're best suited to, they never know when their next meal will be delivered so they strike first and worry about the consequences

later. They're supremely adapted for living in food-poor waters and can survive in creeks that brown trout and rainbows won't even venture into because they can't find enough food. In fact, brook trout can survive in headwater streams that won't even support sculpins or dace.

Because of this inclination to feed almost indiscriminately, you'll often find them very close to the main current, and not as often in backwaters where the delivery of food might be intermittent. They don't like current as fast as a rainbow might be able to handle, but they'll often be right on the edge of faster water. You will seldom find them very far from one of the main threads of current, and you are also less likely to find them in very shallow water that might support cutthroats. Brook trout also appear to prefer to be close to cover, like brown trout, although that cover will preferably be in close proximity to the main current.

Hatchery Trout

Hatchery trout, at least in the first few weeks after being stocked, seem to break all the rules. Raised mostly in tanks with little or no current, they don't know how to handle it. When they first get dumped into a river, they'll find a slow pool that mimics the environment they're used to, and they may circle around the pool

Although brook trout are primarily insect-feeders, where they grow large, in places like Labrador, they feed on mice and baitfish and grow the teeth to handle larger prey. This one was caught on a mouse pattern, and a number of similar-sized fish were caught with streamers. But under the right conditions, even the biggest ones still feed on insects.

I know for certain that this brown trout is of hatchery origin because it was caught in a river that is heavily stocked and does not support wild fish. This trout has the clean fins and red spots that we associate with stream-bred fish, and it is nearly impossible to tell for certain, once a trout has been in a river for a year, whether it is from wild stock or hatchery. Markings, colors, and condition of fins are only a clue and are not totally reliable.

in endless laps, waiting for the mysterious pellets to rain from above. They're not savvy to the dangers of predators because they grew up associating food with a human raising their arms above the water (although many hatchery fish today are fed with automatic feeders, so not all of them will have that association). They may lie in slow, shallow water, right out in the open, in places a wild trout would never consider.

Where hatchery trout are introduced into a river with an existing population of wild trout, stuff happens. They don't know the rules. When they bumble into a spot a wild fish already occupies, hatchery fish get pushed out of the best cover by the tougher wild fish. They're like the ski tourist in a bright puffy jacket in a redneck local bar that innocently chats up the girlfriend of a drunk logger. They don't know the territory. This pushes them into less desirable spots and makes them easy prey for eagles, herons, and ospreys.

Hatchery fish don't often last long. If they don't get eaten by a predator or caught by an angler, they sometimes just die of starvation because those less efficient spots they occupy don't supply them with enough food to balance the energy expended to stay in place. But the survivors eventually get the memo and learn to navigate the hierarchy of the river, although they seldom become as efficient or crafty as wild fish, even if they manage to survive for a couple of years.

The one thing I've noticed about their feeding behavior is that they stay surface-oriented, more so than wild trout, and surprisingly they become extremely selective. This doesn't seem to make sense until you realize that we've *trained* them to be selective. Where wild trout learn to sample different foods as they grow and mature, hatchery trout are raised on one kind of food for the first year or two of their lives—pellets. After they get acclimated to a stream they appear to retain this selective feeding behavior and it's often to midges, I suspect because midges are so abundant that it may be the first food they encounter in their new home.

WHEN THEY DON'T FEED

Do drift-feeding trout get full? It probably depends on water temperature, which affects their metabolism. Robert Bachman's trout on Spruce Creek fed constantly, throughout the daylight hours, and other studies of trout metabolism have shown that with optimum water temperatures in the 60s, a trout can completely digest and evacuate its entire stomach contents twice a day. Bachman observed a single trout eat two large crayfish, after which it continued to feed on mayflies and caddisflies

as if it hadn't eaten for a week. Based on what I have read and also what I've observed, if water temperatures are between 50 and 65 degrees, smaller trout will feed constantly. Fish over 14 inches will also feed regularly, but because they're more inclined to wait for bigger prey to drift by, they may not feed as often.

There are three situations where trout don't feed. One is when water temperatures are too low. I hesitate to give a number because in some rivers trout feed in waters below 40 degrees (although typically with water temperatures on a slight rise) and in other rivers they don't get active until it rises above 50. Another is the case of a large trout that feeds mostly at night or on a rise of water and is just loafing, typically with its head stuck in a logjam or at the bottom of a deep pool. The third and most important reason is when a trout is spooked or frightened by a real or perceived threat.

One of the most underrated skills in reading trout water and finding trout is recognizing when and where trout have been spooked and are just not feeding. When fish are frightened by a bird's shadow, an otter swimming through a pool, too many boats going over their heads, or an angler getting too close or making sloppy casts, they bolt for safety. This is what is referred to as cover, but cover is anyplace a trout could hide. They use only certain places within cover that are called refuge sites.

Trout don't feed when they are frightened. There are two degrees of this fright behavior. The first is when they are mildly alerted—maybe you make a bad cast, or the fleeting shadow of a bird passes over them. Here they'll sink right to the bottom, even lower than when in a normal feeding position, and will stay as motionless as they can—as opposed to a feeding fish, which will sway from side to side and often dart into the current to capture something. Anglers often see trout in this position and say they are "sleeping." Nothing could be further from the truth. A trout like this is very much alert, and if further frightened it will bolt for a previously identified refuge site: under a rock, in thick weed beds, under a log, or in a brush pile where it is completely hidden. This second reaction, bolting for cover, can happen immediately without the intermediate step if they are frightened in an overt manner, like a kingfisher diving

Pelicans are voracious trout predators. How long the trout in this stretch of river will stay spooked is anyone's guess, but you can be sure they won't be happily feeding nearby anytime soon. Sometimes we arrive at the river after predators have flown or paddled over the trout and we can't figure out why they aren't feeding. It may just be that the trout were frightened and won't be playing for a while.

If you see other anglers in a stretch of river, you may have better luck moving somewhere else (plus it's the ethical thing to do). No matter how careful they are, they'll spook some of the fish and by finding a place that has not experienced any traffic lately you'll be more likely to locate feeding trout.

into the water, a rock thrown near them, or an angler stepping into a pool close to their position.

How long does a trout stay spooked? Bachman found that his brown trout, if mildly spooked and just dropped to the bottom, would resume feeding within a few minutes. If they bolted for cover they would not begin to feed again for about 20 minutes. But I have seen trout stay spooked and not feeding for hours—or at least I think I have. I have spooked trout in a pool, left the pool, and come back an hour later with no sign of a fish feeding and no strikes. Perhaps I just had the wrong fly, or maybe the fish were no longer interested in feeding. But for an adult wild trout, one over 9 inches long, I would give the fish at least a two-hour rest before I try that pool again. I think the time a trout stays spooked also varies with the size of a stream and the comfort of the fish. In small, clear streams, where trout are highly exposed, they seem to resist feeding for over an hour. But in larger rivers, where they have both distance and depth for security, they seem to approach that 20-minute time frame observed by Bachman.

When looking for trout, if you spook a fish near your feet and it bolts into the middle of the pool, will that cause a chain reaction and spook every other fish? I've seen it both ways, so you can never be sure. I have seen cases where bumping one fish caused it to bump into another and spook it, and these fish darted past other trout that were spooked as well. You see that in the rare cases where the water is clear enough to watch the whole game of billiards unfold, but often you don't know. The best approach is not to go any further and let the pool settle down. Look for feeding fish. Or wait five minutes and try a few probing casts in likely spots.

If trout are actively feeding, one alarmed fish may not worry the rest of them one bit. I once hit a heavy Trico spinner fall on the Dream Stream section of the South Platte in Colorado where you could hook a fish, let it weave among a pod of other fish, and by the time you released the fish the rest of them would be feeding with abandon, as if they couldn't care less about what happened to their neighbor. But trout that are not feeding heavily remain more alert, and catching or spooking one may create that dreaded chain reaction. When food is abundant, apparently the cost of higher exposure to predators is worth the risk of being eaten, and somehow over the evolutionary journey that trout have traveled, the ones who took advantage of food when it was abundant survived better than their more neurotic peers.

In a normal day on an average trout stream, you can find more productive water by just staying away from other anglers. Even if I see another angler just leaving a pool, I won't fish it. Those fish have been disturbed, and although smaller fish often begin feeding within minutes, any smarter, older trout will remain spooked longer than I care to wait. By not elbowing your way into a pool with three other anglers in it you'll find trout where you suspect them to be and they'll will accept your fly if properly presented. You'll also be a more considerate angler to other people on the water.

One May morning I was wading the heavily fished West Branch of the Delaware at the peak of the mayfly hatches. It was no surprise that the river was crowded, but over the years I have found places to fish away from other anglers regardless of the fishing pressure. On this day, however, even though I walked a half mile from the parking lot and thought I'd be on the water before the heavy drift boat traffic, every spot I had planned in my strategy was occupied by at least two wading anglers or a drift boat parked right where I wanted to fish. I kept walking until I came to a riffle I didn't like very much. It was very shallow at the head, slightly deeper toward the tail, but I had never taken more than a small fish or two from it. I had also never seen a drift boat parked on it—not a positive sign. I have found that paying attention to where drift boats drop anchor is a good way to find places to fish in the future because guides who are on the river every day seldom miss a productive spot.

The water was higher than normal and slightly dirty, which made that spot look even less appealing. But if I wanted to fish without worrying about intruding on someone else's spot, and to fish without hearing some sociable anglers yammering back and forth about everything from rising fish to last night's baseball game, it had to do. And it was on a side channel out of sight of other anglers. A size 14 gray mayfly was hatching, so I figured I should get to it before the hatch was over.

Scanning the pool, the best place, in that day's high water, looked to be a slight curve in the bank just before the tailout that could give trout protection from the current. Getting to it would put me in an uncomfortable situation, midstream in fast current just above my waist. But nothing else was going right, so I figured I might as well challenge myself to some sporty wading. When I got to midstream, I thought I saw a nose wink in the slow water just off the bank. And then another just downstream of it. I would not have even spotted those trout if I had not gotten closer by wading out. I tied on a size 14 Hendrickson emerger and got slightly upstream of the fish so I could throw a downstream slack-line presentation into the slow water along the bank without too much drag.

After a few casts I hooked a large brown trout. It was too fast where I was standing to net the fish, so I had to lead the fish back to the shallows on the opposite side of the river where the fish was feeding. This meant fighting the current again, just to net the fish. But it was worth it, as that fish was just over 20 inches long. After I released him I thought, "Do I want to go back out there in that heavy current again?" I had seen at least one other fish on that bank, so back I went. By the time the hatch was over I had landed three fish over 20 inches, leading each one back across the current, then fighting my way back out for another try. It was one of the best mornings I have ever had on that river. If I had been able to get into my favorite spots, I would not have done as well, but by forcing myself to find water where the fish had not been pestered and were eager to take a fly not only did I have a great day—I found a new spot to add to my list for the future.

If you're in a drift boat fishing an area with lots of side channels, try to pick the least traveled, or even untraveled, channels on days with crowds of other boats on the water. Dave Kumlien, longtime guide in the Bozeman area, once floated me down the Madison at the peak of the salmonfly hatch, which is a large stonefly that only hatches for a few days each season and brings the largest trout to the surface. And it's no secret. It also brings out every angler with a drift boat parked in their yard for hundreds of miles around. Dave's strategy was to look for side channels that were too shallow for a boat, park the boat on the bank, and walk up the side channels fishing big dry flies. The fish in the main channel, and in the wider side channels, were either spooked or had seen about 200 big dry flies already in any given day, and we didn't do very well there. But in the narrow side channels, we rose dozens of trout that acted like they had not seen an angler or another fly all week. I'm sure we weren't the only ones with that strategy, but it paid off anyway.

Thus, in looking for trout, it's not always about currents or water temperature or insects. Sometimes its about finding water where trout do what they are supposed to do. At least by fishing undisturbed water you can find trout that *might* take your fly, as opposed to fish that can't be caught because of something beyond your control.

Current brings food to trout. Where you find the right current, you'll find feeding trout. This is an assortment of tiny mayflies and midges from a backwater on the Missouri River in Montana, one of the richest trout streams in North America.

CHAPTER 2

Currents

Finding those 2-foot-per-second pockets that trout prefer will help you narrow down locations in a river. Developing a sense for this requires a basic knowledge of stream hydraulics, but there aren't any helpful guides to the parts that are important to us as anglers, either in print or on videos. Stream hydrologists are interested in aspects like sediment loads and the effect of currents on the shape of a riverbed, and especially the dynamics of moving water that form river channels and how these channels erode and change shape over time. Those are important if you are trying to figure out how to develop a channel deep enough to move a barge down the Mississippi or if you own property on a trout stream so you can predict how habitat improvements might fare over the next decade. But as anglers we don't care about that. We want to know what the current is doing right now, and how it affects a trout's position. We'll go into specific types of trout holding water later—for now let's look at the dynamics of current so it will be easier to discuss specific trout locations later.

Admittedly, what we're examining in this chapter shows stylized and highly simplified examples. You'll seldom find isolated, perfectly round rocks in the middle of a river or nice symmetrical bends. Nature is messy and even with these simple examples currents can get unpredictable. Imagine what happens when you get multiple rocks in a stream channel with their turbulence bouncing off each other and making predictions even more unruly. But just like to truly understand a complex piece of music you need to understand scales and key signatures and chords, to predict what is happening in the three-dimensional space of a trout stream some knowledge of the physical principles will lead to a deeper awareness.

I've dug into the details of stream hydraulics so you don't have to. My eyes have glazed over with formulas that go back as far as da Vinci, and the modern ones that utilize square roots and logarithms and a bunch of symbols I have never even seen before. I think I understand the Reynolds number, but when the Prandtl-Karman turbulence theory is explained my head wants to explode. Bit by bit, though, I've been able to tease out the more basic, macro-level aspects of stream hydraulics that can explain what we see in river currents and how these can affect trout.

Maybe you don't care about this stuff. It could be too geeky. You just want someone to tell you where to look in a river for trout. I think, though, that to understand what you see swirling on the surface and interpolating that into the three-dimensional space trout live in, you need to have some basic concept of the physical properties of water in motion. It's mostly invisible, and also the little diagrams I show you about where trout might be living are only examples of one place and time, so in order to look at your own trout streams where the rocks and logs and bottom are different, some fundamental and admittedly stylized scenarios are helpful.

As detailed as the science is, trying to predict the dynamics of moving water is about as reliable as predicting where the stock market will be a year from now. Even authorities on the subject have trouble making predictions. I've seen structures developed by the most respected expert in river morphology, designed to hold back and re-channel flood waters on a large western river, fail miserably with the first major flood. So don't think by understanding a bit of basic stream hydrology you're going to turn into a mystical savant who can instantly locate trout. At best it will help you see trout streams in three dimensions, and as dynamic environments that not only change with seasonal flows, but

change every second (luckily those short-term dynamics generally repeat in a cycle in one spot, over and over, so they aren't a big factor in finding fish).

FLOW VS. VELOCITY

Many guides live and die by the flows monitored by US Geological Survey (USGS) gauges on major rivers. Flows can determine whether a river is wadeable or if enough water is present to float a drift boat. They can tell you if dry flies and smaller nymphs will work, or if you'll need to fish big streamers and sinking lines to get to the fish. But knowing the flow won't help you if you don't know the river, and it especially won't give you any idea of the velocity of the water, which is the critical part of finding trout.

Flow is defined as the number of cubic feet of water per second (cfs) moving past the point in a river where the gauge is located. It's estimated by knowing the average depth of a river and the width of the river at that

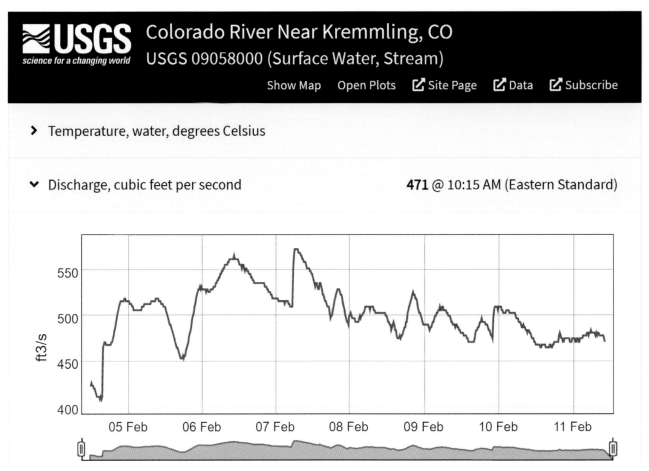

A USGS flow chart for the upper Colorado River. Viewing it graphically like this can show you short-term trends in flow rates, which are helpful in determining where to fish and what technique to use—or even if you should be fishing at all. These fluctuations could be from dam releases, snowmelt, or rain events, and you can see that the river went from a very low flow to some strong peaks and then settled back down into a more consistent flow. Consistent flows in most rivers mean more successful fishing. Also note that you can track temperature fluctuations from this same website.

This tiny Vermont brook (below) is probably flowing at about the same velocity, somewhere around 2 feet per second, as the Yellowstone River (above) in the park at low summer flow. However, their discharge in cubic feet per second is vastly different. So discharge or flow shows you how fast a particular river is moving compared to a few days ago, but doesn't allow you to compare the speed, or the fishability, of one river to the next because the larger river's flow is spread over a much wider and deeper floodplain.

point, and is measured by the height of the water at the gauge station. It knows nothing about velocity, which can depend on the slope of the riverbed, the width of a river, and obstructions on the river bottom and along the banks that slow the progress of the water.

For instance, I just looked at some flows of Montana rivers, all of which are fishing reasonably well and running clear. The little Gallatin is running at 294 cfs. The larger Madison below Quake Lake is at 1,000 cfs, and the Missouri is at 3,450. Up north, the giant Kootenai is huffing along at 10,000 cfs. Comparing a couple of rivers that I know, I can predict that if the Missouri is flowing at less than 4,000 cfs, I'll be able to wade most of the river and have some decent dry-fly fishing. If it's at 5,000 to 6,000 cfs, I'd better find a friend with a drift boat and be prepared to fish some streamers. However, my little local river, the Battenkill, offers better streamer fishing at 700 to 1,200 cfs and wading and dry-fly fishing below 600 cfs.

The one useful aspect of flow if you don't know a river, though, is seeing the recent trend. You'll be able to tell if a river's flow is stable, falling, or rising, and how rapidly the change is happening. If you've heard a river is fishing well and you look up the flow history and see a nice flat, stable flow over the past few days, you can figure the fishing will be about the same. If you see a big spike in the flows, the fishing could be better—or it could be worse—but you know some changes are in store and whatever you found the other day, or whatever report you saw, could be old news. All bets are off.

Another useful aspect of flow is that discharge along a river channel is relatively constant, as long as no new inputs of water like large tributaries enter a river. In the year 1500 Leonardo da Vinci determined that if discharge is constant but the area is decreased, velocity goes up. He called it the continuity principle. We can use this, because if the flow in a river has gone up suddenly, such as increased flows from a dam release, in places where the river is wider, thus more area in the river channel, the chances of finding spots in the river with lower velocity are greater. And during low flows, when some of a river might be too slow to offer enough food for trout along the conveyer belt, you can look for pinch points where the river is narrower, providing some faster water for the fish.

It's the downstream velocity that matters most to us when trout fishing because it affects where the fish can live (and also where their prey can live). The range of velocities in a typical trout stream can run between almost zero near the bottom and along the banks to somewhere about 8 feet per second in the center of a large river with a steeply sloped bottom and few obstructions. The highest velocity ever recorded in a river was 22 feet per second in a gorge on the Potomac River near Washington, DC, in a flood.

IT'S TURBULENCE ALL THE WAY DOWN

In fluid mechanics, flow in a liquid is described as either laminar or turbulent (or some consider a transitional state, which is a bit of both). In laminar flow, particles move in smooth paths in layers, with no mixing of adjacent layers. Everything moves independently, like a deck of cards thrown on a table. The velocity, pressure, and other flow properties remain constant. In turbulent flow, the layers mix and cells of fluid move off in other directions, interacting with each other in a chaotic manner that is nearly impossible to predict.

Although I have seen instances where angling writers write about laminar flow in trout streams, stream hydrologists say it doesn't exist in natural streams on the scale relative to the size of even a trout fry, because the roughness of the bank and bottom, and obstructions in the water, constantly mix the water. In water flowing over a perfectly smooth rock, you can find an almost microscopic layer of laminar flow, but that's as much as you'll find in a natural stream. So even though the middle of a slow, smooth-flowing river appears to be laminar, there is always some turbulence present. It's just a matter of degree. And we can't always predict what will happen. In fact, physicists don't even understand turbulence very well. In a famous but perhaps apocryphal story, Werner Heisenberg, the winner of the 1932 Nobel Prize in physics, best known for his famous uncertainty principle, was asked if he could ask God two questions, what they might be. His answer was, "Why quantum mechanics? And why turbulence? And I'm pretty sure God would be able to answer the first question."

We know that turbulence happens when water slides by a solid object in a parallel direction and interacts with the object first at a molecular level, where water molecules stick to the object. It's called shear stress. Water is a viscous liquid, so this layer interacts with the layers above it, forming globs of turbulence that mix with other layers above it in an intricate ballet. This layer of disturbed flow is called the boundary layer and its exact dimensions are impossible to predict. But at any given point, its upper limit is where the main downstream flow of a river is no longer influenced by mixing and turbulence below. According to ecologist Steven Vogel in his book *Life in Moving Fluids*, "most biologists seem to have heard of the boundary layer, but they have a fuzzy notion that it is a discrete layer rather than the discrete notion that it's a fuzzy region."

Rivers are dynamic, three-dimensional structures, and in order to learn how trout use them you need to try to at least estimate what is going on under the surface. And despite some patches of smooth water in this photo, none of the flow is laminar. It's all turbulent to some degree.

So if all flow in a trout stream is turbulent, and even physicists don't understand how it works, how the heck are we supposed to predict where a trout will be? Luckily, turbulence comes in many flavors, from slight to extreme, and we can predict what will happen on a macro level when moving water interacts with solid objects. And even though turbulent flow is chaotic, it tends to repeat over and over in the same spot with some regularity. If there were no turbulence in a river, current speed would be uniform and we'd have a difficult time figuring out where trout might be. But turbulence slows the downstream energy of the water, creates those pockets of slower water that hold trout, and move the food supply in a stream in predictable alleys that trout take advantage of.

Don't confuse laminar and turbulent flow with steady or unsteady flow. Whether flow is steady or unsteady looks more at the macro level of moving water. Hydrologists classify steady flow as water that is mostly all moving at the same speed and direction, with no change in depth. There is still some turbulence present, but it isn't strong enough to change the average velocity or direction of the current. Unsteady flow is when water passing a given point moves in many directions, the velocity changes from one moment to the next, and

the depth also varies when boils of turbulence raise the level of the surface. Trout will feed in both steady and unsteady flows, depending on the speed of the current and the amount of unsteadiness.

How Much Turbulence Is Too Much?

Slight to moderate turbulence is a good thing for trout. It reduces the downstream velocity of the water, so a trout uses less energy to stay in position. The little eddies and swirls of moderate turbulence may help a trout hold its position, and if you watch a trout at rest it's seldom completely at rest, swaying its body in the current as it constantly adjusts but with a minimum of effort. At a certain point, though, turbulence becomes a liability. Trout prefer predictability, as it's easier to capture an insect drifting in the current when a trout spots its prey and makes a slight move to intercept it. Anything that suddenly veers off a path requires more energy to chase. In addition, if turbulence becomes too strong, it can push a trout back and forth, requiring more overt adjustments than just a slight body movement.

By nature, as we've seen, turbulence is chaotic and unpredictable. How much is too much, and what degree of turbulence will make trout avoid it? From what I've observed, if the cells of the turbulence approach the body size of a fish, it will avoid those places. A trout will chase a streamer into very turbulent water and occasionally even dart into it for an especially appealing nymph or dry fly. But it's a low-percentage place and you'll seldom find trout lying in areas of strong turbulence.

It seems to correspond to body size as well. In small mountain streams with trout seldom longer than a hand span, turbulence cells longer than about 6 inches in diameter are places these little fish avoid. Larger trout seem to be able to handle larger eddies of turbulence, though. Fishing the lower King's River in California on a bright day with clear water, I noticed large rainbow trout hanging suspended and feeding subsurface over very deep water, in midwater where you would not normally expect them. I watched them for a while, trying to figure out why they were hanging in a place I wouldn't expect them, and noticed that the strong turbulence at the head of the pool extended down into the center of the pool where I saw the fish. The cells were so large and, for the most part, repeated in a predictable manner, that the fish seemed to be riding a plume of current like a gull hanging in the air over a seashore, just on the upper boundary of the turbulence cell. They did sway more than normal and needed to adjust their positions with the vagaries of the current, but they seemed to be quite content feeding in the turbulence. When I've noticed trout hanging in strong turbulence they have invariably been rainbows, and I've seen steelhead behaving like this as

From the surface, slight to moderate turbulence looks like this. The water has a bumpy surface but no standing waves and no white water. Trout can hold and feed nearly anywhere in this water.

The heads of the pools
on the Battenkill are
easier to fish, especially
with a nymph, as it's
easier to get a fly down
into the many pockets
formed by varying
depths, more-complex
bottom structure,
and slower pockets
that form below the
areas of turbulence.

This cutthroat trout is holding near the bottom in moderate turbulence. The changes in direction in the mild turbulence slow the velocity of the current and allow the trout to hold in position without expending too much energy.

well. It's rare to see browns or brookies or cutthroats behaving like this.

There's another reason trout avoid more-chaotic areas of turbulence. It's often accompanied by dense air bubbles, such as the white water you see at the head of a deep, fast pool. Although that water is less dense and you would think trout might prefer it, I think they avoid it because they can't see their food. The chaotic current combined with low visibility makes it a tough place for trout. However, these places also make a great spot for trout to hide because the reduced visibility makes it harder for predators to see them. I'll often fish through a pool and then spook trout from under the boiling water at the head of the pool, but I think they bolted there when my bad casts and careless wading pushed them into the foam for protection. I don't think they like feeding there.

At the other end of the scale are places where the surface is pocked with tiny goose bumps, as in a gentle riffle, or wavelets smaller in size than a trout that don't propagate into bigger cells. This too is turbulence but of a more benevolent type. None of the cells are large enough to push a trout around, but the broken surface hides the fish from predators, and it hides gross mistakes in our presentation that smooth water wouldn't allow.

VERTICAL AND HORIZONTAL STRATIFICATION

You probably know that the current near the bottom of a river is slower than at the surface, which is why trout hold there. When water comes in contact with a solid object, molecules of water that touch the solid object stick to it, and the effective velocity is zero. If the bottom of a river was completely smooth, above a certain velocity turbulence would still form because the viscosity of the water forms an internal resistance and

this spreads to adjacent layers, producing mixing and turbulence. But the bottom of a river is not a smooth pipe, so irregularities on the bottom form turbulence at any speed as water bouncing off an object raised above the bottom bumps into water flowing above it, and cells of turbulence form that carry up through the water column, although as it extends farther from the bottom, energy is dissipated so turbulence is lower. The faster the water, the more extensive the turbulence, with bigger cells and a more widespread effect.

In the more turbulent layer, energy is lost through friction with the bottom and downstream velocity is lowered, because instead of moving in a steady downstream direction, some of the energy is direction upward and sideways and backward. This loss of energy creates heat, especially from friction along the bottom, which causes the cells of turbulence to slowly migrate upward, as warm water is less dense than cold water. The heat produced is negligible to organisms living in it because, due to the thermal resistance of water, any temperature increase is insignificant. You don't need to worry about fishing water with heavy turbulence in warm weather because it will never warm the water enough to even be measured with your stream thermometer so it won't hurt the trout—and anyway turbulent water offers more gas exchange with the air, so oxygen content will increase in areas of heavy turbulence.

The difference in velocity in a stream channel, from bottom to top, is not a straight-line relationship. It's more of a logarithmic relationship; in other words, the

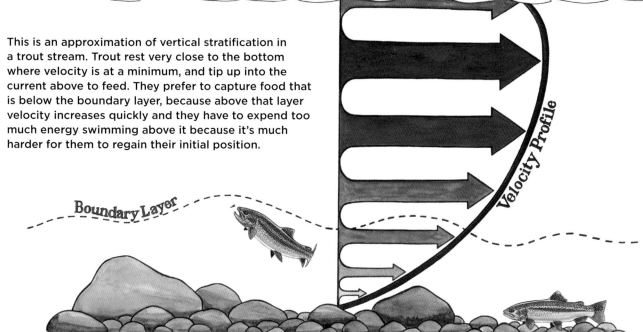

This is an approximation of vertical stratification in a trout stream. Trout rest very close to the bottom where velocity is at a minimum, and tip up into the current above to feed. They prefer to capture food that is below the boundary layer, because above that layer velocity increases quickly and they have to expend too much energy swimming above it because it's much harder for them to regain their initial position.

velocity increases slowly in the boundary layer as you rise from the bottom to a certain point and then it rises quickly to a maximum. The rougher the bottom, the higher into the water column this slower region extends. At the surface is a little variation from a true curve because friction between the surface of the water and the atmosphere slows the velocity a small amount. This slightly slower velocity extends up to 20 percent of the depth, so in 4 feet of water it extends down to almost 10 inches below the surface (although, being a curve, it's most pronounced right at the surface). When fishing dry flies and nymphs, I've always favored a leader that floats (I grease it up with a little dry-fly paste), as I somehow feel this gives me a better presentation, and I think that a sinking leader or tippet extends into the faster water just below the surface and pulls on my dry fly or nymph at a speed faster than the current at the surface, producing drag.

This difference also has important implications in fishing subsurface flies. In fast water, trout hug the bottom where the current is 2 feet per second or less, where fish can maintain their position without expending too much energy. If the current in the middle of the water column is much faster, somewhere around 5 or 6 feet per second, trout will tip up into the layer of slower water where the velocity curve is not as steep, but will avoid going above the inflection point where the curve gets much steeper. This is why, particularly in fast water, you need to get your flies close to the bottom, in that calmer layer, because even if trout see your nymphs or

streamers in the middle of the water column, they'll be reluctant to brave the flow. Not only do they use more energy getting to the faster layer, but once they get there, the current pushes them backward, forcing them to swim upstream to regain their position.

The size of this slower layer is related to the size of objects on the bottom. And unless the layer is bigger than the height of a trout's body, it's difficult for a trout to find protection from the current. In water with an abundance of large rocks, the calm layer extends farther into the flow, but over a smooth bedrock or sand bottom it is narrower. Over a very smooth bottom like a layer of sand or fine gravel, you may not find any trout in the main current unless there is a slight divot on the bottom, at least as long as a trout. Fish lying in these depressions on a smooth bottom are reluctant to move very far into the water column. This makes fast but smooth-bottomed waters more difficult to fish with subsurface flies.

Vermont's Battenkill is one example of this conundrum. The surface velocity in the Battenkill is deceptively swift, and because the surrounding land is composed mostly of glacial till, smaller gravel, there are few large rocks on the river bottom. Getting a nymph down to these fish is a challenge, and over the years I have found that to successfully fish nymphs, I need to find heads of pools, where the fish lie in the pocket just below a riffle, where the water deepens and slows quickly, because it's much easier to get my fly to them here than in the fast, smooth water in the middle or tail of a pool.

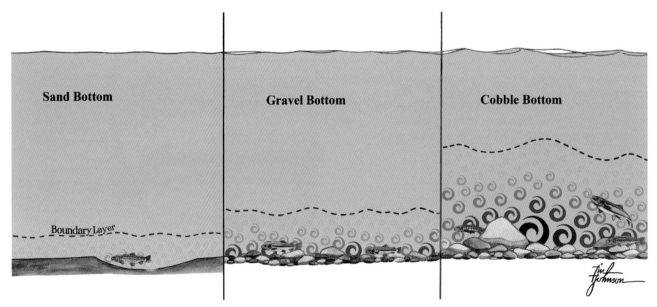

The composition of the bottom, assuming the same current velocity, will determine the size of the boundary layer and how many trout it may support. On a sand or other smooth bottom like bedrock, the only place trout will hold is where you find a depression in the bottom. Rough gravel gives a slightly larger boundary layer and more places for trout to live. A cobbled or bouldered bottom offers the most places for trout to live and an easier place to feed, so it should hold more trout per square foot.

The smooth, flat water of much of the Battenkill is deceptively swift, as you can see by the wake behind Tyler Atkins. It's a tough place to fish a nymph because the fast surface current, unbroken by much turbulence, whisks away the line and leader before the fly has a chance to sink. It also does not hold many trout except for places where a shelf on the bottom or an obstruction like a rock or log slow the current.

In contrast to the Battenkill, the Madison in Montana is carpeted with rocks and boulders of all sizes, and I've found that as long as I stay out of the swift main current in the middle of the river, I don't need to set my indicator as far up on the leader, or can fish a dry-dropper with a shorter dropper. That calm layer extends much farther up into the water column, sometimes right to the surface, so trout here are more likely to venture farther from the bottom when eating subsurface food and are also more likely to take a dry fly, as it does not consume as much energy as it does in a river like the Battenkill.

It's important to note that the shear stress that causes turbulence is proportional to the square of the velocity. So the faster the current, the wider the boundary layer, and it doesn't take much of an increase in current to widen the slower boundary layer below. We worry about trout getting washed away during a severe flood until we realize that the increase in current speed gives the trout a wider boundary layer of slower current to escape the ravages of the torrent.

Water in contact with the banks also forms turbulence and slows the flow of current. Just as a rough bottom of cobbled rocks gives the trout a wider comfortable layer, a rough bank lined with rocks, logs, or dimples

and bays along the shore will offer more comfortable places for trout, especially if the current along the bank is fast. Even a shallow, sloping bank produces some turbulence and slower current, from gentle undulations of the bank and the bottom. The comfort zone of calmer water will extend from the bottom of the river into the shallower water along the bank, and trout will slide into these places to feed. They prefer to feed here because when the calmer zone is mostly uniform, all the way to the surface, a trout can feed in the whole water column without the need to dart into any faster, more difficult current. They can slide sideways using little energy, never venturing into faster current.

One cold, dreary day I was fishing the West Branch of the Delaware, and unusual for that river, I could not find a single surface-feeding trout. I must have covered a mile of water looking for noses poking into the surface film when I came to a large pool I had never fished before. The right bank was much deeper and faster, not a high-percentage spot for finding rising trout, but since nothing was happening I decided to wade up that bank anyway, more to explore it than expecting to find any fish. About halfway up the bank was a slight projection, just a little finger poking into the faster current, and I

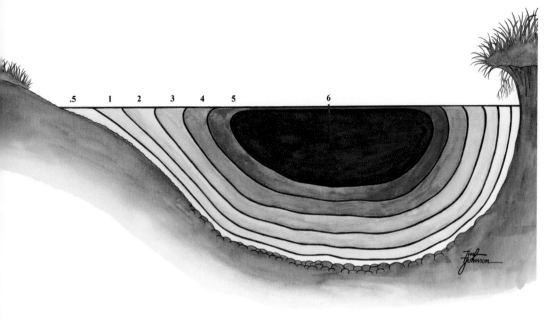

Water in contact with both the banks and the bottom creates isobars of current. Here is a hypothetical and greatly simplified view of the differing currents in feet per second, in a cross-section of a river. Trout are comfortable holding in current less than 2 feet per second, so you can see the places where they'll prefer to hold and feed—close to the banks and close to the bottom. Objects in the streambed or along the banks will change these velocities, but this shows what a non-obstructed section of river would exhibit.

thought I saw the wink of a rise there. As I got closer I saw the fish again, with a slow, broad rise that pushed a wide swath of foam aside as it fed. All I could see on the water were a few size 22 olive mayflies, and as much as I avoid fishing a small fly to large fish, I tied one on. After a few casts the fish took the fly with barely a ripple and I actually landed it, a brown trout of 22 inches measured against a reference point on my rod. It was the only trout I caught that day but the biggest fish of the week.

Floods

What happens during a flood, either from heavy rainfall or from a sudden water release from a dam that produces electricity from hydropower? Truly a lot less than you think. I get this question all the time, both from anglers and non-anglers, after a flood: "What will happen to the fish? Do they all get washed away?" Hardly ever. You'll notice that as the volume of water in a river increases, the height of the water in the channel increases and often the river gets wider. A lot of the flow increase is lessened by an increase in the space the water occupies, thus the overall velocity of the river does not increase much.

Studies of floods in natural river channels have shown that an increase in flow in a river that is ten times the normal flow only doubles the velocity of the water flowing at the surface. And because of vertical and horizontal stratification, the increase in velocity near the bottom and along the banks is negligible. Floods may make wading or boating difficult and it might be tough to get your fly down to those fish hugging the bottom, but they'll stay comfortable even when conditions look brutal.

THE CONCEPT OF SOFT WATER

You may have heard people talk about "soft water" or "soft spots." This is strictly an anglers' term and if you ask hydrologists about soft spots they won't have any idea what you're talking about, nor will they care. A soft spot is that Goldilocks water, not stagnant but not too fast, somewhere between 1 and 3 feet per second, usually with gentle turbulence and a uniform flow. You'll eventually know it when you see it because you'll catch most of your trout in soft water.

Soft water on the surface is easy to spot, but don't forget we're talking about three dimensions here, so there are areas of soft water that you won't be able to see because the soft spot could be close to the bottom, hidden by faster or more turbulent water above. But some understanding of hydraulics will help you imagine what is going on under the surface.

CURRENT AROUND SUBMERGED OBJECTS

The behavior of moving water around an immovable object relatively perpendicular to the current flow (as opposed to the shear stress of current flowing parallel to an object) is called "flow around bluff bodies" by stream hydrologists. Let's start with a theoretical example, a bowling ball submerged in the middle of a river. Water hitting the upstream side of the bowling ball sticks to the ball at a molecular level because of the viscosity of water, and water molecules upstream of that layer also stop moving, similar to a car pileup on a freeway.

In a river in flood, much of the energy from increased flow spills over into the floodplain, so the increased velocity of the current, especially near the bottom and along the banks, is not as severe as you might think. Trout have survived floods for hundreds of thousands of years and have adapted to them quite well.

Although not all soft water can be seen from the surface, this is what it looks like on the surface. It has gentle turbulence, a uniform flow, and is moving about 2 feet per second. Trout love to hold in water that looks like this, and it is also some of the easiest water to fish because the gently broken surface hides mistakes in our presentation.

Hydrologists call this a stagnation point. Some of the traffic is able to slide off into the shoulder to avoid a collision, and water begins to flow around the sides of the bowling ball. On the sides of the ball, parallel to the current, water also slows down due to friction and shear stress.

Just downstream of the bowling ball, water leaves the surface of the ball, called the separation point. And immediately behind the ball is a region of dead water with zero downstream velocity called the cavity region. This is the region where smaller organisms like insect larvae and diatoms live without the threat of being washed away by the current, but it's typically not large enough to protect something as big as a trout. The faster water flowing around the bowling ball is drawn into this stagnation point because the pressure is lower here and lift is created from water flowing over the top of the ball, just like a bird or airplane wing. So with all these conflicting forces vortices, or areas of reverse flow, are formed, and in a perfectly symmetrical object like a bowling ball (ignoring the finger holes) these vortices flow in opposite directions because fluids must conform to the law of conservation of vorticity. As we progress downstream of the bowling ball, the vortices lose energy and gradually get smaller and less violent, although they do continue for quite a distance and begin to oscillate in a sinusoidal pattern.

How do trout use these forces? We know they use the stagnation point in front of a rock because we often find them in front of rocks in fast water. Yet when measuring this point in front of a rock with a current meter, I've found that it seldom extends far enough in front of a rock to protect a trout's entire body from the force of the current. For instance, I measured the flow of a 2-foot-diameter rock in a current where the main flow is 4 feet per second, and the area of reduced velocity in front of the rock is only a few inches. However, with a trout's tail in the stagnation point, it must be enough to allow the trout to hold its position without expending a lot of energy. And a shallow trench is often formed in front of a rock or log, which gives a trout a bit more protection from the current as it flows over a depression. It may also be just a matter of being able to see its prey coming because immediately behind a rock, with all the turbulence and the view upstream blocked, it is difficult to see prey items drifting in the current.

But we know trout live behind rocks in the current, right? They do, but in my observation they don't live right behind rocks, with their noses pushed right up to the rock. First, there isn't much food coming to a

A cobbled bottom, with larger rocks, like that of Montana's Madison River, has the potential to hold more trout per square foot than a smoother bottom of gravel or sand because of the larger boundary layer near the bottom and many little pockets of refuge for trout to hold and feed.

About the only option George Daniel has in this spot is the smooth water directly in front of him. The extreme turbulence to his left swirls in all directions and is unpredictable, making it a nearly impossible place for a trout to hold its position.

fish immediately behind a rock, and the food that does drift behind the rock comes from behind the fish, due to the reverse current caused by the vortices. And the turbulence immediately behind a rock can be too severe for a trout, buffeting the fish in an unpredictable manner. However, as you get downstream of the separation point, the vortices are less severe and begin to draw in drifting food from outside the wake. These less severe areas of turbulence may actually help stabilize a trout, with gentle current pushing in from the sides of the fish, not so strong as to push the fish around but enough to give it gentle shoves. So when looking for trout below objects in the current, look for the place where the wake narrows. Here the force of the current from above is still reduced by the gentle turbulence but not enough to push a trout off balance.

I first learned about where trout lie behind rocks long before I knew anything about hydraulics. When I was a teenager, I tied flies for a fly shop owned by a gentleman named Carl Coleman, who taught me lessons in fly fishing I still use today, fifty years later. The first time Carl took me fishing, we walked into a spot on a river he had fished since childhood. There were three evenly spaced

rocks in a deep run and Carl parked me downstream of them and told me there were several nice brown trout right in front of me. So naturally I made a cast right to the downstream side of the rock because trout hide behind rocks, right? "Not like that," Carl said. "The fish are farther downstream, not right behind the rock. If you cast your line all the way up to the rock you'll put your fly line right on their heads and they might spook. Plus you don't need such a long cast. Make your casts farther below the rock."

After a few casts in the right place I hooked what was likely my biggest trout to date, around 14 inches long. We were fishing nymphs with a floating line, straight upstream with no indicator or sighter. These were the days before anyone used indicators or Euro nymphing and fishing these flies was still a dark art because the only clue to a strike was a hesitation in the tip of your floating line. "I think there might be another fish in the same spot," Carl said, and sure enough I caught a second fish well below the rock. Carl then took over and fished the other two rocks just upstream of the first one, pulling three trout from the same relative location behind the rocks. It was a lesson I would never forget, and I sheepishly admit that whenever I fished that stream, the first place I would try was the run with those three rocks and I was seldom disappointed. The trout were always in the same place.

You can get a general idea of the size of a stagnation point in front of a rock or other object by the amount of the object that is perpendicular to the current. A square concrete block will have a wider and more desirable (for a trout) stagnation point in front of it than a bowling ball of the same size, and a triangular block that has a point that projects upstream into the current will offer the smallest stagnation point, and also a smaller wake downstream. A rock with a large surface perpendicular to the current will also have a wider wake below, and trout may be quite a distance below it. And, counterintuitively, a rock with a rough surface will have a smaller wake and less turbulence behind it than a smooth rock. It's the same principle that reduces air friction on a dimpled golf ball.

The force of the current and the size of the rock dictate how much turbulence occurs in the wake behind it, bearing in mind that the shear stress is proportional to the square of the current velocity. With a smaller rock, one maybe twice the diameter of the body width of a trout, in moderate current, there will still be a reduction in flow, but the turbulence will be light. In this case you might find a trout very close to the downstream end of the rock. If the rock is wider, or if the current is faster, you might find a trout farther downstream.

Different water depths also create different kinds of turbulence and micro-habitats for trout. Imagine a large rock with 2 feet of water between its upper surface and the surface of the water. Here, you get turbulence at the separation point on each side of the rock where the vortices form, as well as turbulence because of the increased pressure of water coming over the top of the rock mixing with the low pressure of the slower velocity behind the rock. As water levels drop, if the upper surface of the rock partially protrudes out of the water, more chaotic turbulence ensues as white water, and as the water mixes with air bubbles it can be as much as 60 percent less dense than water without entrapped air bubbles. Trout may even have trouble holding neutral buoyancy in this area, and when salmon jump a falls, they don't use white water as a launching spot because they can't get enough purchase against the current to make a leap. It also decreases visibility for the trout even more. Trout may be found even farther downstream from the rock in this situation.

If the water drops a bit more and the entire upper surface of the rock is exposed, the amount of turbulence behind the rock lessens, but the cavity region becomes larger and almost stagnant, offering little food for a drift-feeding trout. Just because you caught three trout 10 feet downstream of a rock two weeks ago doesn't mean you'll find them in the same spot if the water level changes. Trout will move up or down to find the

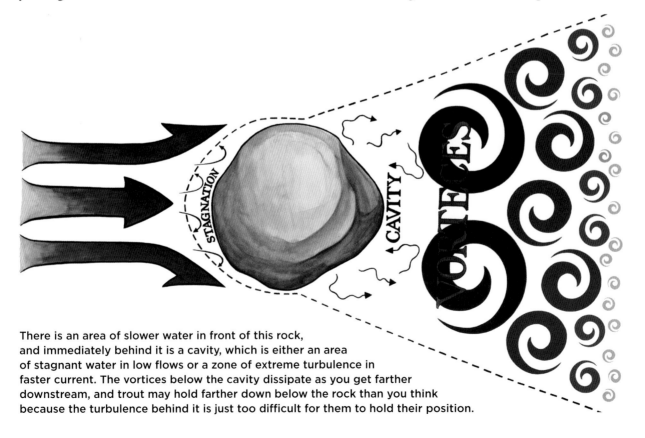

There is an area of slower water in front of this rock, and immediately behind it is a cavity, which is either an area of stagnant water in low flows or a zone of extreme turbulence in faster current. The vortices below the cavity dissipate as you get farther downstream, and trout may hold farther down below the rock than you think because the turbulence behind it is just too difficult for them to hold their position.

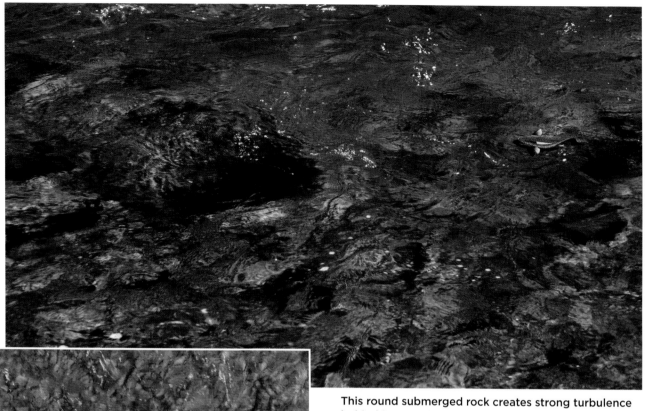

This round submerged rock creates strong turbulence behind it, even though it's not totally apparent from our perspective. Trout won't be immediately behind the rock but will be farther back where turbulence is less.

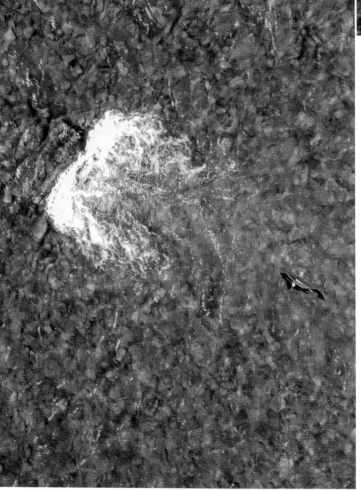

This partially submerged rock creates a lot of bubbly turbulence, which makes it even harder for a trout to hold its position. Thus a trout here will likely be farther from the rock than if it was fully submerged.

best feeding and resting spot as the water circulation changes. Your best bet is to look for the spot where the severe turbulence starts to lessen and level out, and the swirling vortices become less apparent—regardless of its distance from the rock.

When a rock on the bottom of a stream approaches the size of a trout's body, as opposed to a large boulder or a collection of boulders, trout use these smaller rocks in an entirely different manner. Instead of an object for protection from predators and for funneling food to them, trout use these rocks as pillows. I don't know what else to call them. The rocks I see used for this purpose typically range from baseball size to a bit longer than a trout's body and can be round, rectangular, or triangular. Flat rocks seem to be preferable to round ones. The rocks are invariably positioned with the upstream edge a bit higher than the downstream edge. I see this so often that I suspect there is a hydraulic reason for trout choosing these, as the rocks aren't big enough for protection and don't provide any more food than a flat stretch of bottom close by.

You'll see trout about a third of the way downstream from the leading edge of the rock with their head almost on the rock and their body trailing in the current above the rock slope. Trout don't huddle right on the bottom;

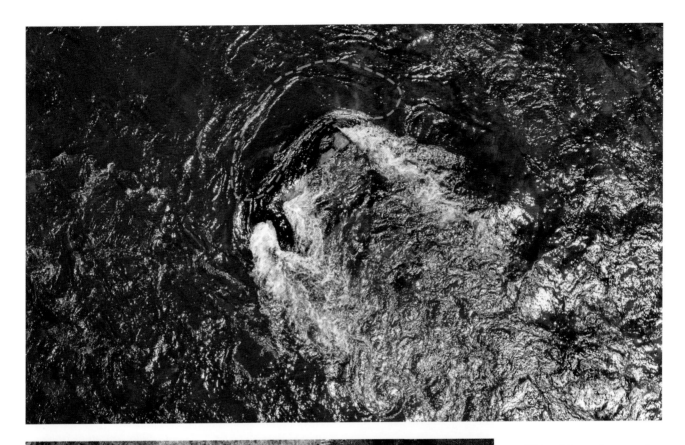

This wide rock presents a bigger surface to the current, and you can see the extensive stagnation point in front of it. There is a lot of severe turbulence behind the rock, and I'd expect that the spot in front of it is more likely to hold trout.

The area downstream of this large rock is a dead zone. You can tell it's almost stagnant because of the fine silt and sand that has accumulated behind it. I don't think you'd find trout feeding anywhere in the immediate downstream area of the rock. In front of the rock and along its outside edge? Absolutely. Behind it? Not likely.

This brook trout is holding just off the bottom, using the smaller rocks here as pillows. I suspect that the slight turbulence just behind the rocks supports the back end of the trout's body and helps it hold in the current. This is a shot of an undisturbed, wild trout taken with a remote camera and the trout is exactly where it wants to be—it's not a fish that was just released and resting.

In the wake of a large rock, trout are more likely to feed in front of it, along its sides, or back in the focal point where the turbulence slows down. With a smaller rock, the turbulence is not as severe and trout may hold and feed much closer to its downstream edge.

they like to be suspended just above the bottom for better mobility and the ability to rise up to intercept food in the water column when drift feeding. A rock perch gives them this vantage point. My theory is that the slight turbulence creates an upwelling on the downstream end of the rock that balances the trout's head on the upstream side. A trout will choose a particular rock and use it for hours at a time, returning to the same rock day after day. This is, I believe, why trout anglers learn that a cobbled bottom will hold more trout than one with a gravel or sand bottom. The fish just find more comfortable places when they have lots of options.

BENDS AND HELICAL FLOW

Bends are formed in a river one of two ways and sometimes a combination of the two. One is when a straight piece of river encounters an immovable object like a rock ledge or a higher piece of ground that is not easily erodible. The other way, more common in valley areas where a river is free to explore its floodplain, is when meanders form from the erosion of material from one side and deposition of material on the downstream, opposite bank. Bends nearly always form deep pools with complex currents that are confusing if you just look at surface currents.

I didn't truly understand bends until many decades into my trout-fishing life. The place that made me slap my forehead in recognition of my lack of observation was a small tailwater river in Utah, off the beaten path and full of large brown trout in very clear water. I had fished nymphs up through a series of bends in the river without success, which frustrated me because I knew this river was full of trout and I was sure I had fished over many decent fish without the hint of a strike. Coming up to one bend but hanging back so I could observe, I noticed the glint of a trout, feeding subsurface on the inside of the bend but facing broadside to the main flow of the river.

Trout can't hold their position when perpendicular to the flow for long, but this fish continued to feed calmly and with seemingly no effort while remaining in that strange position. I realized that if most of the trout were feeding like this, not only was I putting my flies in the wrong place (on the outside, deeper bend) but I was spooking every fish in the clear, shallow water. When a fish has one of its flanks facing you instead of its tail, it gets a much better look at the scenery downstream of it—including people waving sticks in the air.

The water's surface above the fish, though, seemed to be moving steadily downstream with the rest of the flow, and I still could not understand how it could hold

A natural meander in a river caused by constant erosion and deposition of streambed materials. These are typically more gentle bends, and the pools formed may not be as deep and dramatic as pools formed when a river's course hits an immovable geologic obstruction.

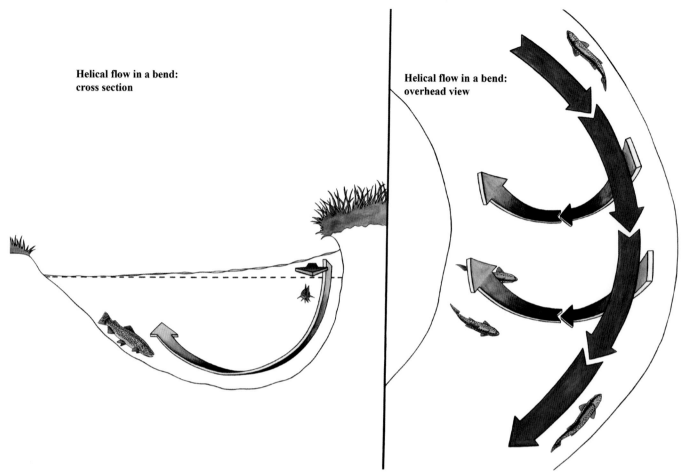

Helical flow in a bend: cross section

Helical flow in a bend: overhead view

It's important to understand the concept of helical flow at a bend because it tells you which direction trout will face and how to approach them and present a fly. Fish in the upstream part of the bend will be facing directly into the current you see at the surface. However, just below the bend, fish on the inside of the bend will face into a subsurface helical flow that is caused by water piling up against the far bank. They'll be facing in what appears to be a sideways direction, but as always they're facing into the current.

its position. Then I remembered that a couple of times, when my indicator was drifting down through the main flow, I was surprised when I picked up to make another cast that my nymph had drifted way off to the inside, at right angles to where my indicator drifted.

Digging back into those dreaded hydrology textbooks when I got home, I discovered the concept of helical flow. When water is pushed up against a bend, part of its surface gets superelevated. Gravity pushes this higher column of water toward the opposite bank, but the flow is mostly under the surface, and in an upward yet decelerating motion. Centrifugal force turns it into a spiral. This is how deposits of sand and silt build up on the opposite side of a bend (because the slower current allows suspended particles to drop out), and it's also why trout like the inside of a fast bend. Most anglers pay attention to the inside of a bend, knowing trout are found there, but what most of us don't realize is the trout can be facing at an angle that we might not expect unless we understand this subsurface helical flow. And

that's important to how you approach a pool and how you position your flies.

Now sometimes this kind of flow is obvious, as in a large, very fast bend where you get a reverse flow and a whirlpool on the inside of the bend. In many cases, though, this helical flow is not strong enough to form a visible whirlpool. But it still happens below the surface.

SEAMS AND AREAS OF FOOD CONCENTRATION

Let's talk about seams, probably the first thing a trout angler learns about reading the water. Seams are distinct boundaries between fast and slower downstream velocities, and most fly fishers know that trout predictably feed there. We're told that trout are more comfortable in the slower water, where they use less energy, but they like to be closer to faster water, which brings them food at a higher rate. But looking at seams with some knowledge of hydrology, there is even more to them.

The bend pool below these anglers was formed by the river running into a sheer cliff. This pool will be quite deep because the force of the current erodes the bottom when it can't dissipate energy along the bank.

Jesse Haller fishing a small seam line in a pocket below a rock. Seams are not always large features, and you may need to investigate the water carefully to find them.

First, why is there even fast and slow water? The faster water comes from the main channel of a river or a current thread, where momentum and gravity keep it moving. But where does the slower water come from? It's been slowed by friction with the stream bottom or a bank.

Imagine a fast seam on the edge of shallow water. The shallow water is typically slower because more of it is in contact with the bottom or the bank, and most of its volume is still influenced by friction and turbulence, even though it looks placid. Then imagine a seam against the far bank, which is deeper but the bank itself slows the water and the seam is typically much closer to the bank—and the deeper the water along the bank, the closer the seam will be to the shoreline.

But other stuff happens here that is not directly related to bottom and bank structures. When fast water meets slow, there is some friction between the two flows because of the viscosity of water, and spirals of turbulence form—they might be smaller than the cells formed by a big rock, but they still slow the flow of the current. Food gets trapped in this slim area of turbulence, its downstream progress is slowed, and trout have an easier time plucking it from the flow. If the faster current has circulating current, which

it probably does because faster water encourages more turbulence, opposing spirals will form in the slower water because of the conservation of vorticity. The area of turbulence formed may be too narrow to fully protect a trout from the current, but it does concentrate food. Just watch as mayflies flutter down the surface of a fast run. Most of them gradually get drawn into the seam, and you'll see them concentrated in this narrow band.

You've probably also been told to look for the foam line or bubble line in a trout stream to find feeding fish. Seams trap bubbles and debris as well as insects, so tracking these lines will help you determine where trout food is concentrated. These lines become even more important during periods of low flow, when much of the water is too slow to provide food at a fast enough rate for drift-feeding fish.

During low water, the foam line indicates the center of the fastest flow in a river, and it doesn't just carry insects that hatch in the middle of a riffle. Because of the friction along the banks that slows water currents and forms cells of turbulence, these rotational patterns carry anything that falls into the water toward the center of the river, and they actually cause a slight convex shape

A major foam line and two other minor ones flow through this pool. These give you a good idea where to find feeding trout, and my pick of the best spot here would be where the major and minor foam lines intersect—especially because it's also a place where the water shallows, concentrating food into a narrower band.

to the surface of the river, with the lower point in the middle. This is important even when fishing imitations of insects like ants and grasshoppers. Most people fish them only next to the bank, but an ant that falls into the water along a bank is soon drawn into the center of a river, so don't rule these patterns out for midwater fishing.

Foam lines also are useful just for spotting the flow patterns of the water in general. They'll show you areas of high turbulence and are especially handy for spotting areas of reverse flow that circulate behind places with hydraulic jumps because of the intense turbulence.

A single foam line through a pool often traces the *thalweg*. It's a German term (most of the early studies in limnology were done in Germany) and is the line of the deepest channel along a river's progress downstream. It's usually the deepest part of a river and the line that carries the fastest water or the main current thread. But it's not always the deepest spot. Sometimes, back eddies off the main channel are even deeper than the thalweg, as I've sometimes found when wading close to the bank and found myself in over the top of my waders.

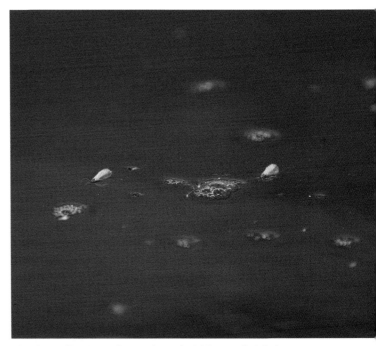

The foam line is a place where bubbles and debris collect—but it's also the place where hatching insects, or insects that fall into the water, collect.

READING INTO SURFACE CURRENTS

At this point you have a better idea of how the hypnotic revolutions of currents have formed, and hopefully a better approximation of what's going on under the surface. Whenever you see riffles or swirls on the surface, you know the turbulence formed along the streambed is carried all the way to the surface, and the middle and upper parts of the water column have less downstream energy and are better able to support a trout hovering in the current instead of being glued to the bottom. When you see a relatively smooth surface, the water is either too deep or too slow to form turbulence cells able to reach the surface.

The size of each little surface disturbance also tells you how attractive the current is to trout. In a wide riffle with a gravel bottom, wavelets are small and close together. Water is swirling in all directions because of turbulence and its downstream force is lessened, but the globs of turbulence are small enough that they don't push a trout out of position. If the turbulence cells are large, it's a combination of fast current and larger objects on the bottom. There may be trout hugging the bottom near the larger objects on the streambed, but as the cells are large enough to reach the surface, they are probably reaching all the way to the bottom and may prevent a trout from resting or feeding comfortably below them.

Hydrologists classify current velocities as subcritical, critical, and supercritical. The determination of this is

dependent upon the ratio of inertial forces to gravitational forces, where the gravitational forces encourage water to move downhill and the inertial forces (like turbulence and the viscosity of the water) resist gravity. You can tell if a flow is subcritical or supercritical by placing a stick in the water. If you see a little wake upstream of the stick and the angle of the wake behind it is relatively wide, the flow is subcritical. If there is no wake in front of the stick and the angle of the wake behind it is less than 45 degrees, the flow is supercritical. Critical flow is where the angle of the wake is 45 degrees but it's a narrow band of velocity, merely there to determine the difference between subcritical and supercritical.

You don't need to measure or even care whether a flow is supercritical or subcritical, but there are two scenarios associated with these concepts that alert you to places to avoid in a trout stream, where you'll seldom find feeding fish: hydraulic jumps and hydraulic drops. They're easy to recognize even if you don't know anything about hydraulics.

A hydraulic jump is when flow suddenly transforms between supercritical and subcritical flows. A waterfall is the perfect example. As water approaches the lip of a falls, it speeds up, gaining energy, then suddenly drops vertically and its downstream energy drops to near zero. This releases energy in the form of strong turbulence and standing waves often form, with flows reversing in the turbulence. Although the standing waves in a hydraulic jump are used by migrating trout and salmon to gain additional energy to help them jump a falls, they aren't places a trout will tarry for long, because the strong turbulence keeps them off-balance and makes drift feeding difficult.

Hydraulic jumps don't just happen at waterfalls. They also happen behind boulders or other objects like bridge pylons in fast flows. Thus, if you see standing waves in the current, you won't find trout directly under them. They may be off to the side of a standing wave, but as trout fishing often requires precise casts, avoiding standing waves will keep you from making unproductive casts.

You have no doubt seen bumps in the water's surface downstream of midstream rocks and other obstructions. Sometimes the bumps are quite distinct; other times you'll see just a slight bump with a wake behind it. The bump will be visible a bit downstream of the obstruction, so if you're trying to target a trout lying in front of a rock, take care to place your cast well above the bump because the hydraulic jump behind a rock gets pushed downstream of the current. And the width of the wake behind the bump tells you how attractive the spot behind the rock may be for trout. A wide wake indicates subcritical flow, turbulence will be less severe, and trout might be closer to the rock. A narrow wake (less than about 45 degrees) indicates supercritical flow, and trout, if present at all, will be further downstream from the rock.

Hydraulic drops are when flow quickly transforms from subcritical to supercritical. In other words, a chute. You've seen this on rivers, where the slope of the riverbed changes from moderate to steep, and the water changes from either smooth, slow flow or gentle riffle to very fast and usually quite smooth. Typically the flow

A waterfall is a classic hydraulic jump. The sudden release of energy forms strong turbulence at the base of the falls and decreases downstream velocity. The slower water just beyond the turbulence is the result of that decrease in downstream velocity.

The bump formed by a submerged rock will show on the surface downstream of the rock. There is strong turbulence just behind the bump, and it lessens just downstream of that point—which is the place you are most likely to find a trout.

The narrow wake (less than 45 degrees) below this rock tells you it is in supercritical flow. There will be strong turbulence below the rock, and trout are not likely to live immediately behind it.

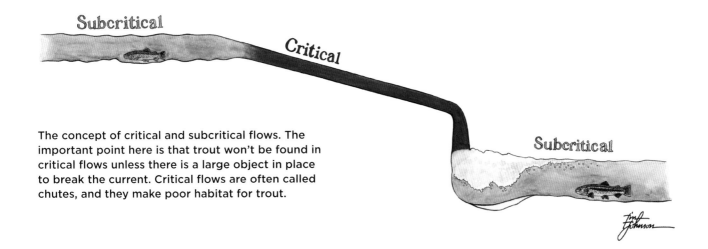

The concept of critical and subcritical flows. The important point here is that trout won't be found in critical flows unless there is a large object in place to break the current. Critical flows are often called chutes, and they make poor habitat for trout.

is so strong that it pushes rocks or logs farther downstream, so the bottom is flat and featureless. There are few places for a trout to hold in a hydraulic drop because there is no protection from the supercritical flow, except behind the occasional large rock that refuses to budge in the strong current. Invariably, when the hydraulic drop meets a deeper pool of riverbed with a lesser slope, a hydraulic jump is formed. Below that jump, where turbulence lessens, is where you'll find trout. You can judge that spot by looking for the place where the standing waves dampen into gentle riffles.

Everything you've read in this chapter is stylized and theoretical, and it's seldom as clean-cut as a diagram in a book. When you get on the river, you'll notice that many of these scenarios happen in concert with others, further complicating all the stuff we don't know about river hydraulics. But I think having a basic understanding of hydraulics will still help you find trout—and, just as important, rule out where they are unlikely to live.

The wide wake behind this rock indicates subcritical flow. Trout could be found closer to this rock because there is less turbulence behind it.

Just a quick glance at this spring creek tells you the water temperature will remain relatively constant year-round, the water will be on the alkaline side, and trout growth will be rapid because of the abundant food supply. And because trout find it comfortable nearly anywhere in a stream like this, reading the water can be tough unless you see them in the clear water—which you often do.

CHAPTER 3

Temperature, Water Chemistry, and Growth

S urprisingly, the productivity of a running water ecosystem can also help you predict where to find trout. How fast a trout grows in any given stream may not tell you where to find them, but it does tell you if there is a potential in a river for finding very large trout—and they *do* have places they like more than others. Plus, it's just interesting, geeky stuff about these fish that fascinates us.

WATER TEMPERATURE AND DISSOLVED OXYGEN

Water temperature is everything to trout. Like most cold-blooded animals, they are stenothermic, or adapted to a narrow range of temperatures. For most trout, the range they can survive is from the freezing point of water up to the high 70s. However, they have an optimum range, where feeding, activity, and growth are at a maximum, and this temperature range is from about 50 degrees to 65 degrees. When water temperatures are over or under this range, trout will move, if they can, to warmer or colder water.

Some species have slightly different preferences—for instance, brook trout have a slightly lower optimum and lethal temperature—but it's difficult to put an exact number on these temperatures because some trout populations can acclimatize to higher or lower temperatures. For instance, rainbow trout in a hatchery in Virginia were raised at different temperatures and their optimum temperatures were then observed. Fish raised at 42.6 degrees preferred water from 41 to 55 degrees. At the other end of the scale, fish raised at 75.2 degrees preferred water from 66 to 77 degrees. Yes, it was an experimental setting and those numbers might not happen in the wild, but it does show us a trout's ability to acclimate to local conditions. And, in fact, races of rainbow trout have been found in desert environments that can tolerate water temperatures up to 85 degrees—10 full degrees above what we normally think of us their lethal limit. And trout in high-altitude streams and lakes where water temperatures seldom get above 50 degrees have a much lower optimum feeding range.

You can catch trout in the winter, almost down to the freezing point of water, but you'll need to keep an eye on water temperatures and fish for them in specific water types to be successful. Trout don't feed as often or as regularly in cold water, but they do feed a bit almost every day.

Sources of Water Temperature

Water temperature in a river does not just come from the water in the river's main channel but also from other sources, and the amount these sources can add over a river's course can vary depending on their inputs. Talking to US Forest Service biologist Becky Flitcroft, who is based in California and studies the effects of fires and other disturbances on fish populations, she reminded me that the water in a river, and thus its temperature, has three inputs. Induction is the water coming from upstream, and this is often the main driver of temperature. But also factored into the equation is insolation, which is the amount of sunlight hitting the water and even includes the color of the rocks on the bottom of a stream, as dark rocks absorb more heat than light rocks. A third input, which we often ignore because it's hard to spot, is the hyporheic zone, or where groundwater infiltrates the riverbed.

In cold-water periods, just a few degrees difference in water temperature can bring fish more out in the open and into feeding positions, and any time the water warms even slightly the fish will be stimulated to feed. One sunny winter day I was fishing the upper Roaring Fork in Colorado with my friend Patrick McCord. When we got to the river the water was 41 degrees, and Patrick explained to me that only two more degrees of warmth would get the fish on the move. Sure enough, by mid-morning the water hit 43 degrees, and in places that seemed lifeless a couple of hours ago the fish were eagerly eating small olive nymphs and we even saw a few rise.

Knowing this can help you find trout in winter. Look for places where the sun hits the water early and stays on the river for as long as possible. Meadows and rivers with wide floodplains will offer the best fishing. Long stretches of canyon water where the sun doesn't reach the water or narrow floodplains lined with conifers won't give the water as much solar heat. Pay attention to the areas downstream of these open spots as well. Water has a high thermal resistance, which means it gains and loses heat with difficulty, so just a small patch of sunlight won't do you much good. You need a few hundred feet of exposure at least, but it also means the water will hold its heat well downstream of the sun exposure, even if that water flows through a shady canyon.

Streams in narrow valleys or in deep canyons may not get much sun during the winter, so check the surrounding topography before a winter expedition to make sure at least some sunlight gets to the water. Otherwise, the water might not warm enough to get trout actively feeding.

Steam rising from a river on a subzero morning usually indicates the presence of a spring, which releases warmer groundwater into the channel. This part of the river will be slightly warmer in winter, thus trout may move into this zone and feed. These spots are important to note for other times of the year because they'll also be cooler at the height of summer.

Looking for hyporheic zones is a lot trickier than finding places where sun hits the water but can be even more important in finding trout in both winter and summer. Groundwater reflects the mean annual temperature in any given region, which means this water is warmer than surface water in the winter and colder in the summer. In most of the trout zones in North America, groundwater temperatures are between 45 and 55 degrees, slightly warmer in the more southern tailwater zones. When you have a trout stream in the dead of winter where the induction temperature is in the mid to high 30s, an influx of groundwater at 48 degrees can offer the trout the equivalent of a vacation to Florida. Ten degrees at these temperatures is a dramatic increase to a cold-blooded aquatic creature, and as a result their metabolism and feeding activity will escalate. And the more they eat, the more likely we can catch them.

How do you find these places? One way is to look for surface springs entering rivers. On one southern Vermont stream that is open year-round (most Vermont streams are legally closed during the winter), Pete Kutzer and Shawn Combs took me to a spot that had been

producing well even in the dead of winter. We felt lucky to catch a few wild browns and rainbows in one short stretch, and when I asked Pete why he thought the fish were feeding in this pool, he pointed across the river. There was a hint of green where a bed of watercress poked through the snow along the banks, masking a diminutive spring entering the river. The trickle of water at the surface probably belied a more substantial volume entering the river below the surface. It was enough to keep the fish happy.

Groundwater that enters a river below the surface, directly into the streambed, is almost impossible to spot unless you swim or wet wade in a river during the summer and suddenly feel a cold burst of water around your legs. But I have found a way to find these places in the dead of winter, on days so cold you wouldn't dare fish. On very cold mornings, 10 degrees or below, you can walk or drive along rivers, looking for steam (I guess it might be better described as ice fog). Groundwater entering a river is so much warmer than the air that it causes ice crystals to condense above the surface, sometimes rising many feet into the air and giving away a warm spot in a dramatic manner. As I understand it, the warmer water has a higher saturation vapor pressure, thus condensing above the surface into ice fog. So take a trip to your favorite river on the coldest mornings of the year and make a note of where you see steam rising. Not only will these places be better fishing during the winter because of the warmer water, but they'll be better fishing in the heat of summer when these spots will offer colder water, and thus more oxygen, than other places in the river.

If you're lucky enough to fish for trout in tailwater rivers at the southern limit of trout abundance (actually farther south than the historical range of trout, because many southern tailwater fisheries lowered summertime water temperatures to a range hospitable to trout), trout won't always be restricted only to deep, slow pools. On rivers like the White and Little Red in Arkansas or the San Juan in New Mexico, water temperatures flowing out of bottom-release dams are even colder than groundwater. This is because cold water is denser than warm water and sinks to the bottoms of these reservoirs during the colder months when the ambient air temperatures

are cold, and because of the insulating nature of water these cold temperatures can last throughout the summer. So even though groundwater temperature in Mountain Home, Arkansas, is 62 degrees, the water coming out of the bottom of Bull Shoals Reservoir on the White River is between 50 and 60 degrees year-round. It's still a decent temperature for winter fishing but affords even more relief for trout in the blazing heat of southern summers, when rivers that don't have a cold tailwater release on them would be lethal to trout.

Cold Temperatures

Trout are cold-blooded, and the temperature of the water they're suspended in determines their metabolism. Trout will feed right down to the freezing point of water, but they'll do so sparingly, their feeding activity rising as their metabolism goes into higher gear. Exactly how active a trout will feed in lower water temperatures, below 45 degrees, varies with the amount of food available and even with local races of trout, because a trout living year-round in very cold water, like in a glacial stream, can adapt to feeding at lower temperatures

A spring seep running into the Madison River in Montana at the height of a drought. It will give trout an added boost of cold water in the summer and warmth during the winter months. Sometimes these springs aren't easy to spot, but keep your eye out for them because they can point to concentrations of trout in winter and summer. In winter, they are sometimes easier to spot because they'll be the only spot of green in an otherwise brown and frozen bank.

You can see one reason trout move into deeper water in winter. If they stay in shallow water, they risk getting slammed with pieces of floating ice and slush.

than trout in more temperate rivers where they have the opportunity to feed in warmer water later in the season.

Trout need *some* current to wash dissolved oxygen over their gills and to remove their own waste products, but in cold water they'll usually choose slower, deeper water. Because holding in a current requires energy expenditure, when a trout feeds sparingly it needs to find slower-water refuges so its energy budget does not go negative. In most populations in winter, trout may exhibit a slight decrease in weight or just maintain their body mass, which they make up in spring and summer with warmer water and more abundant food.

In partially frozen rivers, trout also seek slower, deeper water to avoid floating ice and slush. This is not an inconsiderable problem. If a trout spends the day dodging chunks of ice and slush, it will soon waste away, burning energy without gaining any calories in return. Thus when looking for trout in the winter, look for places protected from the main flow and deep enough to provide sanctuary from floating ice above. Even if no floating ice is present, imagine places where trout will not be exposed to this danger. Pools or pockets of slow water deeper than 3 feet will provide this kind of protection.

In a study in the Bitterroot drainage in Montana, cutthroats and bull trout made downstream migrations to find suitable winter habitat, as much as three-quarters of a mile. Their movement was greater in the shallower middle reaches of the streams because periodic freezing and thawing displaced the fish. The researchers found that some fish preferred beaver ponds and pools with large amounts of woody debris, while others used pools with large boulders. They also found that trout decreased their use of submerged cover once surface ice formed—but a fat lot of good that does us in finding trout in the winter!

This does not mean trout in winter will always hide deep in root wads or mud deposits, in suspended animation or otherwise inactive. In two separate studies of wild trout in winter, one of rainbows and browns in California and one with brown and brook trout in Ontario, empty stomachs were found in only 4 percent of the fish in both studies. Most stomachs were found to be about 50 percent full during the winter, but as it takes three to four days at 36 degrees to fully evacuate a trout stomach, it's difficult to determine exactly when and how much those trout fed. But feed they did, on insects and small crustaceans like scuds from the drift, and you can't feed on drift when your head is tucked into a root wad.

So in winter, look for trout in places with deeper, slower water off to the side of the main current thread in the center of the channel (because the current may be too fast there), but don't look for them in stagnant places with no current at all because trout need a bit of current for feeding and for survival.

If water temperatures warm during the day, due to a warm rain or plenty of sunlight on the water, trout may move into riffles and faster water to take advantage of drifting food for an hour or so. My money would still be on the deeper, slower water, but this water is tougher to fish than shallow riffles so if you see a few insects in the air or on the water, a bit of time spent on water we don't normally think of as winter habitat might be worth a few casts. They won't move far, though, so look for riffles at the head of deep, slow pools, where trout can easily slide up into them.

Author and guide George Daniel of central Pennsylvania considers water temperatures in the high 30s or low 40s "very fishable," but the very best conditions for finding trout in winter, according to George, is when you get warm weather that gradually melts snow but is not substantial enough to cause flooding. And he says, "Fishing goes off the charts if you get a warm rain. As long as it doesn't flood and as long as the snow melts slowly, so it doesn't lower the water temperature, it can be the best fishing of the winter." So when winter fishing, finding trout is often as much a matter of watching the weather as it is looking at pools and riffles.

One additional feature to look for when locating trout in winter is proximity to some secure cover. I just told you a trout won't feed with its snout tucked into a root wad, but that does not mean root wads and other structure are not important. Most of a trout's serious predators are warm-blooded, so their activity levels and ability to chase a trout in cold water gives them an advantage over a sluggish trout. Mink, otters, herons, mergansers, eagles, and ospreys don't hibernate and need to feed actively in cold weather. The places I find trout in the winter always have a secure hiding place close by. So if a slow, deep pool has a smooth bottom with no rocks or logs in it, even if it's the right depth and speed, it's unlikely to hold trout. Look for slower, deeper places that are a couple of flips of a tail away from hiding places and you'll be more likely to find trout.

The places trout find to be safe during the winter are limited in most rivers. Habitat with enough slow current, depth, and cover, plus protection from drifting ice, may be found in only a few places in a given mile of river. Trout seem to lose a lot of their territorial behavior

In cold water, trout move into winter refuge areas where the water is slower and deeper. They need some current, but prefer less than at other times of the year because they try to conserve energy when their metabolism is lower.

On a sunny day, if the water temperature warms slightly, trout may move into faster water to feed. Smart money is still on the slow, deep stretches, but there is always hope . . .

under these conditions as well, so you may find them ganged up in places.

Rainbow trout in particular seem to form winter pods, so if you catch one rainbow from a pool, chances are there will be more in the same spot. And those spots can change with a change in water levels or ice formations. I was delighted to find seven rainbow trout in one small pocket in my backyard river in January of 2021. It was too early for a spawning aggregation, so I assumed the trout were there because the spot offered good winter protection. It wasn't the deepest or slowest of the pools in this part of the river, but it did offer a nice root wad just downstream of where the trout congregated. With a sharp cold spell, the level of the river dropped and the fish disappeared. I never saw them again and assumed they found a deeper spot, somewhere more difficult for me to detect on a sunny day. Or maybe they moved so far that they weren't along my daily dog-walking route.

One added note of caution when you go searching for winter trout: Because the amount of available habitat is limited during winter and trout may burn a lot of

In winter, look for places with wide floodplains exposed to the sun. The water will warm quicker and trout will be more likely to feed.

energy when being played by an angler, be careful how you play these fish. Get them in as quickly as possible. This lessens the amount of energy they burn, but it also gives you a better chance to release them close to their winter refuge. If you lead a fish downstream through a riffle into the next pool, that fish will be forced to work back upstream to its refuge—or may even waste a lot of energy looking for a new refuge if it can't get back.

Do trout move upstream or downstream during the winter? I don't know of any scientific studies that examined wild trout movement in winter, but I suspect most fish move downstream, because as you move down through a river's course, you are more likely to find those slow, deep overwintering pools. Trout may even move into marginal habitat in the lower reaches of rivers, where the water gets too warm and depleted of oxygen in the summer to support trout but contains plenty of oxygenated water in the winter because cold water holds more dissolved oxygen than warm water. I know of a local river that is strictly smallmouth bass and pike water most of the year but has a number of coldwater tributaries, and trout move down out of these tributaries in the winter into the larger river, where they can find slow, deep water with lots of cover. We catch these trout occasionally in late fall when fishing for pike, and they are large enough to grab the 6-inch pike streamers we use.

Optimal Conditions

When water temperatures climb into the high 40s, magical things happen in trout streams. A trout's metabolism increases, and at the same time mayflies, stoneflies, and caddisflies begin hatching, and minnows, crayfish, and scuds become more active. The cold-blooded creatures of this world begin their periods of peak activity, and it's not an accident that trout become more active at the same time as their prey.

The optimum temperature for trout, when most of their activity and all of their growth happens, ranges

Optimal temperature time: Insects are hatching, water temperatures are in that prime 50- to 65-degree range for trout feeding and activity, and trout can be almost anywhere. This is where your stream-reading skills come into play because it's possible to find trout in a wide variety of water types. You have to determine which ones will be the best.

between 50 and 65 degrees, depending on the species of trout and what a local population of fish is acclimated to. Trout move out of their slower, deeper winter refuges and into riffles and runs and pools—just about any habitat that offers moderate current and at least a foot of water over their heads. It makes fishing more productive, but now your stream-reading skills and knowledge of what trout need are critical. With optimum temperatures trout will be found almost anywhere, and sorting out exactly where they're feeding can be a challenge. A fun challenge, of course.

The period of optimal activity is when we do most of our fishing and what most of this book is about. In most places, it happens between April and October, except for some high-altitude streams above the tree line in mountainous regions or places like Alaska and Labrador, where the optimum period may be shorter, perhaps from late June through August. During these temperatures you can count on trout feeding, or at least willing to feed. If you don't catch trout during these temperatures, it's wise to either change your fly and presentation or find another spot, because if you're casting over water where trout live, they should be willing to take a fly.

Some tailwaters and spring-fed streams host dense growths of aquatic vegetation, and in these streams,

fishing in the evening, after dark, and early in the morning can be slower than you might expect, despite near-optimum water temperatures at the height of the trout season. With sunlight on the water, plants increase the oxygen concentration of these streams, which are often slower moving with fewer riffles and white water than typical trout streams. However, respiration occurs 24 hours a day, and after the sun leaves the water, plants withdraw oxygen from the water. Trout also decrease their activity when the dissolved oxygen content of water drops, possibly feeling much like I do in a boring meeting in a closed room with little ventilation. Once the sun hits the water in the morning, their activity and feeding picks up.

When I was a teenager, I fished a very productive spring creek that hosted mostly small trout but I would see the occasional very large brown trout bolt out from a dense weed bed. My fishing buddy Leigh and I had done a bit of productive night fishing on other rivers, but we'd never attempted it on this stream. One day we hatched a plan, not only to night-fish the spring creek but to do it on a bit of heavily posted water owned by a private club. That fact alone made it more interesting. We sat in a diner drinking coffee until well after dark, and then snuck into the posted water, with a cautious eye

In rivers with lots of aquatic vegetation, trout won't be as active in the evening or early morning because plants respire all the time but only produce oxygen when sunlight hits the water. Trout get slightly more lethargic when oxygen levels are lower.

on the house where Joe, the caretaker, lived. When the lights in his house winked out, we began fishing. And we fished all night without a single strike. I know we fished over a number of large trout, and I can only theorize that the low oxygen content because of the profuse beds of chara (a multicellular alga that has stems and leaflike structures) and watercress lowered the activity level of the fish.

Warm Temperatures

Warming waters present challenges for trout and anglers at the upper end. Trout require somewhere between 2 and 4 parts per million (ppm) of oxygen to survive, but as the water warms, it holds less dissolved oxygen. During the colder months, when water temperatures are between 32 and 65 degrees, dissolved oxygen levels in a trout stream are saturated and in the 10 to 12 ppm range. As waters warm later in the season, oxygen levels can get low enough to stress trout, or at the extreme of around 80 degrees, kill them outright. It's not just temperature, because organic material from pollution or from logging slash removes oxygen from the water as it decomposes. (In a study in Oregon, logging slash in streams reduced the normal 10 to 12 ppm of oxygen down to less than 1 ppm—well below the lethal limit for trout.) But temperature is the main driving factor.

The problem trout face is that as water temperatures increase, their respiration rate increases, using up more oxygen. They need more food at high temperatures but can't get it because the exertion of finding enough food increases their oxygen demand even more. This is why it's quite easy to catch trout at water temperatures above 70 degrees, but it's not a wise decision and many trout waters legally close when water temperatures get too high. The stress we put a trout through when playing it only piles onto their increased oxygen demand at a time when water doesn't hold enough oxygen for them to get what they need. A trout you catch at 72 degrees might swim away fine, but it's likely that fish will soon suffocate under a logjam from lack of oxygen.

When water temperatures get above about 65 degrees, some trout migrate to find cooler water and more oxygen. Some stay in place, or are unable to move because low water conditions prevent them from migrating. Trout respond to suboptimum temperatures in what is called reactive behavioral thermoregulation—in other words, in response to short-term water temperature changes, they move to find more optimum temperatures. And it's unclear if they move to find cooler water from past experience, which could be more of a factor among older fish that have learned over the seasons, or if they just bumble around until they feel a cold water influx and move to it.

As anglers, this presents us with an ethical conundrum. It's one thing to find a stream, or a section of a stream, where cooler water has encouraged a high

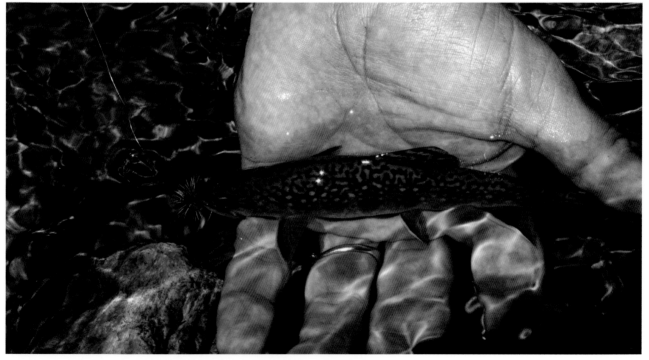

Brook trout are the most sensitive to warm water temperature of all our common trout species and will be the first to move to find cooler water. Where it's best to stop fishing for other trout species at about 68 degrees, if brook trout are present you should probably quit when it hits 65.

Even though good practice suggests we should stop fishing for browns, rainbows, and cutthroats at 68 degrees, rainbows have been shown to be highly adaptable to extremes in water temperature and isolated populations have been shown to be quite healthy at water temperatures into the 70s. However, you never know, so it's always best to quit at 68.

concentration of trout over a stretch of 100 yards to several miles. I think that's fair game. It's quite another to find a pod of twenty trout with their noses all tucked into a tiny cold spring inflow, or at the mouth of a cooler tributary stream. Fishing for those fish is akin to an adult fishing in a tiny pond that has just been stocked for a kids' fishing derby. So when looking for trout in warmer weather, I think it's OK to look for them in places that offer cooler water if water temperatures in the main flow of a river are in the mid-60s, but at 70 degrees, even if you can find trout in small pockets that offer cooler water, you'll likely have to play them through 70-degree water and that could be lethal. Just find someplace else or go chase bass or carp or bluegills.

In the days before we knew so much about the effects of high temperature on trout survival, we were a lot more cavalier. On my first trip to the Rocky Mountains in the 1970s, I just had to fish the Firehole, even though it was late summer and water temperatures in the river, because of all the thermal activity, were well above what is dangerous for trout. But that river is probably the most intriguing trout stream in the world, surrounded by geysers, mud pots, fumaroles, and hot springs. A friend who lived and guided in West Yellowstone told me to

fish Iron Spring Creek, a tributary of the Firehole that enters just below Biscuit Basin Geyser. As I waded up the Firehole, marveling at the small unmarked thermal features along its course, I saw no trout. But as I turned right and followed Iron Spring Creek, within 50 yards of the main river I found a concentration of about a dozen browns and rainbows packed into a small pocket. With a size 18 Pheasant Tail nymph, I was able to pluck half of those fish from the pod until the challenge from those vulnerable trout faded. I walked back, feeling like a used car salesman in a lot full of trust-fund college students with credit cards.

Sixty-six degrees seems to be the avoidance temperature of most trout, and you can expect them to shuffle around at this point. Even brook trout, which are not known to survive in higher water temperatures as well as browns, rainbows, and cutthroats, are quite happy at 66 degrees. But the char genus, of which brook trout (as well as lake trout and bull trout) belong, is not as adaptable to increases in water temperature beyond that point. True trout—browns, rainbows, and cutthroats— once acclimated to a higher temperature, can adapt to higher temperatures for survival, but brook trout do not have this adaptability and will die or migrate once temperatures reach the high 60s. For instance, hatchery rainbow trout, when acclimated to 69.8-degree water temperatures, didn't seek avoidance of warmer water until it reached 73.4 degrees. This was, however, in a hatchery where the stresses of life in the wild and finding food were absent, but although it took place in an artificial environment, it did show the potential adaptability of rainbows.

Finding Cooler Water

Stressing again that you should look for broad sources of cooler water, not tiny refuges, what can you do to find active trout that you can ethically stalk, catch, and release? If the main stem of a river is in the mid-60s, where trout have moved to get into more comfortable temperatures, you might find trout within a short walk or drift. If the stream you intend to fish is above 70 degrees, though, it's not a matter of just walking along the bank or moving downstream in your raft or drift boat. To successfully find safe places to fish in hot weather, you'll need to pick up and move, sometimes many miles away.

You'll find cooler temperatures as you move upstream, or if you explore a major tributary. Headwaters and tributaries are closer to sources of groundwater, are higher in elevation where air temperatures are cooler, and are often less developed and more shaded than the downstream reaches of a river. You may have to explore many miles upstream, but a drive or hike along a river, taking temperatures as you go, will help you find more active trout that you can fish for without fatal stress.

In some river systems, there's a possibility of finding cooler water in downstream reaches because of active groundwater influxes along an alluvial plane. The middle section of the Battenkill in Vermont, halfway between its headwaters and the wider, riffled section that runs into New York State, is often cooler than its very upper reaches in hot weather. The broad Valley of Vermont is porous glacial till and the mountains framing the valley force groundwater to the surface, within the bed of the river, cooling its middle reaches and offering more oxygen and comfortable temperatures.

The power of the Snake and Yellowstone Rivers, in their alluvial plains, forces water up against tight bends

Smaller tributaries are typically colder than the larger river they enter and may offer a cold-water refuge. Their influence may extend for quite a distance downstream, but in very warm weather it's not a good idea to fish at their mouths, because trout may be concentrated there and quite vulnerable.

The tight bends in this meadow stream help keep it cooler during the summer. Water will be forced underground at each bend and will be cooled by the soil as it seeps back into the riverbed.

in the river, where some of the water runs underground for a distance, cooling as it progresses, and then emerges back into the main channel as much as 10 degrees cooler. The famous spring creeks in both watersheds are a combination of true groundwater springs with some influence from seeps off the main channel. Any river with numerous bends probably exhibits some of this as well, so look for places where a river has numerous tight bends instead of long, straight stretches. I've often located these spots on rivers where I see a tiny patch of watercress, because this plant thrives in cooler water. It looks like a spring entering a river but it's not a true spring, just a cooler seep from the upstream side of a bend.

Groundwater can be a mixed blessing. Although it will cool river stretches where it enters, the groundwater itself can be very low in dissolved oxygen until it mixes with water exposed to the air. Biologist Becky Flitcroft told me that she needs to constantly remind river managers that they need to look at oxygen levels and not just temperatures, because bacteria and other creatures live in the substrate underground and they can use up most of the oxygen by the time it reaches the surface. Nitrogen supersaturation, in groundwater and in cold water coming into a river below a dam, can also be detrimental to trout, similar to the way divers are affected by the bends.

I grew up fishing a spring creek that emerged from the ground at about 10,000 gallons per minute within 100 yards of its source. Occasionally I would fish right up to the source of the springs, but I always found the trout population there to be extremely sparse, and the few fish I caught were in poor condition—long and snaky, lackluster fighters, and often with bulbous, goggle eyes like cartoon characters. Until the creek flowed a bit and oxygen saturated the water and nitrogen bubbled out of it, fishing wasn't worth the effort. You'll see similar issues in tailwaters if you fish right at the base of the dam, and you'll find better trout habitat farther downstream from sources of cold water, where the cooling effect is still felt but the water is richer in dissolved oxygen.

With water temperatures in the 60s, trout will often relocate below the mouths of colder tributary streams. At these temperatures, it's not so much that trout are

Riffles add oxygen to places that might be lower in oxygen because of higher water temperatures. How far that influence travels downstream is a matter for speculation.

in danger or starved for oxygen, but the slightly cooler water slows down their metabolism slightly, and in periods when they're not feeding they don't lose as much energy. Even if a tributary has gone dry in low-water periods, don't assume it lacks enticement for trout. The flow that was rushing in the spring is still trickling underground below the streambed, cooling the main river. This cooling effect can extend many yards below the mouth of a tributary. A quick check with your thermometer can give you an idea how far downstream it extends.

The importance of deep pools in providing thermal refuge for trout is probably overrated. Water in rivers is never deep enough to truly stratify as it does in lakes, and because the constantly moving water gives off heat at such a slow rate, the temperature at the bottom of a deep pool will be nearly the same as the rest of the river. However, because the bottom of a 6-foot-deep pool is well below the level of the banks and closer to a potential groundwater flow, there may be hidden springs seeping in. I think that deep pools, in times of low flow and warm temperatures, may offer more protection from predators than they do cooler temperatures. We'll talk about this more when we examine the importance of cover.

In a similar vein, a short portion of shade provides no thermal relief. You will absolutely find more trout in the shade during high summer, but only because it hides trout from things that want to eat them, not because it's cooler. Coming back to the concept of high thermal resistance of water, it takes a long expanse of shade to offer cooler water. While a mile of heavily shaded river, whether from the deep recesses of a canyon or a heavily forested area, might lower the temperature of the water a degree or two, a bathtub length of shade along an exposed stretch of river won't lower the temperature a bit.

During low, warm water you'll find more trout in riffles. Conventional wisdom tells us the trout are there because of the increased oxygen supply, as the churning of the water in riffles increases the gas exchange. I'm not so sure that's the reason they move into riffles. I don't know how long it takes the increased oxygen concentration to drop off below a riffle, and it probably depends on many factors, like the temperature of the water and air and the flow velocity, but I suspect this increased oxygen may carry well below riffles. I *do* know that the faster flow in riffles provides a steadier supply of aquatic insects than slow, flat water, and that riffles provide much protection from overhead predators

Although the water just below a dam release on a tailwater will be warmer in the winter and cooler in the summer, it may also have a lower oxygen concentration when drawn from the bottom of a large reservoir. For best fishing, it's sometimes best to get a few hundred yards below the dam so that the water has time to absorb more dissolved oxygen.

A deep pool might offer protection from predators during the summer, but it won't do much to cool the water, as rivers don't stratify as lakes do.

because trout are harder to see under the broken surface. I can't find any scientific literature on this, and the biologists I've talked to don't have an answer. I actually looked into buying a dissolved oxygen meter so I could measure the oxygen content within a riffle and then continue to measure it farther downstream to see how much it attenuates. But meters cost as much as a good camera and it seems silly just to prove my point. Trout will be found in riffles in low, warm water regardless, and that, I guess, is as much as we need to know.

Finding cooler water in summer may just be a matter of timing. Trout rivers reach their minimum temperature at about dawn and warm throughout the day, well into the evening. I'm constantly hearing about "fishing in the evening when the water cools down" but water temperatures are slow to give off heat—again because of that thermal resistance issue. After being baked in the sun all day, a river that was in the 70s during the day may cool down a degree or two in the evening, but really not enough to make fishing a smart move. Aquatic insects, which aren't as sensitive to high temperatures as trout, may hatch profusely in the evening during the summer, and trout may feed on them, but that does not make fishing for the trout a good idea. This is why Montana, and increasingly other states, has instituted what are called "Hoot Owl Restrictions." Under this regulation, which

can be temporary for a few days or for an entire season in dire circumstances, fishing must stop between 2:00 p.m. and midnight. Currently the lower Madison River is permanently under Hoot Owl Restrictions from July 15 through August 15, and other rivers are temporarily affected when daytime temperatures exceed 73 degrees for three consecutive days.

So regulations or not, fishing in the morning during hot weather just makes sense. In fact, in my own experience, even in the height of summer, there is a peak in feeding activity around midmorning when water temperatures rise. The water may be coolest at dawn, but trout seem to respond favorably to rising water temperatures, which makes sense because their metabolism increases. Aquatic insects also respond to these increases by hatching as the water warms slightly, and also terrestrial insects become more active and fall into the water as the sun warms them in the morning.

Colder water is essential in summer fishing, but a sudden drop in temperature may make it difficult to find trout in an agreeable mood, even if the temperature drops from marginal to optimal temperatures. Some fishing buddies and I once met the great Joe Humphreys on the Delaware River for a few days of fishing. The West Branch of the Delaware had been running at 66 degrees, a decent temperature for fishing. However, hot weather had driven water temperatures in the lower main stem of the river above 75 degrees, and river managers called for a release of cold water from Cannonsville Reservoir on the West Branch to help mitigate the temperatures farther down the river. The day we arrived, the cold-water releases on the West Branch dropped the temperature to 58 degrees, a near-perfect temperature for trout fishing. However, the sudden drop in temperature put the fish into near-torpor, and in a river where even in summer you can expect to catch a half-dozen fish or more in a day, I think two of us caught a fish and the rest were blanked. Of course, a day or two after we left, the trout acclimated to the colder temperatures and fishing was off the charts. So water temperature as a snapshot is not as important a predictor of finding trout as is change in water temperature, and warming water will always predict better fishing as long as the warming trend does not push water temperatures into the 70s.

HOW WATER CHEMISTRY PREDICTS WHERE YOU WILL FIND TROUT

Knowing a bit about the water chemistry in a trout stream is not one of the most important aspects of finding trout, but it can help. It's also a factor in how big trout will grow in any given river because it affects their food supply, and just knowing that a stream will hold big trout does give you some hints on where to fish.

Most biologists who have studied the effects of water chemistry on trout have concluded that habitat trumps chemistry in gauging how productive a stream will be, which makes sense. Food supply is usually not a limiting factor in a trout population, as trout set up feeding stations where they will be safe from predators and where they can feed without wasting too much energy. They then take what they can get from the drifting food, and if they get a lot of it, they grow bigger. But it's not like a trout lying downstream of a bunch of other trout will starve because they eat all the food before it gets to the lower fish. Trout don't graze like cattle, thus they don't overexploit their food supply—at least drift-feeders in streams don't. Trout in lakes and ponds that feed mainly on baitfish can diminish the food supply to dangerous levels, but this book is about finding trout in moving water.

The amount of invertebrate food available per a given square foot of bottom determines whether a river is relatively sterile or rich. It's a continuum, from a stream with water so pure that it's almost distilled water, as in

Don't confuse aquatic mosses with high productivity in a trout stream. Moss will be more commonly found in tea-colored, acidic, infertile streams. The water color alone gives you a clue that fish here won't have much food and will only be found in places that give them the best access to drifting insects.

There is obvious spring influence in this stream, as you can see the spring pouring from the mountainside in the background. The stream is full of rooted aquatic plants like watercress and ranunculus, indicating high alkalinity and high productivity. Trout in water like this can be almost anywhere, especially since spring creeks usually have moderate currents.

a melting glacier, where food is scarce, to a streambed covered with caddis, mayfly, stonefly, and midge larvae, plus the addition of crustaceans like crayfish and scuds and sow bugs. And richer streams with more invertebrate food will also support more baitfish that grow those outsized trout that can't get enough calories from drift feeding on insects. In those streams you need to pay attention not only to drift-feeding locations, but also to deeper, brushy lairs where big trout may be lying in wait to ambush bigger food.

Why is this important in finding trout? Because in an infertile stream, trout can't get enough drifting food unless they are in the main current, so you'll only find feeding trout close to the main current threads, in the prime locations that give them enough food. In a very rich or fertile stream, those marginal places farther from the main current will also offer enough drifting prey to support a trout, so you'll not only find more trout, but you'll find them in unlikely places like backwaters and slower current. Infertile streams can be fished quickly, just "skimming the cream" off the water and only fishing

the prime spots. In a richer, more productive stream, you'll need to pay more attention to every nook and cranny because trout can be almost anywhere. You still need to know how to read currents and understand what good habitat looks like, but it can affect the pace at which you fish and where you can expect to find trout.

The one instance where just guessing at the relative richness of a stream can throw you off is where you have a substantial allochthonous food supply—in other words, stuff that gets into a river that does not live in the water. Most of the drift food in a trout stream is autochthonous or bred in the stream, like the aquatic insect larvae and crustaceans that live there. However, prey that drops into the river, like terrestrial insects, mice, and frogs, can provide a substantial source of food. In fact, there's a theory that if trout have a short window of feeding at near-optimum temperatures with a substantial food supply for that period, they can grow very large because the rest of the year they kick back and don't feed much, thus wasting little energy chasing food because they already got enough for the year. This could be why brook trout in Labrador grow so large—for a very short period in summer they gorge on large mayflies and mice, and the rest of the year, in these cold, infertile streams, they coast. It's been suggested as well that the huge trout in New Zealand that live in crystal clear, relatively infertile streams get so big because they gorge for a short period each year on large beetles and cicadas.

To put this into a less exotic scenario, if you fish an infertile stream in August where you'd expect trout to be close to the main drift lanes and you see lots of grasshoppers along the bank, remain vigilant and look for trout in places you might not find them earlier in the year. Let's get mildly geeky for a bit and look into why some streams are richer than others. Then we'll put this into a more practical perspective—how you can eyeball a stream to guess at its richness.

The terms pH, hardness, conductivity, and alkalinity are all related, and give us an indication of how productive a watershed might be. This needs to be qualified, though. Because we're interested only in trout here, we need to assume that both water temperature and habitat diversity (in other words, the abundance of large and small rocks or large woody debris) are within acceptable limits for trout, because they are far more important than water chemistry. But provided those needs are met, water chemistry can tell you something about the trout population. These chemical factors can either affect trout directly or affect the quality and quantity of their food supply—and where in a stream they feed.

pH and Acidity

As you may remember from your high school chemistry, pH measures the concentration of positive hydrogen ions in a sample of liquid—in other words, its acidity or alkalinity. A pH of 7 is neutral, and in trout waters anything above 7 until about 9, which is realistically the limit of trout streams, is alkaline. Anything below 7 is acidic. Trout waters can be as low as about 3.5; any lower than that, trout survival is unlikely. Brook trout are the most tolerant of acidic waters and can live and spawn down to that lower limit. Browns, rainbows, and cutthroats can be found in waters down to about 5 but they can't successfully spawn in waters lower than 6.5, so although you can find these species in waters with a pH lower than 6, they were either spawned somewhere else and moved into that area or were stocked from a hatchery.

Acidity in water is bad for trout and most of the stuff they eat. Even brook trout are healthier in waters with a pH above 6, despite the fact that they can tolerate much more acidity. But in higher acidity they'll be smaller and skinnier than in more alkaline waters. It's also important to note that pH is on a logarithmic scale, so a pH of 6 is ten times as acidic as water at the neutral level of 7.

Where does the acidity in water come from? Pure distilled water is neutral, but rainwater and groundwater pick up various compounds as they come in contact with air and soil. First, rainwater naturally reacts with carbon dioxide in the air to form weak carbonic acid. Even in a pristine world, untouched by man, rainwater is naturally acidic both from this reaction and from volcanic eruptions, where sulfur dioxide in the air forms weak sulfuric acid. Nitrogen and sulfur compounds from burning fossil fuels also react with rainwater to produce weak nitric and sulfuric acids. Decomposing organic material in the soil adds acidity via humic acids.

Man-influenced acidity in rainwater has improved from a peak in the 1960s and '70s. Adirondack lakes, many of which held robust trout populations based on surveys in the 1920s, became so acidic that they could not support trout—in fact, most aquatic life disappeared. Similar effects were seen in Scandinavian lakes and streams because they were downwind of coal-burning plants in England and central Europe. Unfortunately the Adirondacks lie downwind in the bull's-eye of plumes from coal-burning midwestern power plants, but the Clean Air Act improved pollutants in the air and acid levels have been dropping since about 1984. Some trout lakes and streams came back from the dead. Besides the countless health benefits of cleaner air, we need to stay vigilant to make sure these laws remain strong, or we'll begin to again lose these priceless trout resources.

You don't have to look very far to find other instances of the detrimental effects of high acidity in trout streams. In places where mine effluent has raised the acidity of trout streams, the fish disappear, yet mitigation of acid mine drainage results in dramatic improvements in trout survival. At very low pH values, such as in very acidic rain events or acid mine drainage, another aspect of acidity comes into play—the release of aluminum ions into the water. Aluminum in neutral or alkaline waters is insoluble, but under acidic conditions the aluminum becomes soluble and it's toxic to aquatic life. Like I said, acidity is bad.

Measuring pH exactly is not practical for anglers. The inexpensive pH kits you can fit in a pocket are not reliable, and pH meters you can trust to give you an accurate reading are expensive and bulky—not something you want to carry around in a fishing vest. I own one but I've spent a lifetime studying water chemistry, and it helps me do research for books like this. But there are ways to get a close-enough estimate of the relative pH of a trout stream just by looking at the water.

The profuse growth of filamentous algae in this spring creek is a sure sign that aquatic food will be abundant. Not only will it host lots of insects, but they'll be supplemented by a high density of freshwater crustaceans like sow bugs and scuds.

The easiest way is to just look at the color of the water. Tannic or tea-colored water is invariably on the acidic side. The tannins in water come from the decomposition of organic matter, especially conifers, and in water that is unbuffered (more on that in a bit) it stays in the water. The combination of naturally acidic rainwater, humic acids, and a lack of buffering in the streambed delivers water that is low in pH and less productive of the invertebrate foods trout need to grow quickly. You'll find this type of water in areas with bogs and beaver ponds, where much organic decomposition happens, and in places with an abundance of conifers, especially when the water flows through insoluble bedrock like granite, gneiss, and sandstone.

Crystal clear water can also be on the acidic side of neutral, although typically not as acidic as tea-colored water. This is most often found in headwater streams before they have flowed through lowland areas, which can contribute buffering capacity. Rainwater is acidic and most groundwater is naturally acidic because of decomposition in the soil, and if there is nothing in the watershed to neutralize this acidity trout, and the invertebrates they eat, will be sparse. Crystal clear water can

be deceiving, though, because spring creeks that arise from limestone springs are strongly buffered, and clear water that comes from a reservoir in a tailwater can also be buffered because the landscape around the reservoir often leaches acid-reducing minerals into the system.

One way to tell if clear water is on the acidic side is to look at the aquatic vegetation. The only aquatic vegetation you'll find in acidic streams is mosses. Streams on the alkaline side of neutral will host an abundance of aquatic plants like watercress, chara (a filamentous alga), and ranunculus, which all thrive in alkaline waters. But you don't need to be a botanist. If a clear-water stream has plants in it and the plants aren't mosses, you can be reasonably sure it's on the alkaline side.

Just to review and to make sure we don't lose sight of our objective—predicting where we'll find trout—if you suspect a trout stream is acidic, it can be totally devoid of trout, or if they're present may be small and skinny. You are unlikely to find any large trout here unless they've been stocked. The trout will be relatively easy to catch because they don't see a lot of food and will grab almost anything that looks remotely edible. Trout will also be concentrated only in the prime places that offer access to drifting food, close to the main current. And if you don't catch any trout in a given area, it's a good idea to keep moving, because there won't be a high density of fish and you could even be fishing over barren water.

Dissolved Solids, Hardness, Alkalinity, and Conductivity

Let's look at the more alkaline, more productive side of the water chemistry equation. Streams with a pH of 7 or above provide us with a lot more opportunities, both in numbers of fish and sizes of them. Once it hits the ground, rainwater can be buffered by chemicals in soil to reduce the natural acidity. Groundwater emerging from springs, high in carbon dioxide and thus carbonic acid, can also be quickly buffered, and in places with limestone, dolomite, and marble it is naturally alkaline because of the geology it flows through. These rocks are high in calcium and magnesium, which we'll see are the primary elements that aid in buffering acidic water.

Here's how it works: Acidic rainwater or groundwater comes in contact with calcium or magnesium carbonate (mostly it's calcium). These compounds are normally insoluble in water, but in the presence of even the weak acids in rainwater, they dissolve as bicarbonate. The calcium bicarbonate in solution is an effective buffer system that neutralizes the acidity in water, as anyone who has ever had an upset stomach can attest. Plants also utilize bicarbonate ions, so this encourages the growth of aquatic plants, which is the reason you see so many aquatic plants in streams running through limestone bedrock. The famous chalk streams of England and France run through nearly pure calcium carbonate, but limestone, marble, and dolomite are also high in calcium and give the same effect, although not quite as dramatic.

After the carbonate/bicarbonate/CO_2 system reaches equilibrium, the soluble bicarbonate precipitates out in the water, forming a layer of calcium carbonate on plants and rocks. You'll see this in high-alkalinity streams as a thin, pale film of calcium carbonate on the rocks, and can sometimes feel it as roughness in the plants. But this solid calcium carbonate is now available if any acidity remains in the current, so the stream continues to be buffered by the precipitate for many miles, even if there is no additional source of buffering. In many of the so-called limestone streams of the mid-Atlantic, with abundant limestone belts in the bedrock, the water in the streams will be perennially chalky-looking, about the color of dishwater, because of the suspended calcium carbonate in the water. You know these streams will have a rich food supply and likely an abundance of trout just by the color of the water.

You'll hear this described as hardness, high conductivity, or dissolved solids. These are all related because most of the dissolved salts, measured by the conductivity of the water, are calcium and magnesium salts, with other salts sometimes coming into play. To get an idea of how hard or alkaline the water is in your favorite river, you can buy a very inexpensive total dissolved solids meter, which measures the concentration of dissolved chemicals in the water, which is often mostly calcium and magnesium. It's a rough estimation because iron and sodium ions, which don't contribute to the buffering of water, are also included. But it will give you at least a ballpark figure. Or you can take a bath in the river to see how easily the soap washes off.

The encouragement of plant growth, both rooted plants and algae, increases the primary productivity of a stream so that it can support a larger supply of food because the invertebrates that trout eat browse on plant matter in the stream. Instead of just relying on leaf litter that falls into an acidic stream, aquatic insects have a supercharged food supply. And because of this more abundant food, baitfish are also more abundant, which supports the growth of bigger trout. The calcium in the water also supports aquatic crustaceans like scuds, sow bugs, and crayfish, which further boosts the trout food supply.

Trout living in streams with a richer food supply will behave differently. Because they have food available all the time, they may pick and choose and not grab every morsel that goes by. Often they'll wait for an opportunity, like a hatch, when easier prey (insects trapped in the surface film) is available. And you will find them in

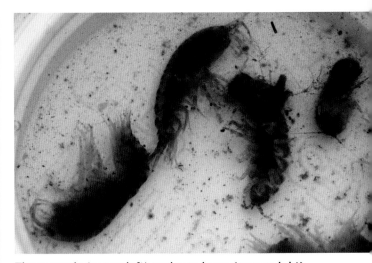

These scuds (upper left) and sow bugs (upper right) were samples from the throat of a brown trout in a spring creek. They need high concentrations of calcium to survive and are a year-round source of food for trout. Some of these crustaceans have begun to turn pink, which they do when they die or are acted upon by the digestive juices of a trout.

In the heavily forested eastern part of North America, profuse plant growth utilizes much of the nutrients in the soil, and as a result the waters are not as productive as they would be in a more arid region.

different types of water, not just in places close to the main current, because there is food everywhere. So when looking for trout in a stream you suspect is alkaline, you need to move slower, assume almost every little pocket can hold a trout, and be prepared to be surprised anyway.

Streams are not just highly acidic or highly alkaline, as you probably suspect. It's a continuum, with trout in spring creeks running through calcium-rich bedrock on one end to tannic brook trout waters that flow out of bogs at the other. The Battenkill, one of my home rivers, is an extreme case of a schizophrenic trout stream. It runs through a valley that, on the Green Mountain side, is fed by acidic tributaries with low productivity. This mountain range is characterized by ancient Appalachian metamorphic rocks that were once part of an enormous range that has eroded down to insoluble quartzite and gneiss bedrock. Streams running down its slopes are acidic and tea-colored. Yet the feeder streams from the other side of the valley are born in the Taconic mountain range, with marble bedrock and high calcium content. These tributaries run clear and alkaline. Because the

Green Mountain side is fed mainly by snowmelt and rain, in the early season the water looks tannic, yet as flows drop in late spring much of its flow comes from springs on the Taconic side, so the water is clear and often without a hit of color unless rain brings more flow from the Green Mountain side.

How does that affect where you'll find trout? The Battenkill must be dominated for the most part by its acidic side because it's not a particularly rich river, so trout populations are not dense and fish seem to be found near main current flows. However, the spring flows from the Taconic side keep the river cool for a river its size in a valley, and with a good population of sculpins and crayfish because of its alkaline nature in summer, it does produce some large trout. Springs are also highly desirable for trout spawning, so the river has excellent natural reproduction. But as I mentioned at the outset, habitat is a stronger limiting factor than chemistry, and I think the main reason the Battenkill does not have a dense population of trout is because of a lack of large woody debris and deep pools in many parts of the

In much of western North America, low rainfall combined with sparse plant growth means that more nutrients are available in the soil to be leached into rivers. On the average, they are more productive than rivers east of the Mississippi.

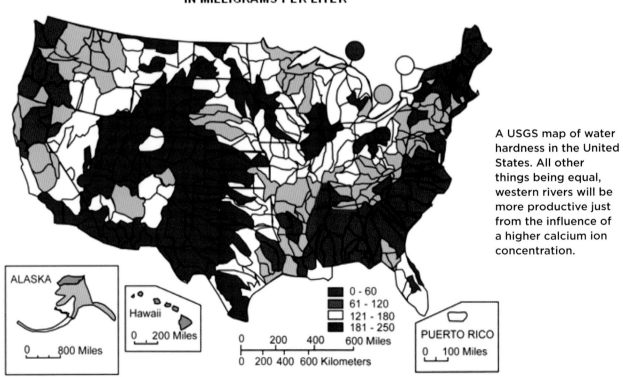

CONCENTRATION OF HARDNESS AS CALCIUM CARBONATE, IN MILLIGRAMS PER LITER

ALASKA

0   800 Miles

Hawaii

0   200 Miles

0   200   400   600 Miles

0   200 400 600 Kilometers

- 0 - 60
- 61 - 120
- 121 - 180
- 181 - 250

PUERTO RICO

0   100 Miles

A USGS map of water hardness in the United States. All other things being equal, western rivers will be more productive just from the influence of a higher calcium ion concentration.

river, so the number of feeding spots safe from overhead predators is limited.

One reason the rivers of the Mountain West have higher trout populations than eastern rivers is perhaps because of the relative arid conditions around many of the western rivers, resulting in more nutrient inflows. Whereas the lush, heavily forested East has depleted nutrients in the soil for millions of years, often these nutrients are still abundant in the soils of the West, where plant growth is not as dense. To get a look at this, you can view the USGS map of water hardness throughout the United States. The East Coast shows mostly low hardness values, below 60 mg/l, while the Rocky Mountain states are in a zone where the average water hardness is high, between 120 and 250 mg/l.

One other aspect of water chemistry that can determine the character of a trout stream is the amount of phosphates and nitrates entering a river. Soluble compounds of these elements are essential for plant growth, and the higher their concentration, the more abundant the rooted plants and algae you'll find in a river. And because of the higher primary productivity within the river, the invertebrate population is more abundant. More food encourages more and bigger trout.

How Water Chemistry Affects Trout Growth and Abundance

As with most ecosystems on earth, humans have had a strong effect on water chemistry, and it's not always negative from a trout's perspective. Chemical fertilizers, manure spreading, and sewage and septic outflows increase the productivity of a trout stream. Unfortunately, with agricultural runoff, unless it is from an organic farm, along with the nutrient enrichment comes insecticides, fungicides, and herbicides that can be deadly to a trout stream, especially to the aquatic invertebrate population.

When fishing a new river in a populated area, if I know the river has trout I'll look for a sewage treatment plant and fish downstream of that location. I know I'll find more and bigger trout there, but I need to remember not to wet my knots with saliva and to use my nippers instead of my teeth to cut tippet material. I'm addicted enough to trout fishing to ignore the odor for a few hours of great fishing. The Bow River in Alberta has a famously robust trout population, and much of the credit for its density goes to sewage treatment plants in Calgary. Studies have been done by biologists that credit "cultural enrichment," as the euphemism goes, for increasing trout populations, and the removal of these treatment plants has been shown to decrease trout populations.

A river flowing through an agricultural valley can exhibit higher productivity because of fertilizers entering the stream; however, oxygen levels can be degraded from increased algae, and decreased vegetation along the banks can raise water temperatures. Pesticides are always a concern as well.

High in the headwaters of a stream, very few nutrients have entered the water yet, so productivity will be low and trout will be concentrated in the very best places.

The problem with this cultural enrichment is that the increased plant growth also puts pressure on the biological oxygen demand, or BOD, in a river. Plants and algae die and decompose, and this uses up oxygen. This is not a problem if a river stays cold enough to hold sufficient oxygen despite the increased BOD, but as you go downstream and a river warms, it becomes a problem. And when the river eventually flows into a lake or the ocean, the increased nutrient load encourages algae blooms that can be deadly. It's a mixed blessing for the entire ecosystem. And sewage flows can be high in other chemicals from birth control pills and other prescription drugs that have unknown and possibly deleterious effects on trout growth and reproduction.

Numerous studies have shown that altitude has a negative impact on the size and number of trout in a given stream. In other words, as you move downstream you'll most often find larger and more numerous trout, until you get to the point where water temperature becomes too high for trout, and bass and other warmwater species take over. This is probably intuitive, because in the headwaters of a river, water flow comes from rainwater, snowmelt, or springs, and unless the springs are from calcium-rich bedrock, the productivity of the water is low. As a river flows down its course, nutrients, from natural and man-made sources, enter the river and productivity increases. You'll find more and bigger trout here, assuming the habitat quality in the headwaters and the lower reaches are equal. There will be more insects and baitfish to support trout growth. If you want solitude and just want to catch trout, move to the headwaters of a river. If you want more and larger trout, and you want to concentrate more on insect hatches than fishing attractor flies, you'll be better off moving lower in the watershed.

How do tailwaters fit into this scheme? In most cases, a tailwater, or river flowing from the base of a reservoir, is far more productive than the upper end of the river that feeds into the reservoir. Nutrients, both natural and from agricultural activity, flow into the reservoir and get concentrated there, so the water flowing out below the dam has a high concentration of nutrients. Even if the reservoir has profuse aquatic plants, they'll only be concentrated in areas reached by sunlight, so the nutrients that wash into it are not used up.

A reservoir will also support both phytoplankton and zooplankton, organisms that live in stillwater environments but not in flowing water—plankton in flowing water just gets washed away, so it cannot develop a stable population. Filter-feeding insects, especially caddisflies and midges, take advantage of this rich soup in the outflows of reservoirs and can form incredibly dense populations. Tailwaters support healthy trout populations because, of course, of the cold, constant-temperature water flowing from them, but also because of the rich food supply.

Tailwaters can even boost production because of larger organisms that live in the reservoir above and get sucked into turbines. Many of them are killed and wounded in the process, and the famous shad kill on rivers like the White in Arkansas is a prime example. When the water gets cold in late fall, below 42 degrees, shad are either killed or stunned and get drawn into the outflows, which offers exciting fishing and giant trout because the fish wait for the easy, high-calorie prey below the dam.

Mysis shrimp, an introduced crustacean in some western lakes, also fall into this category and produce giant trout that sit in the food trough below dams and gorge on this nutritious food. The large trout of the Blue, Taylor, and Frying Pan Rivers in Colorado are primarily due to Mysis shrimp that were introduced into reservoirs feeding these rivers. It's ironic that the shrimp were introduced into the reservoirs to serve as a food supply for the salmonids there, but the plan backfired because the shrimp had life histories that kept them out of the zone that lake-dwelling trout prefer and they upset the food pyramid by preying on the native daphnia that young trout needed for growth. No one expected the dramatic effect on the river trout below the reservoirs, but this unexpected consequence benefited fly fishers looking for trophy trout.

Knowing a bit about the geology and water chemistry of a river system is fascinating to me and helps me understand what makes trout streams tick. I was first influenced by the effects geology has on the character of the landscape (and, by extrapolation, its rivers) by John McPhee's book *Annals of a Former World*. It made me realize that nearly every aspect of a river's environment is influenced by the rocks it pours through. I don't think this knowledge will necessarily help you catch more trout, but it goes a long way to an understanding of why each river has a unique fingerprint.

In tailwaters, concentration of nutrients in the reservoir upstream will boost the productivity of the water, giving them a richer food supply for trout and confounding our stream-reading efforts because trout can and will live in more locations in the river. If food is nearly everywhere, you're not as picky about where you live.

Wherever possible, try to get the long view of a river before stepping in the water. Look for hidden subsurface structure, cover, and especially the flow of current through a pool or run, which will tell you where the food supply—and feeding trout—will be found. This shot was taken from a bridge, but you can use a hillside or even a satellite view on a map to plan your fishing day.

CHAPTER 4

Landscape, Cover, and Water Levels

This chapter is a bit misplaced regarding how you should approach a strategy on finding trout, as an overall, bird's-eye view should be your first observation. But I wanted to give you the details on other aspects of finding trout first, so you know what to look for. Decisions you make on where to find trout should be made from a distance first. Look at the entire watershed, then zero in on specific places in the location you pick. An internet satellite view, combined with a topographic overlay, is best for pre-planning. Then, once you get to the river, try to find a high vantage point where you can examine the river at its current water flow, because you never know the conditions at which a satellite view was taken. It could have been in flood at that time, or at a historic low. A hill, highway, or bridge may work. They are not always handy, but get the best view you can.

GET THE LONG VIEW WITH A MAP

A topo map combined with a satellite view is almost essential when planning to explore a new river or a stretch of a familiar river you've fished before. First, look at the valley the river flows through and the contour lines along its banks. A broad valley with widely spaced contour lines indicates a low-gradient river. Flows will be slower, and unless there is some groundwater influence in the river, it will warm quicker in the summer. With long expanses of slower water, a river like this may also be harder to fish because the fish will be spookier and will get a better look at your fly.

These qualities should not scare you away, though. With generally slower currents, trout won't need to work as hard to get their food and will grow larger in a shorter time period. There is typically more abundant baitfish life in these areas as well, so trout have a food source that helps them reach a bigger body mass because they don't need to rely just on insect food. And in places with wide meadows, grasshoppers and other large terrestrial insects will be abundant. In addition, in times of floods or high flows, and in early spring when water temperatures are low, this type of water can be your best option. It may be easier to

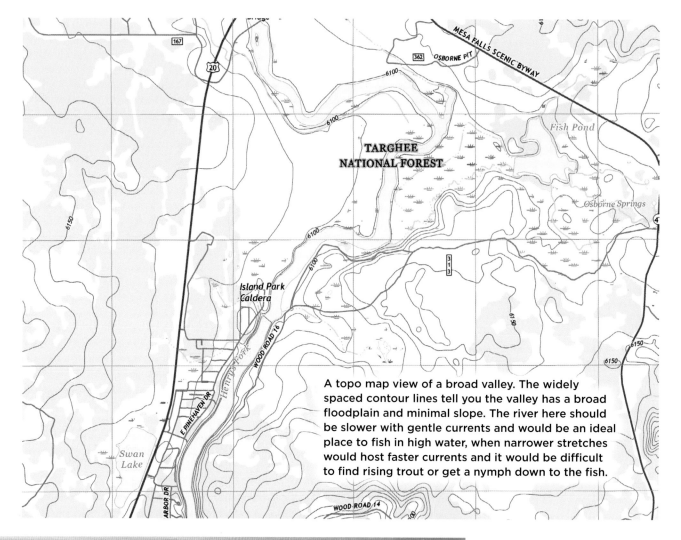

A topo map view of a broad valley. The widely spaced contour lines tell you the valley has a broad floodplain and minimal slope. The river here should be slower with gentle currents and would be an ideal place to fish in high water, when narrower stretches would host faster currents and it would be difficult to find rising trout or get a nymph down to the fish.

The same stretch of water in real life. The water here is as expected—slow currents, meandering bends, and lots of places for trout to feed in all kinds of water, even in high water.

The same stretch of water as in the topo map below. You can see the effect of a narrower floodplain, which, as expected, produces a river with faster current and lots of white water. The increased current and added oxygen might make this a great place to fish in midsummer—and the trout will be easier to catch in the faster current. It might be a place to avoid in high water because of the raging current.

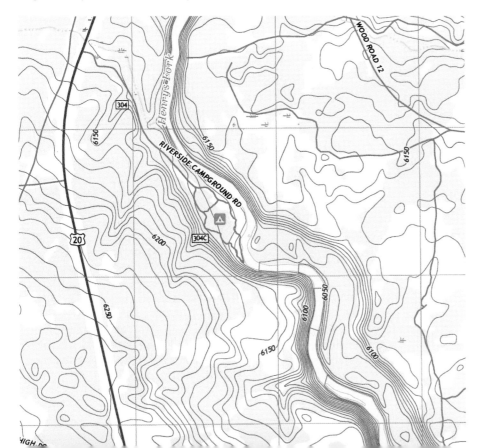

Here is the same river as in the photo on the opposite page but just a mile downstream. Here, the narrow contour lines along the banks suggest that it will offer faster current, steeper slope, and lots of pocket water.

get a nymph or streamer down to the fish in the slower current, and the first place trout will feed on the surface on insect hatches will be in this slower, flatter water.

At the other end of the scale, trout streams in narrow valleys, with steep contour lines on one or both sides of the river, will have faster currents, deep plunge pools, and most likely lots of pocket water. Although you can effectively fish these stretches at any time of year, even in high water if you look for slower pockets around large rocks and along the banks, these should be your go-to places during the summer months, especially in low water. The deeper pockets and rocks provide protection from predators, and the deeper water of plunge pools also offers the protection of depth. Even though the fish will likely slide into shallower water to feed, they have the security of deeper water, where they are less visible, should danger threaten. The more abundant white water also introduces more oxygen into the water, which may help trout survive when water temperatures warm. And narrow valleys often offer more shade, which also keeps

the water cooler provided there are long expanses of shade and not just a few patches.

A good option in the summer if you have the physical ability is to climb down into a canyon. If you do, you'll likely find fewer anglers crowding your space, though the walk into a steep valley means a bit of rock hopping and a grueling walk out at the end of the day. Remember always, though, to quit fishing when water temperatures warm above 68 degrees (65 for brook trout) so the fish you release will be able to survive the stress of playing and landing them.

Diversity of Habitat

When exploring a new trout stream, I always look for places with a diversity of habitat. I don't know what type of water trout may prefer in a particular river until I start fishing, and I can't predict what kind of insect hatches will be abundant. Is most of the food trout prefer here in the form of midges or crustaceans like scuds and sow bugs? In that case, slow water might be best. But maybe

Satellite images can often be helpful in finding places with diverse habitat, which are always smart to try when you don't know a river. Here we have a tributary coming into the main river at 1, fast water and riffles at 2, an island with riffles at 3, a wastewater treatment plant at 4 (for possible enrichment of the water), and deep pools at 5. The river also has a nice bend, which is always helpful in creating deeper pools and more diverse habitat. Imagery © Maxar Technologies, USDA Farm Service Agency, Map data © 2022 Google

The same stretch of water from ground level. Jesse Haller is enjoying the options of fishing the faster riffles, and if they don't produce he has the option of moving downstream into a deep pool.

these fish feed more often on mayflies, stoneflies, and caddisflies. If so, I'll look for riffles and fast runs and pocket water. But I don't know ahead of time, so looking for diverse habitat in one stretch of river predicts that I should find some productive water.

If you look at a map and see long stretches of slower water, indicated by a broad valley, you might get stuck in water that doesn't hold many trout. Or, if you see a stretch of water that looks fast, based on steep contour lines, but it's a straight shot for a long distance, there may not be many places for trout to sit in protected areas away from the faster current. On a topo map, look for stretches that combine wider valleys with pinch points where the river narrows and quickens. On a satellite view, look for spots that combine riffles and pools, pocket water, and runs with the occasional long, slow pool.

I'm reluctant to fish any new water without some sign of riffles because not only do they indicate a diversity of water speeds, but they also produce most of the insect life that trout depend on. Riffles are quite apparent in satellite views unless the river is so narrow that it's covered with foliage. Even so, a river will occasionally peak into view and you might get an idea of the diversity of habitat.

Bends in a river always introduce diversity of habitat and varying currents, and they are another feature I always look for. Regardless of whether a piece of water flows through a wide valley and may be relatively slow or runs through a narrow canyon where the current is mostly swift, bends offer a lessening of current in fast water and they speed up current in slow water. Bends also invariably dig deeper pools because of the turbulence created on the outside of the bend, and they collect large woody debris that provides cover for trout. I always look for a stretch of water with as many bends as possible, because each one is a hotspot where I'm sure to find good habitat—and trout.

This one's a bit more difficult to estimate from a map and sometimes easier to eyeball in person—vertical drop. It applies mainly to rivers with a steep gradient, where the current may be so swift that trout can only hold in places where large rocks break the current, or along the banks where friction and turbulence slow it down. Habitat can be limited here, as well as an abundance of trout. On a map, look for places where the steep gradient flattens out, where the contour lines broaden just a bit for a brief period before pinching back into tightly spaced lines. When you're close to a river, if

Look for plateaus, especially in smaller streams, where the slope of the land flattens just a bit. These are places where you'll find slightly slower water and deeper pools.

you step back you can see little plateaus. The water will get slower and deeper here, providing better habitat for trout. In one mountain brook trout stream I fish, I know I can catch little trout in the steep sections, in little pools in front of and behind rocks. Sometimes I fish these spots just to see what's there, but if I have limited time or want to cover a lot of water I'll climb through them quickly until the terrain flattens out. I know I'll find better pockets and bigger trout in the plateaus.

Tributaries

A trout stream with few or no tributaries is always suspect. Tributaries are often the main spawning areas for wild trout, and especially closer to the spawning season, brook and brown trout in the fall and cutthroats and rainbows in the spring will be concentrated close to them. Fishing near them does not mean you're fishing over spawning trout, which many people think is unethical. Trout will move toward these tributaries a month or more before beginning to spawn.

In a stream I often fish, the brown trout spawn in November. Yet in August I'll see large browns, sometimes a male beside a big female, sitting in a pool in a relatively open spot without cover, which is uncommon during the day for brown trout. I suspect these fish are moving, as I can't see another reason for them being so exposed other than stopping to rest before moving farther upstream. They are usually gone the next day, which gives me more confidence in my theory. The same river has wild rainbows that spawn in early April, and I sometimes see a half dozen of them milling around in a pool in February, exhibiting what looks like pre-spawn behavior. Again, the next day they are nowhere to be found. I am sure they are headed to the tributary where they emerged from eggs a few years ago.

Tributaries are usually composed of a greater percentage of groundwater than surface water. This means places below them will be warmer in cold weather and cooler in hot weather because groundwater maintains a near-constant temperature throughout the year. The shorter the tributary, the more likely it's composed mostly of groundwater because it doesn't have the floodplain to accumulate much surface water. Longer tributaries, more than a mile in length, are more exposed to atmospheric temperatures so are more likely to be closer in temperature to the main flow of a river. So if you are fishing during extreme temperatures, look for places with shorter tributaries entering them.

Tributaries can also be places to avoid. Sometimes they run through intensively farmed reaches or just through terrain with unstable banks, which adds mud and silt to them and reduces visibility where they enter.

Soap Creek on the Bighorn and the Taylor Fork on the Gallatin are both notorious for adding muddy flow, and sometimes it seems like if you stand over them and cry, letting a few tears drop in, they'll get muddy. You can't really tell which tributaries will be muddy from looking at a map, although the longer the tributary, generally the greater chance of it muddying up after a rainstorm. You'll want to fish a river above where a muddy tributary enters if you're concentrating on nymph and dry-fly fishing, but muddy flow can also induce larger trout to move into the areas of lower visibility and hunt large prey. So it wouldn't hurt to run a streamer through water like this.

If a tributary flows out of a lake before it enters a trout stream, you can estimate one of its effects from a map and the other you'll have to visit it in person with a stream thermometer. If the lake is relatively close to where the tributary enters the river, you can assume it will run clear, as most lakes run clear because silt settles out quickly even after a rain. However, lakes expose a lot of water to the sun and atmosphere, and if the weather has been hot, that tributary could be warmer than the main flow. In high altitudes this is not as much of a problem as at lower elevations.

I was exploring a small mountain stream one summer and was not even sure it held trout. Fifty yards above the bridge where I entered the stream I caught a fallfish, a large minnow that prefers warmer water than trout—not a good sign. However, around the next bend a minuscule tributary entered the creek, and I knew from looking at a map that it flowed out of a shallow pond and was probably quite warm. Once I got above that tributary it was all trout—wild browns, rainbows, and brook trout, some of which were much larger than I would have suspected. I never caught another fallfish, which must have been lying in the warm water plume that flowed out of the pond.

How Will You Get to the Water?

When planning a fishing trip, a critical consideration is getting to the water without trespassing. If you're on public land, of course, you won't have any problems, as you can just look at a satellite view and find pull-offs near where you want to fish. I like to look for reasonable parking areas that aren't too close to the river, and where the river flows away from any roads or trails for a distance so I can get away from other anglers. Not only is it not good ethics to fish close to other people because you might disturb their fishing, but you'll find better fishing where someone has not thrashed the water for hours because the fish won't be spooked and will be more inclined to feed.

Know your access regulations. They vary by state, and not all access points, either public or private, are as well marked as this area. The use of a phone app with property boundary overlays is handy when exploring new water.

Where private land or a mixture of public and private land surrounds the river you want to fish, things can get tricky. Every state has its own access laws, and you need to find out if you can cross private land or even if you can walk in a river through private land. In states like Wyoming and Colorado, a landowner can own the bottom of a river and if they own both sides, you may not even be able to drop an anchor when floating through the land in question. Vermont, Idaho, Pennsylvania, Montana, and other states have much more liberal laws, where as long as you can get into a river at a public access point like the right-of-way at a bridge, as long as you stay in the river or walk the banks to the high-water mark you can fish wherever you want. But again, every state is different. The best way to research state stream access laws is to use Backcountry Hunters and Anglers' publication *Stream Access Now*, which can be downloaded from their website. It details the laws of stream access in each state.

Even knowing state laws and where official public fishing streams are located can be tricky. Decades ago New York State secured easements on rivers like the East Branch of the Delaware and has posted yellow "Public Fishing Stream" signs along the banks. Unfortunately, they did not have the funds to actually get *access* across private land to some of those streams, so as you

drive along the river you see "Posted No Trespassing" signs right alongside the "Public Fishing Stream" signs. And you can't get to the river for miles in some areas. Colorado also has confusing public and private reaches that are not well marked or not marked at all, and you can be in and out of private land without even knowing it—until you get arrested for trespassing. It's always a good idea to research where you'll be fishing by using online property maps or apps like BaseMap, which offers a landowner overlay. Fly shops in the area are also a good source of legal access areas. If you want to fish private land you can contact the landowner, although it's anyone's guess if you'll receive permission. A promise to pick up trash or a gift of a nice bottle of spirits can't hurt.

ONCE YOU GET CLOSER

When you get to the river, before you begin to eyeball possible places to fish, before you even start looking at riffles and pools and rocks and logs, continue your broad evaluation of conditions. Water levels are a big factor in the best places to fish, and even knowing, if possible, where the water levels were a week or a month ago. When fishing a tailwater it's important to know if the water level is managed with daily pulses of high water for electrical generation or if it is managed as a "run of the river" flow, which means it will mimic a natural seasonal variation of floods and low water, depending on rainfall and snow melt.

One thing you should check, before your trip at home or when on the road, is the flow in the river, how it compares to normal flows at that time of year, and whether the river is steady, rising, or falling. This is easily eyeballed in a matter of seconds by looking at the USGS stream flow data online. The graphs are tremendously handy at determining the kind of water conditions you'll encounter, and if you fish a river regularly, I'd bookmark the page so you can refresh it quickly without doing a long search. The problem is not all rivers, especially smaller ones, have USGS gauges on them. One way to estimate the flow in a non-monitored river is to check the closest monitored river, as it has probably experienced the same weather patterns. If the river in question is a tailwater, you might also be able to check the release schedule for the dam you'll fish below. Some dam regulators are great about this and even tell you what they expect to release over the next few days. Others just tell you the current release and are not as helpful.

You'll also want to check the flow yourself, especially on smaller rivers with no gauges. Look along the edge of the river for emergent grasses and sedges. They typically grow right at the edge of the water at a normal or base flow. If the waterline is well below them, you're faced with low or dropping water levels. If the grasses are covered with water, you can estimate how high the water is compared to a normal flow. You'll also be able to tell whether the water is rising or dropping. If the bases of the stems are clean, the water is steady or rising. If there is a dirt line on the stems above the water line, the flow is dropping. Streamside rocks can also give you a clue. If there is a damp or wet line above a rock that is partially submerged, it's probable that the water is dropping. If the waterline is dry, the flow is either steady or rising.

High Water

When a trout stream is in flood, it's difficult to generalize where trout will be found. Some fish just stay in place as the water rises above them, especially if their location already has protection from the current. During floods, the velocity near the bottom and behind objects stays roughly the same, as all the energy of the added flow is directed into the main, unimpeded part of a river, or is absorbed by water flowing into flat pieces of land along the riverbed. It's also a matter of scale and geography. Slow, meandering rivers merely direct the excess energy into the surrounding floodplain, so the velocity in the main channel of the river speeds up but by a smaller increment. However, streams with a steep drop and narrow canyon walls offer no other place for the water to go than downstream, and these can increase in velocity to the point where trout will be pushed into the few slower-moving spots at the bottoms of deep pools or where the valley plateaus a bit and the current lessens.

Discharge, cubic feet per second
Most recent instantaneous value: 12300 02-21-2022 09:30 CST

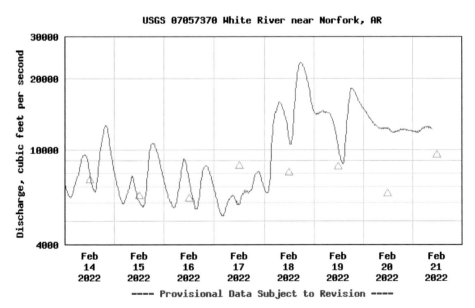

This USGS flow chart shows a tailwater that pulses daily, but also shows an increase in overall flow, probably due to a rain event in the middle of the week. Keeping an eye on these charts before you go on a trip will tell you what kind of water conditions to expect.

When you see grasses along the edge of a river submerged, you'll know the flow is higher than normal and it's easy to get an estimate of exactly how far the river has risen. You'll need to adjust your fishing expectations and strategies.

In high water, look for places with flatter water or gentle riffles. Trout will often move closer to the banks, especially if there is some structure there for protection. The log along this bank would be the first place I'd look.

Trout are tough and able to handle nearly any flood thrown at them. In late August 2011, Hurricane Irene parked itself above Vermont for days and left a trail of destroyed homes, roads, bridges, and apparently trout streams in its wake. A few weeks after the hurricane, I visited a favorite mountain brook trout stream, a tributary to the Battenkill, that runs through a narrow canyon. The road and many houses were completely washed away, and the riverbed changed dramatically. I could not see how a trout could have survived, and with all the riparian vegetation ripped away, I told friends the river would probably not come back to normal in my lifetime. That fall I fished the river and caught some trout. They were skinny and covered with scratches, apparently from being surrounded by moving rocks. Yet by the next year, and in subsequent years, the wild brook and brown trout population bounced back better than ever. And the Battenkill, a larger river in a broad valley with a wide floodplain that allowed the flood energy to dissipate, suffered little to no damage.

In many rivers, trout will move into the shallower, slower water along the banks to get away from fast current and also to find food. These are your best targets in floods, because it may be difficult or impossible to get your fly to those fish that stayed deep. The ones along the bank, though, are in there to feed and you can have surprisingly good fishing as long as you concentrate on slower, shallower water along the banks. Look for any projections like little points of land, fallen logs, or large rocks. These will be especially attractive to trout because they slow the current even more—and they offer protection from predators when trout are in shallow water.

Trout in tailwaters with pulsed hydroelectric generation are a similar story, except the trout are even more conditioned to moving into shallow water during a rise of water because they experience it nearly every day. Jamie Rouse has been a guide on the Little Red River in Arkansas for many years and has learned to fish its moods. In this river, water will rise and fall a full 10 feet during electricity generation, which creates a contrast between a raging torrent and midsummer lows in a 24-hour period. Jamie has learned that in high water, trout, especially the larger trout that can handle the heavier current, will push into the banks and will be found in very discrete places along them. He looks for what he calls "micro points" along the bank—again any projection or object that breaks the flow just a bit more and produces a comfortable feeding spot. Not all trout move to the banks in the Red, but enough that he'll experience some of his best fishing in high flows because the fish are predictable.

Jamie then finds when the water drops, fish are much more spread out in the river and are spookier and harder to locate, and he looks for them at the edges of moss beds and drop-offs into deeper water. So although most fly fishers prefer low or moderate water levels instead of floods, there are places where they produce excellent opportunities.

High water can concentrate trout in discrete places, especially along the bank. This high-water brown trout ate a flashy streamer.

From my experience and that of experienced fly fishers I've talked to, whether the water is rising, steadily high, or falling can determine the best ways of catching trout. Streamers or large wet flies swung in the current seem to be best on rising water. Minnows and crayfish get disoriented, and trout go on the prowl as water levels rise to try to take advantage of this because under normal flows, these critters are too agile and maneuverable for a trout to capture. Look for these fish in ambush spots where the water is slower and trout can corral their prey.

Once the rise has subsided, nymphs and even dry flies are more successful because the trout that chased the bigger prey items get full and seem to rest and digest their food. Smaller trout, and those that prefer drift feeding, are now able to see their drifting prey better. And the higher water levels wash worms, small crustaceans like sow bugs and scuds, and cranefly larvae into the current, and in the dropping water these smaller foods are easier for drift-feeding trout to spot. This kind of fishing is best in gentle riffles where the current is broken but not as swift because the current from all the rocks in a riffle adds turbulence and slows the flow. That's only a generalization, though, and you could experience great nymph fishing on rising water and a decent streamer bite on falling water. Nothing is certain in trout fishing.

Low Water

Low water, lower than the base flow or "normal" flow of a river, presents different challenges. We've already explored how high water temperatures, often associated with low flows, can make fishing difficult or ill-advised. But low flows can happen in cool weather, or earlier in the year, when temperatures are optimum. Trout will be spookier and harder to approach. But where do you even look for them? If you keep two things in mind, depth and current flow, you'll be able to find trout in low water conditions. Yes, cover is also important and we'll cover that shortly, but without some depth and current flow the best cover in a river will remain barren of trout. That nice overhanging tree with submerged logs, if in 4 inches of water and in stagnant flow, won't be attractive to trout.

In low flows, look for water that is a foot deep, or deeper. And in water that's only a foot or two deep, look for adjacent places where the water is deeper and available to trout when they bolt for protection. Trout like to feed in this shallower water but seek out this depth only

During low water, look for places with depth nearby. The fish may not always feed in or around the deep water, but they'll stay close to a place of refuge and depth (as well as large rocks like this one) to make sure they have a place to get to quickly when danger threatens.

In low water, you'll want to look for places with some kind of current. Even if you're not close to an obvious riffle, look for that foam line that indicates where food drifts. I'd stay away from places where the surface is clear and without any foam.

where they have room to run and dart into deeper water when danger threatens. A small depression that is a foot deep and only 8 inches wide by 2 feet long won't hold a trout long unless it's migrating. Trout may move into a riffle where their backs are almost out of the water to feed during low water, but only in riffles backed up by deep pools above or below.

If you just do your research using a satellite image, you might be startled by low water conditions. You don't know what time of year that satellite photo was taken, and it's very hard to determine depth from directly above. My buddy Shawn Combs once told me about a secret stream, very lightly fished and full of large brown trout, that is on the way to my mother's house five hours away. One summer when visiting her I decided to take a detour on my way home to check out his stream. He had given me coordinates for the best parking spots and I pored over Google Earth, planning how I would fish the little river. It looked like plenty of riffles and pocket water, and I thought I would find trout everywhere.

Once I got there, though, I discovered that the riffles and pocket water I saw in the satellite view were long expanses of flat shale bottom, with little structure and minimal depth. I tried them anyway, without a single

strike or rise. I found I had to hoof it a half mile between places where the river turned a bend or there was a large fault in the slate, with enough depth to hold some trout. I did find them, and I lost one large brown trout on a nymph at the tail of a pool that still haunts me. I would have loved to have gotten it a bit closer just to see how big it was.

Current is a critical determining factor in low water. No matter how deep a pool is and how much cover it offers, you'll only find feeding trout in enough current to bring them food at an acceptable rate. What's acceptable to trout? I'm not sure, but I do know that if you inspect a pool and watch for the main current thread, indicated by bubbles and debris carried along by the current, you'll also find where insects are drifting. In higher flows, there may be current flowing from one bank to the other and here it's not as important. But in low water, in a slow pool it can be less than a foot wide. It can also move back and forth from bank to bank, so it's critical to pay attention to the bubble or foam line. It will tell you exactly where trout are likely to feed.

Riffles are always a great place in low water because they provide cover from overhead, add more oxygen to warmer water, and are where most of the insect food is produced in a trout stream. I try to avoid fishing any stream in low water that does not have riffles. I have a friend who specializes in chasing unicorns. He talks to the state biologists and find rivers that support populations of large brown trout, found after they do their electroshocking surveys. He keeps bugging me in the middle of the summer to check out a stretch on one river that is closer to my house than his and he says hold piles of brown trout over 20 inches. I know it and have fished it before, unsuccessfully, and to fish it in the middle of summer would be an exercise in frustration—at least for my skills and patience. This piece of water is long, slow, and flat—and very clear—without a single riffle. Trying to approach these trout on a sunny day would be nearly impossible because the fish can see your every move. And trying to blind-fish water like this with a nymph or dry would end up spooking the fish because you never know exactly where they are and you end up putting your fly line over countless unseen fish. I'm going to wait until I can hit it just before dark, during a hatch, or when the water rises and gets moderately dirty.

What happens when a stream has been low for weeks in the summer and suddenly grows in volume because of heavy rains? Even after the water clears, spots that look attractive may be devoid of fish, so knowing where the riverbed was at previous flows (by looking at streamside grasses) may help you avoid unproductive water. In larger rivers, with the security of deeper pools and riffles close by, trout may move back into spots that were dry last week—but not always. Trout that settle into deeper water during low flows will likely stay put or at least stay close to those places of security even when the water levels rise. They may slide into the shallower areas to feed, but if you suddenly have a nice run with 2 feet of water in it after a summer rain but it's isolated from deeper pools by 50 or 100 yards, trout won't magically appear. Their summer homes have already been set by previous low water.

This is especially true in small streams, where deep pools may be separated by a quarter mile or more of water. In my experience, trout won't move out of these places and repopulate other parts of a stream even if the water comes back up to spring levels, where they might have lived a month or more before. We had a summer in the East where June was the hottest and driest on record and fish in the small streams retreated to areas of refuge—deeper pools and cooler water. Some appeared to have moved downstream where the pools were deeper, and others moved further into the headwaters in search of cooler water. Then July arrived, with heavy, steady rains and cooler weather. Many of the places that were barren of trout in June because of the low water suddenly looked good again, with plenty of

depth and current to hold fish. Yet when I fished these small mountain streams, I only found trout close to those deeper refuges or way up in the headwaters. The rejuvenated places were still barren of trout.

The earliest low water of the season seems to set the stage for the rest of the season, until brown and brook trout begin migrating upstream to spawn in the early fall. Knowing what has happened earlier in the season is essential for ruling out unproductive water, either by looking at historical flow gauges or by asking the experts at a local fly shop how low the water got earlier in the year.

Water Color

Looking at the color of the water probably won't help you find trout in any given location, but it might help you decide when to move on and find another place to fish. Visibility and color combined can tell you a great deal about how the fishing might be.

If the water is the color of coffee with heaps of cream in it, chances are fishing will be poor. If mud running into a river from plowed fields or eroded places on the bank reduces the visibility to 3 inches or less, I'd look for another place to fish. Trout just won't be able to locate your fly unless you plunk it right on their nose, and because you can't see structure on the bottom and most certainly can't see any fish in the water, you have no idea where they may be. You might catch a trout using a bulky black streamer (black is the most visible shade in dirty conditions) with a deer hair head to set vibrations in the water, or even one with rattles to help a trout track your fly with its lateral line sense. You might also pick a fly with lots of flash in it to catch their attention. But it's usually not a winning strategy. And if you see large debris like logs and limbs floating in the current, it's game over. With obstacles banging down the river, trout will move out of the way into very protected places and it's unlikely they'll be interested in feeding at all. You may find a fish or two in protected places, in backwaters well away from the main current, but even here trout may be faced with moving debris.

Better to keep moving upstream in the hope you can find the source of the mud and debris and get above it. You may have to move almost to the headwaters of a river to find better conditions, but it's better than not fishing at all. Sometimes a cloudburst will hit one tributary and muddy up a river below its confluence, and the river above the entrance of the tributary can be much more hospitable. If there is an impoundment on a river system like a lake or reservoir, the still water can often settle out mud and silt, and fishing downstream of these places may help you find better water.

A grayish color to the water is not as detrimental to fishing as a light brown shade. Often a grayish tinge comes from limestone influence, and some of these streams retain their light gray tinge even in low water conditions.

When water becomes this color, lower your expectations. A black streamer might work, but your best option is to move upstream to see if you can get above the source of the mud. Sometimes a single tributary blown out in a rainstorm is the culprit, so getting upstream of it could put you into better conditions.

Tailwater rivers can have a greenish tinge, even during a drought, because of the suspended algae in the water from the upstream reservoir.

Once visibility clears to about 6 inches, fishing gets better in a hurry. The color of the water will probably change, too, from milky coffee to a more grayish or greenish shade. Some limestone streams and tailwaters are always this color and never perfectly clear due to all the suspended matter in the water. In limestone streams the gray color comes from suspended calcium compounds, and in tailwaters the greenish tinge comes from the algae in the reservoir above. But in a typical freestone stream, when the water changes from brown to green or gray, you'll have a better chance with your flies. I would still stick to bigger flies, and it's probably better to either strip a streamer or swing a nymph or wet fly than the typical dead-drift presentation. There will still be finer pieces of debris drifting with the current, and you'll want your fly to stand out with a propulsion of its own so trout don't mistake your offering for another twig or piece of leaf.

Once the water clears to about 20 inches of visibility, standard offerings like nymphs and even dry flies will be productive. Although I've seen trout rising in backwaters with only about 6 inches of visibility, that's rare unless a heavy hatch lures them to the surface. But with 2 feet of visibility, you're likely to be back to normal conditions,

Water with a tannic color actually has decent clarity and should not hinder your fishing efforts. Sometimes the tannic color becomes more pronounced in low water.

where you can nymph, blind-fish a dry fly, or fish a dry-dropper combination.

Tannic waters, those the color of weak tea in normal flows, may get darker and browner because of a greater percentage of water running off coniferous forests as opposed to a mix of surface water and clear groundwater in normal flows. Visibility is usually not hindered that much when tannic waters get more stained, but you should probably still hedge your bets and use a black or dark fly with some flash in it. Chartreuse, orange, and yellow can also be productive colors in stained rivers. Either incorporate these colors into your streamers or use a nymph with a hotspot in one of these colors to attract the attention of the fish and let them know your fly is not debris.

COVER

Cover is essential for a trout's survival. Its importance in finding feeding fish is often overestimated, though. Yes, a trout needs protection from predators, a safe place to dart to when danger threatens, a place that predators either can't get to or have difficulty attacking a trout within. But trout don't always live in these places most of the day, and quite often don't feed there. It's tough to get drifting insects with your head stuck in a logjam. And that overhead cover, bushes or trees close to the surface, is not always located in a prime feeding spot. Sometimes it is, and a spot that offers both protection from predators and the right current speed for feeding is often called a "prime lie" because it offers a trout all it needs to survive without moving. Those spots are not as common in many streams as we (or the trout) would like, so trout need to navigate between feeding spots and hiding spots.

If you talk to a fish biologist that has electroshocked a river, they will tell you that all the trout, except for the very tiny ones, live in the heaviest cover. If you listened to them you'd ignore a lot of great places to fish, because you'd only cast around logjams and large rocks. But have you ever watched an electroshocking crew at work? First they all arrive at the sample location and stand on the bank getting ready. Then they bang around with aluminum canoes, loading generators and buckets to hold the

The area in front of this log is a prime lie. A prime lie is a place where a trout has immediate access to cover and is a great place to feed, in a current lane that brings a steady supply of food. Some feeding lies don't have immediate access to cover and are more open, but they'll always have access to food. Trout may use cover in a place where feeding is not optimal, but they'll only use those places to stay away from danger. And if they're trying to hide they won't feed, so cover without a clear feeding lane is of little use to us as anglers.

Electroshocking crews will tell you all the decent trout are found in heavy cover. Of course, that's where they see them. When you put a crowd of people into a river with nets, banging around in aluminum canoes and sticking probes in the water, where would you expect to find trout? Some of the trout they find in cover may have been happily feeding many yards away from that logjam cover but bolted there when disturbed.

fish into the canoes. Then a dozen people or more slog into the water, pushing big waves way up to the head of a pool. Then, walking abreast, they move up through the pool, and—surprise—they find all of the trout trembling under big rocks or in heavy logjams, or at the very least in the deepest part of a pool. There may have been trout feeding throughout that pool quite happily, but as soon as the entourage begins its work, every fish that can swim against the current will find a safe place to hide. What the biologists find regarding the size and numbers of trout is still valid because the fish almost never leave a pool or run when scared, but they are not exactly stealthy and so are not a reliable source of *exactly* where to find fish. They can point you to the best pools, but probably not where to find feeding trout.

If a trout is to survive it needs cover, unless a river has absolutely no predators. I can't think of a single trout stream in the world that has no predators, but even if one existed, trout are hardwired at birth to bolt when

a shadow crosses the water or unusual waves disturb a pool, or they sense movement above the water that was not there before. This cover should be a quick swim away, and trout like it to be in as straight a line as possible so they don't waste time or energy darting around obstacles. They typically won't swim through shallow riffles or very fast water to get to this security, and they may bolt upstream or down to get to it. But they always know exactly where it is from months or years of practice.

When you spook trout, and you invariably will, you will often see them darting away because your peripheral vision catches their movement easily if the water is clear. The natural reaction is to remember the logjam or rock the fish swam to for future reference. And the fish could very well be there at times but hidden in cover, and it may not be as receptive to eating your fly as it would be when actively feeding. The fact that the fish swam from *somewhere* to the cover means at that time it

Trees that extend just above the surface of the water seem to provide the best cover. If trees are too high they provide perches for certain fish-eating birds, and if they touch the water they appear to disrupt the surface so trout can't see their food.

was feeding *elsewhere*. So maybe a smarter move would be to estimate where the fish came from and remember that spot. You may not always see where the fish began its flight, but if it came from behind you, turn around and look for places that have optimum depth and current, regardless of whether it offers cover, because if the fish already had cover close by, it wouldn't be swimming 20 feet to get to it—the fish would merely melt into its sanctuary.

Types of Cover

When most of us think of cover, we imagine a tangled root wad or trees that overhang a river, and these are both good cover but for different reasons. The overhanging trees keep herons from walking in the shallows to stalk trout, and they also make it nearly impossible for an eagle, kingfisher, or osprey to dive-bomb an unsuspecting trout. Submerged root wads are more effective, though, if the primary predators in a stream are mink, otters, or fish-eating ducks like mergansers. An overhanging tree prevents no problem to these swimming predators. You won't always know what flavor of predators live nearby, but if you see an abundance of osprey nests it makes sense to look for water with overhanging trees. And if you see a mink or otter scampering along the bank, the most productive pools will have tangled logjams.

TREES AND BRUSH

When we think of cover what comes to mind immediately is overhead cover, which makes sense given the meaning of the word in non-trout instances. This is usually composed of trees or brush that hang over

the water. Trees provide both physical and visual cover. As physical cover, trees block the ability of birds that plunge into the water after trout from having a clear shot. The closer the branches and leaves are to the water, the better the cover is for trout, because a tree with only high branches will allow birds like kingfishers a place to perch before diving on a trout. Branches close to the water don't give the bird enough momentum via gravity to make a decent plunge. Branches just above the water are great, but branches that trail onto the surface don't seem to make a spot as attractive for trout. I suspect the surface distortion makes it tough for trout to see their food drifting by.

Branches hanging right over the water make getting a fly in there difficult but usually not impossible, and many people pass up these spots because they worry about losing flies. The trout under those branches, though, feel a little more secure and aren't fished over as much and may be easier to catch with some planning. A direct overhead cast, the one most people use, won't work. You can learn to make a shallow-angle side cast and fire the fly under the branches, but often just casting into the clear area above the overhanging trees and letting your fly drift underneath is the best option. And you are less likely to lose flies.

Just because this area has shade and overhanging trees does not mean it will be a place that holds trout. The water is too shallow and the current is too weak, so no amount of cover will make it a better place to find fish feeding.

This trout was tucked into the shade line along the bank. It wasn't there because it has a dislike for sunlight or because it was cooler in the shade (it wasn't). The trout was there because it was less visible to overhead predators.

A trout feeding in shallow water, out in the open, in bright sunlight. They'll feed in the current they find most efficient for feeding regardless of cover as long as they are not disturbed. But you can bet this fish has a rock, log, riffle, or deep water that it can bolt to in less than two seconds.

Trees also provide visual cover by forming shade. In a stream I fish a lot in midsummer, fish slide out into the main current in the center of the pool and feed on small mayflies and probably terrestrial insects that fall into the river. They line up just downstream of the shade line, and as the sun crosses the horizon and the shade line across the pool becomes smaller, the fish slide downstream to keep pace with it until they run out of room around midday, at which point they slink into deeper parts of the pool until dusk. This stream hosts a number of herons and kingfishers, and by staying in the shade the fish are far less visible to birds than they would be in bright sunlight. I don't think fish have trouble seeing in bright sunlight, so don't overlook a spot on a sunny day just because it does not offer shade. I've seen many wild trout, all times of year, feeding eagerly in bright sunlight. They'll take shade if they can get it, but shade is not essential.

I used to fish a small spring creek that flowed into the Snake River in Wyoming that had a single three-strand barbed wire strung across it, to separate BLM grazing land from adjacent private land. The stream was full of large cutthroats that rose every morning to PMD mayflies, and every one of those big fish positioned itself right under the barbed wire, strung out across the creek like a football line of scrimmage. The wire offered no shade from the achingly bright Wyoming sun, but it did make life difficult for the local eagles and ospreys that I imagine would sometimes circle overhead in frustration. I could give you many more examples, but that one always comes to mind because the effect of just a tiny but formidable piece of overhead cover was so dramatic. Keep your eyes peeled for cover that might look insignificant but can mean life or death for trout.

ROCKS AND LOGS

Objects in the stream offer cover and most often it's a rock or a log—or jumbles of them or a mixture of both. Because they are immovable objects they also give trout protection from fast current if they are positioned just the right way, so these objects can make prime lies.

From my experience, logs are better than rocks for a variety of reasons. First, unless rocks are large and not totally flush to the bottom, they might break current but when it comes to providing a place to hide, they may not give complete concealment. Logs, however, typically get pushed parallel to the current where they offer the least resistance, and because trout also must be positioned parallel to the current they fit alongside or under a log easier. Logs often have branches sticking out from them, which only add to protection from predators. Regardless of whether a log is fully or partially submerged, it

Rocks offer a great break in fast current to help trout hold their position and feed. They are sometimes not as reliable as logs for protection from predators because there may not be a cavity or depression at the base of the rock to hide fish.

Logs lying parallel to the current may not offer as much protection from fast current as rocks, but if they are already in a place where the current is moderate and food is abundant, they offer better protection from predators. Logs like this also collect debris during floods, which adds further to their appeal to trout trying to stay out of trouble.

will be attractive to trout—fully submerged, especially if accompanied by branches or brush piles that have gotten trapped along with the log, for protection from both underwater predators and overhead threats, and partially submerged for even more protection against overhead predators.

Logs are also softer. I am not absolutely sure if this is a reason for making them more attractive, but over the years I've paid close attention to how trout use rocks as opposed to logs along the bank and logs always win when available. In my part of the world, slate is abundant and cheap (scrap is free from local slate quarries), and dairy farmers use it to armor their banks to prevent loss of valuable cropland from erosion. Yet I've noticed that trout are not abundant along piles of slate, even when the slate extends into a nice deep pool with perfect current. When I find a log or a logjam in a river, though, it always holds trout, and usually bigger ones. The edges of the slate are sharp, and even with years or water flowing over them, the rocks stay relatively sharp. I think trout just don't like sidling up to sharp edges when they're hiding, even though the slate appears to offer superior protection.

It's no surprise that when smart biologists plan and install cover to improve the habitat and thus the number and size of trout found in a stream, you'll hear them talking about large woody debris, or LWD. Just dumping piles of rocks, even in a carefully engineered design, can sometimes modify current flow to deepen it and make it more attractive to trout, but just rocks by themselves are seldom used. Instead, habitat designers use LWD anchored by large rocks, so floods don't push the logs out of position. And logs are surprisingly resistant to rot when submerged because most of the insects, fungi, and microbes that evolved to break down wood in a forest don't live underwater. In a study of habitat improvements on the Battenkill, a study stretch of large woody debris combined with rocks for anchors increased the trout population over 500 percent in a matter of just a few years. And all of the structures survived Hurricane Irene, which caused the most intense flooding in Vermont since the 1930s.

Not all rivers have woody debris in them, and trout do just fine using cover from other sources. But in a river that has both rock and log cover, you will find more trout, and often bigger trout, in areas with logs, root wads, and submerged brush. Trout won't always feed right next to them, but your luck will improve if you concentrate on water that offers this type of cover close at hand.

These are man-made structures on the Battenkill designed to work as trout habitat enhancements, at both high and low water levels (this is at extreme low water). They are constructed mostly of woody debris, using large rocks mainly for ballast to keep the logs in place. Notice that they have also let the natural floods of the river assist by collecting other woody debris that drifts down. Not only have these logs been shown to increase trout populations in the area by as much as 500 percent, it's difficult to tell they are man-made so they fit in well with the natural environment of the river.

This is a piece of water I know intimately. When trout feed here they gravitate to the log, and when frightened they use the protection of the log to the exclusion of the slate used to armor the bank. Rocks with sharp edges like this don't seem to be as appealing to them as rounded rocks.

DEPTH

We all lust over trout streams that contain deep pools. We imagine giant browns lying on the bottom just waiting to inhale our nymph. Deep pools are a source of refuge, and particularly in streams that get low and clear during the summer, deep pools are essential. Just not for feeding.

Deep water is a source of refuge where trout can remain hard to see and hard for some predators to attack. But only certain predators. Deep pools offer protection from herons and ospreys and eagles because fish in 5 feet of water are beyond their ability to reach, in the case of herons, and dive upon, in the case of raptors like eagles and ospreys. If the water is deep enough, these predators won't even be able to see trout. But swimming predators like mergansers and otters can easily prey on trout in deep water, so where these animals are around a productive pool for trout fishing will include both deep water and some type of physical cover like logjams or jumbles of rocks.

Rainbow trout use depth and riffled water as opposed to physical structures more readily than other species. I notice this on streams I fish that contain populations of both wild rainbow and brown trout. During the day, if the water is clear enough, I can count the number of rainbows in a pool by standing on a high bank and peering into the water. All the rainbows in a pool will dart to the deepest water and scurry back and forth, obviously frightened but seldom darting to the security of a large rock or log. The browns, however, are either not visible or if I spook them, they bolt for the nearest piece of structure and stay there. I know the brown trout are around because I catch them regularly, but they're just not visible during the day unless there is an ample supply of food like a hatch or a swarm of flying ants to bring them out in the open. And even when both species are out and feeding, when spooked the rainbows head to the deep water and the browns for the brush piles. Unfortunately these streams are also frequented by mergansers, which have a field day with the rainbows because they are easy to corral and prey upon by a flock of these fast-swimming ducks. In summers where the merganser population is dense, the following year I see about the same number of browns but far fewer rainbows.

How much depth is enough to provide cover? It depends on water clarity, but if the water is too deep to see individual small rocks on the bottom, it is probably deep enough to qualify as cover. Eagles and ospreys have better distance vision than humans, but light-scattering in water, due to currents and suspended matter, makes it difficult for any predator to see trout in water over about 5 feet deep, even in clear water with bright sunlight. And ospreys and eagles can only reach

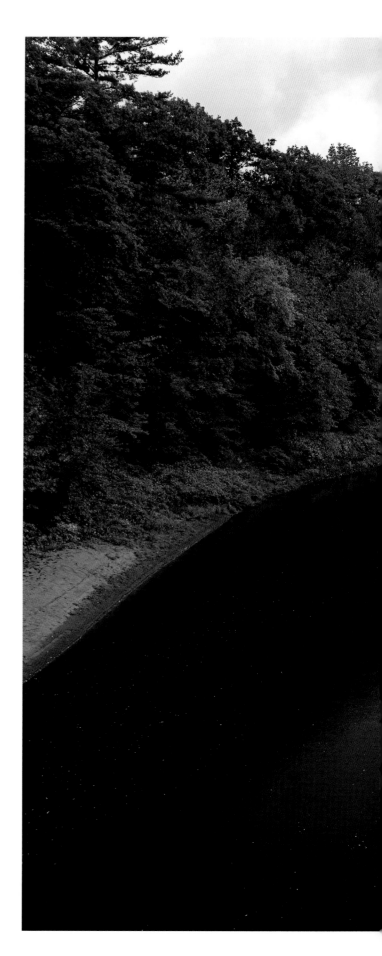

It's difficult for predators to see trout in water deeper than 5 feet, and eagles and ospreys diving can only penetrate about 3 feet of water, so any water deeper than 5 feet will offer protection for trout from all but swimming predators like otters and mergansers. Having structure on the bottom like large rocks or logs will also offer protection from the swimming predators. Trout may not feed in water this deep, but they like to have it nearby as a refuge.

fish in about 3 feet of water, so anything deeper than 3 feet, even in clear water, probably offers enough security for trout in most circumstances.

Trout won't always feed in the deeper places and will move up or down into shallower water to feed, so don't feel like you need to always fish in deep pools. But in low, clear water, especially if there aren't many rocks or logs in the water, look for trout in the proximity of deep pools, where they can easily reach the depths without swimming through shallow riffles or other obstructions. They need a quick, straight shot to that security.

RIFFLES

Riffles aren't often in our thought process when we look for possible trout cover, but they are more important than many anglers think in this regard. The turbulence and bubbles formed by riffles distort our ability (and that of predators) to see into the water. In fact, even in slower pools, a bit of surface disturbance is often enough to provide cover for trout. It's true that riffles also produce most of the insect food trout eat, and in late summer they replenish dissolved oxygen in warmer water through interchange with the air, but I'm not certain that is the most important reason trout live in riffles during the summer.

Once oxygen gets dissolved in water through riffles, I don't think it comes out of solution that quickly, at least to the point where 10 feet below a riffle that oxygen would be depleted. Trout don't breathe the air from bubbles in riffled water—they need it to get into solution first so they can utilize the dissolved oxygen through their gills. And the insects produced in riffles drift down into the slower water in the pool of flat water below. Yet even in colder rivers, where oxygen concentration is not a limiting factor, you'll still find trout right up in the riffles during low water. The only reason for them to fight the current there must be the protection broken water offers them.

If you ignore even shallow riffles during the summer, you could be missing some of the best fishing, because trout are easier to catch in broken water. Don't assume they'll only be in deeper water. They'll be where they feel secure and invisible to predators.

BANKS

Banks provide trout with many options for prime lies, because the current is generally slower and the physical properties of banks make them rich sources of protection. Unless a bank is very shallow and sloping, it offers shade at some point during the day and probably rocks

Besides providing much-needed oxygen at high water temperatures, riffles offer cover to trout because predators can't see them well through the broken surface.

Besides offering breaks in the current, banks also offer shelter in the way of rocks, logs, and shade. In many rivers they are the best places to find trout, and they often provide prime lies that give the trout both food and immediate protection in the same place.

Never pass up an undercut bank. This is one that has produced numerous large trout for me over the years. You don't necessarily need to get your fly back under the bank, as trout hide beneath the bank but look for their food in the current just beyond the bank.

This 18-inch brown trout was caught just on the edge of an undercut bank in a stream where the average trout is 7 inches long.

and logs, breaks in the current, and in many cases cover directly overhead to keep trout out of sight of predators. In fact, if I approach a stretch of water that has a 5-foot-deep center of a pool and a 2-foot-deep stretch of water up against the bank, I'll fish the bank first because the odds of finding trout, and probably larger trout, have always been greater there in my experience.

Undercut banks, where the water flows underneath the bank, are some of the finest places to find trout, especially where the undercut bank offers other cover like rocks or logs or overhanging brush. They are typically close to the main current, which is the reason the bank is undercut because the force of the current at high water digs into the soil beneath the bank but not the upper layer of the soil, which is held in place by vegetation.

A few years ago I found a spot in a local river with a rare undercut bank. The spot is above and below nice deep pools that most anglers fish, but I suspect most of them have not really investigated the undercut. In a stream noted for its abundance of 6- to 12-inch browns and rainbows, the first time I drifted a nymph close to the undercut I caught a 16-inch rainbow. I let the pool settle down for five minutes and tossed my nymph closer

to the undercut, where it was grabbed by a brown trout a few inches bigger than the rainbow that promptly broke my 5X tippet on the log that covers the bottom of the pool. The next time I fished it, I dropped down to 4X and landed that big brown, as well as another large rainbow. Every time I fish that little slot I can count on at least one fish twice the size of the ones I catch anywhere else in that stretch of water. And I haven't shared that spot with anyone, even my best fishing buddies.

When exploring a trout river, trying to decide where to fish, look for spots with continuous cover. In other words, if you find a nice pool that has enough depth for a trout to feed but no water over 3 feet deep, no overhanging trees, no large rocks, and no submerged logs, it may not hold many fish, even if the next pool upstream offers plenty of cover. Biologists have determined that the trout streams that host the largest trout populations have long stretches of water with continuous cover, not in isolated patches. These places will hold the most fish of all sizes, and you may find trout feeding throughout a pool or run because they have a safe place nearby. More trout feeding in more places means a better chance of catching a few.

PART 2

READING THE WATER

By now I hope I have given you a solid overview of what wild trout need in order to survive and grow in a stream, and how the physical and chemical environment determines where they might be found in a broad sense. You might think those aspects alone will help you find trout, and they will. But when you put on your waders or shove your boat off from the put-in, at first you won't be looking at individual rocks or current seams; instead, you'll be faced with the broad physical assemblies of trout streams that are formed by drops in altitude, the character of the stream bottom, and the limits placed on stream flows by the banks that hold the water in place.

We divide these into arbitrary groupings such as riffles, pools, runs, pocket water, and flats. For instance, you might be faced with a broad piece of water with a gentle turbulence on the surface that would be considered a riffle. But on one side of it sits a group of large rocks that could be called pocket water. So these categories can overlap and sometimes you don't know whether to call a piece of water a run or a pool, and that's OK. I'll try to describe them as I categorize them and hopefully you'll agree. But you may come up with your own terminology, which is just fine. One of my fishing buddies uses terms like "buckets" and "tubes," which I've started to use in my own descriptions of water features. We're always learning and expanding our lexicon, and as long as these terms make sense and don't cause too much confusion, I'm all for them.

When describing these categories of trout water, there are some elements that are common to all of them, like banks and midstream rocks and bends. Rather than describing them over and over in each section, in order to reduce redundancy, I've placed them where they seem to be most appropriate. For example, I've gone into detail on bends in the "Runs" chapter, on midstream rocks in the "Pocket Water" chapter, and banks in the "Pools and Flat Water" chapter. So even if the water you fish does not have any pocket water, I'd advise you to read that chapter for a deeper understanding of the effect of rocks.

For each grouping, I'll give you an idea of where trout may be found at different times of the year and at different water levels, and how much or how little trout may move within them in a given fishing day. I'll also give you an idea of what techniques seem to work best in this type of water, although I won't explain how to accomplish them—you'll need to learn how to strip a streamer or drift a nymph through other means, of which there are plenty these days. And, of course, I'll give you those hypothetical fish dropped onto a water feature but be very careful—trout are unpredictable creatures and just because Tom showed you that most trout in the head of a pool will be found just where the lip of a riffle drops off into deeper water, don't assume they won't be in other spots, and if you see fish pushed up into the shallow part of a riffle with their backs almost out of the water where I said they wouldn't be, file that away in your mental library or make a note in your fishing log. I don't know everything, I'm learning new stuff every time I go fishing, and trout are often fickle creatures.

Riffles are the insect producers in trout streams, and also home to most of the baitfish and crayfish. They're typically easy to fish because the broken water hides your casting mistakes, and trout have to grab quickly in the fast water. Not all riffles hold trout of a decent size, so you'll need to know what to look for.

CHAPTER 5

Riffles

DESCRIPTION AND HOW THEY ARE FORMED

Riffles are a standard component of most trout streams, and hydrologists and biologists like to talk about the pool-riffle ratio in a stream, but to them riffles are a broad group that might include what as anglers we call pocket water or runs. They consider any faster-moving water a riffle, but we'll get more granular in our categorization because where you may find trout is different in what we might call a riffle versus similar types of faster current like pocket water or runs. Here's how I describe a riffle: a section of fast water that is relatively shallow with few or scattered bigger rocks or other obstructions. To me, a riffle has just small patches of white water and most of the turbulence is gentle, not enough to form a lot of white water or standing waves.

The Madison River in Montana between Quake Lake and Ennis is often described as the "50-mile riffle" because it forms virtually no large pools and seems to just hustle along without pausing. But to my eye, it's much more than that, with a complexity that is a delight to fish because there are so many places that offer perfect habitat for trout. To just call it a riffle is misleading. This long stretch of water includes stretches of pocket water, runs, chutes, channels, and miniature pools. Sure, it also offers lots of riffled water, but to call it one big riffle is a slur on this amazing piece of water. And fishing tactics need to be adjusted based on its complex structure. If you look for trout in this stretch of the Madison in the same places and use the same techniques all along its 50-mile course, you'll be missing a great deal.

Riffles are formed when the slope of a streambed steepens enough to form gentle turbulence in its flow, but this flow is mostly over smaller rocks and gravel so the turbulence is manifested in little goose bumps on the surface without standing waves or white water. Riffles are typically found in wider places in a river. They can be a few yards long, as they are in small streams, or you might find one on a big river like the Delaware or Missouri that extends for a hundred yards. They eventually flatten out into a pool or a long flat where the slope of the river decreases, as rivers don't exhibit consistent changes in slope because of the constant, dynamic tension between erosion and deposition.

A view of the Madison River just above the famous Three-Dollar Bridge. It's called a "50-mile riffle," but in this one spot I see a riffle, a run, pocket water, and even a few miniature pools.

This is what I would consider a riffle. Gentle turbulence, not an abundance of large rocks, and small patches of white water.

WHERE TO LOOK FOR TROUT UNDER NORMAL FLOWS

I love fishing for trout in riffles—in fact, when I can find trout in them, they are my favorite places to fish. The broken surface lets me get closer to fish than I can in the still water of a pool because trout can't see as well through the broken surface. The moderate current brings food to trout quicker than in flat water so they have less time to inspect a fly, and the disturbance of a fly landing on the water is less likely to alert them. And because riffles usually exhibit more uniform flow with few conflicting currents, drag is much less of a problem here than in more broken pocket water, where lots of eddies and counteracting flows make getting a drag-free float a challenge.

Unfortunately, under normal flows riffles may be devoid of adult trout. A combination of a steep slope and no large rocks to break the flow can make a riffle not worth your effort, but don't feel these areas are wasted water and in need of man-made improvements or diversions. Riffles are the nursery areas of trout streams because they offer habitat for smaller, young-of-the-year

trout up to 4 inches long, as the broken water hides them from predators, and by staying in shallower water they can avoid being eaten by larger trout. Riffles are also the places where most of the insect life in a trout stream is produced, because the numerous small rocks on the bottom offer a diverse habitat for aquatic insects and keep dissolved oxygen levels higher because of the constant interchange with air.

The slope of a riffle can tell you a great deal about its trout-holding potential. Step back a bit to try to get a sense for how quickly the elevation changes in a riffle. If the slope is moderate, or if there are places where the slope of a riffle pushes up into a slight plateau, the water may be deeper and a bit slower, thus holding more trout. If the riffle falls within a steep slope and seems to be in a great hurry to reach the next pool without pausing, it may be great for producing insects and holding young-of-the-year trout under 4 inches long, but not for anything bigger.

But where a riffle deepens enough to present trout with enough depth to feel secure, they can be hidden gems passed up by most anglers. These pockets are especially productive because not only do most fly

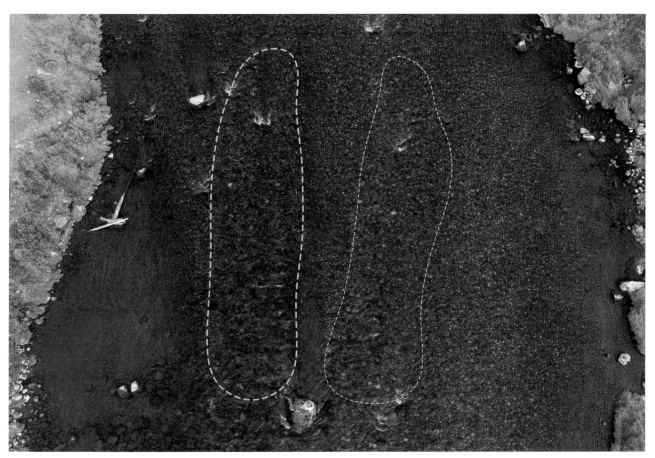

A major pocket in a riffle on the left, and a smaller but potentially productive one on the right. From ground level, these may or may not be apparent depending on light levels and glare. Both of these pockets are close enough to the large rock that trout can bolt to its protection when frightened.

This riffle, at first glance, looks uninviting and is water many anglers would pass up. Yet in the part shown in this photograph, I worked upstream with a dry-dropper and caught over a dozen trout. None of them were monsters, but it sure made for a pleasant hour. You can have a great time in water like this when pools or other hotspots are crowded.

fishers pass them by, but bait and spin anglers, who are more likely to harvest trout, don't notice them and have trouble fishing them with their methods anyway. You'll need to do some careful reconnaissance to find these spots and may even need to wade or float close to them, because these pockets are not always visible from a distance and can't be seen if the light is low or the surface has a lot of glare.

The trick is to find the pockets of water that are 2 feet or deeper. In addition, these pockets need to be long or wide enough so a trout has room to bolt when a predator threatens. If a pocket in a riffle is only a foot long, it's unlikely to hold anything but tiny trout because a larger fish has nowhere to run and no room to maneuver. But lengthen that pocket to about 5 feet and it has potential. The longer or wider, the better. Better yet is a pocket that lies under an overhanging tree, next to a log, adjacent to a large rock, or along the bank. All of these provide additional protection from predators. Best is interconnectedness with deeper water, such as a riffle at the head of a pool or above or below a deeper run or section of pocket water.

Find these pockets by carefully looking at the surface. Riffles are caused by smaller stones in shallow water, which perpetuate turbulence to the surface. Where the riffle deepens, the turbulence may not reach all the

way to the surface, or the turbulence will appear attenuated, which gives the water a smoother look, like little lenses or slicks. Because the depth drops off, the water loses energy in these deeper spots and the current will be more comfortable for the trout, as they'll need less energy to hold their position.

You may find more than just deeper, isolated pockets in riffles. Sometimes one entire side of a riffle may be deeper than the other side, holding trout that benefit from adjacency to the food-producing qualities of a riffle without the need to remain exposed in shallow water. A riffle may also form the head of a pool, perpendicular to the main flow of the current, especially when the slope of a river is more gradual and does not tumble into slower, deeper water but just ambles along until the water is deep enough that the current slows and loses much of its turbulence.

Trout concentrate in places where riffles drop off into deeper water. Where the deeper water is parallel to the current flow, trout will most often be found in the seam between shallow and deep water, which you'll see as a line between bumpy water and smoother water, or by a color change that indicates a change in depth, with deeper water darker in color than the shallows. They'll typically lie right on that seam in a narrow band. Where a shelf is formed perpendicular to the main flow, where

In riffles, look for the smooth lenses that indicate slower, deeper water. These are the pockets most likely to hold feeding trout.

Bumps in a riffle indicate larger rocks on the bottom, big enough to harbor a trout. Remember that the bump is reflected a bit downstream of the rock itself, and that trout may lie in front of these rocks or a considerable distance downstream of them. When placing your fly, the worst place to drift one is right over the bump, so strategize to get a good drift well above the bump or downstream of it.

a riffle drops off into a pool, trout can be found in a more expansive region, sometimes from one bank to the other, and throughout the region where the water begins to slow and drop off. In gentle current they may lie just at the boundary between faster/shallower and deeper/slower water, lined up along the edge. But in faster water, indicated by more pronounced turbulence, they seem to be more widely distributed and will be found not only on the edge of the shelf but well down into the slower water.

If a riffle is mostly deeper with numerous large rocks we call it pocket water, and because that type of water has some special considerations, I am going to treat it as a separate chapter. But you may find a few rocks in riffles, as riffles are often not just composed of gravel or small rocks on the bottom. Whether those rocks offer a likely place for trout depends on their size. A single rock the size of a bowling ball might break the current enough to hold a small trout but it probably won't offer enough security, especially when it's surrounded by water less than 2 feet deep. It will probably also not dig a trench in front and may not offer enough break from the current behind it. From my experience, a rock good enough to hold a 12-inch trout should be at least 2 feet in diameter. That gives a trout enough real estate to hide beneath the rock when danger threatens. Even better is a

jumble of rocks, because once a single rock gets jammed on the streambed, it often collects others as spring floods move larger rocks downstream.

If the rocks are submerged and you suspect their presence by a bump in the surface and swirls behind it, be aware that the bump will be a short distance downstream from the object and if you suspect a trout may be lying in front of the rock, make sure you cast far enough above the bump to drift your fly into position. Otherwise, you'll be placing your fly right on a trout's head or even behind it. And in the area directly behind the rock, if you see strong, swirling turbulence, trout may be found farther back than you might suspect. The break in current behind a rock or jumble of rocks can extend beyond where you see swirls on the surface, so pay special attention to the spot immediately downstream of where the swirls end.

WHERE TO LOOK FOR TROUT IN HIGH OR LOW WATER

High Water

Riffles are generally wider than runs, so the energy of high flows is dissipated over a broader area, giving trout more places to hold in moderate current than in a narrow

During high water, or when a riffle has a steep slope, most of the trout will be found along the bank or in the larger lenses of slower water created by large objects like boulders.

In the low water, trout will more likely be found with their noses right up against a riffle. They live here because there is more oxygen in the water, there is a quicker delivery of food, and the broken surface of a riffle helps to hide them from predators.

run. Thus riffles are high-value targets if a river is in flood stage, either from heavy rainfall or the release of water pulsed from a dam. Trout that would only be found in slots or along deeper shelves in normal flows may spread out into the riffle, and the entire riffle, as opposed to just select pockets, may hold feeding trout. Under normal flows the edges of riffles, close to the bank, slope gradually and are often too shallow to hold trout. During higher flows, though, little pockets along the bank can be prime spots to find trout moving away from the faster current in the center of the river.

You may not be able to see the color changes in a riffle that usually indicate deeper, slower water, because the higher water levels and often the more discolored water that goes along with higher flows may obscure them. But you should be able to find the slower pockets. Look for smooth spots in the surface that can betray a slower pocket. These places might have been too shallow or too small when the water was lower, but with a rise in water they can become prime spots. Look for a smoother surface without swirls, where the current is moderate.

Low Water

When flows become extremely low, riffles can still be productive places for fishing, even though the number of spots will be limited. Riffles hold higher oxygen content than pools because of their constant mixing with the atmosphere, and since high water temperatures are often associated with low water, trout will find it easier to live in riffles where they can get more oxygen. Riffles also provide overhead cover from predators because of their broken surface. A trout in a still pool needs rocks or logs for protection and to stay out of sight, but riffles offer built-in protection, even in the center of the river. You just need the spots that are broken enough, and especially deep enough, for trout to feel secure enough to feed.

You're going to be limited in low water. Look for those places that offer moderate enough current to bring a steady food supply to trout, because at their margins, riffles can move too slow in low water. Look for depth, which will be even more apparent than at any other time of year in low water. The best places in riffles will be those edges along deep shelves, either where a riffle slides along a deeper pocket off to one side or where a riffle drops off into deeper water. Unfortunately, you may not find any of these spots in a drought. Some riffles, although they continue to keep oxygen in the water and produce insect food, may be entirely devoid of trout if you can't find a pocket that's at least 2 feet deep and a couple of feet square.

WHEN TROUT MOVE IN THIS WATER

Trout that use riffles on a daily basis seem to follow this pattern: As insects begin hatching, they'll move upstream from deeper, slower water to where they can capture food at a faster rate, closer to the source of the hatch. They'll sometimes keep moving until they can't go any shallower. I remember the first time I fished the South Fork of the Snake in Idaho with my friend Joe Bressler, who grew up on that river. He pulled his drift boat along the side of a shallow riffle upstream of a cavernous pool, sat back, lit a cigar, and cracked a beer. "Put on a PMD dry size 18," he told me. I looked around and didn't see a single rise. "You sure?" "Yup," he said, "just wait."

I finally saw a few PMDs twirling in the current and got ready to cast. "Not yet," Joe said. "Let them move shallower. They're easier then." Sure enough, a riffle that had been completely lifeless 30 minutes ago (it was shallow enough that I could have seen fish if they were lying there) came alive with big Snake River cutthroats, all magenta and burnished gold in the sunlight. Snouts, backs, dorsal fins, tails repeated in a rhythm that would have been hypnotic to anyone at all interested in natural wonders. To me it was like a cup of coffee after a week of caffeine deprival.

We caught a bunch and at the peak of the hatch, the fish had crowded up into the riffle until they didn't have enough draft to swim any shallower. And as the hatch petered out, we could watch the trout gradually drop back into the deeper water until they disappeared into the depths. Most trout streams don't exhibit the same kind of dramatic behavior, but during an abundance of insects, they'll do it to some degree. Evenings, when low light levels keep trout more protected from overhead predators, are often a prime time to find trout moving into riffles, but if the food supply is tempting enough, they'll even do it in bright sunlight.

To find a riffle that offers this type of opportunity, there must be a secure highway from the protection of depth or a logjam to the shallow riffle. Look for that interconnectivity. A 3-foot-deep pothole in the middle of a shallow riffle, isolated by 50 feet of shallow water from cover, won't be a great place. And trout seem to move *up* into riffles from protection as opposed to dropping down into them. It may be that they follow the food upstream, or possibly that when they are threatened it's easier to bolt downstream with the current than fight the current to get back to safety.

You may also find large trout moving into riffles at dark and after dark. Bigger trout, especially brown trout, often turn into predators after dark and will hunt for baitfish, crayfish, frogs, and other large prey by moving

This big Snake River cutthroat worked its way up into the head of a shallow riffle during a heavy PMD hatch. There is nothing much better than catching a large trout on a dry fly in a shallow riffle, because everything is visible and the fish creates quite a ruckus in thin water.

If a riffle has connectivity to deep water or heavy cover, you may find large brown trout hunting there at night.

around instead of waiting for the current to bring food to them—unless there is a sudden suicide exodus of mice at a river crossing, trout can't afford to wait for bigger prey to come to them. They'll search out easy current and water that is not over a couple of feet deep so they can trap their prey and move around without expending a lot of energy. So if a riffle has a slow, wide area that has easy connectivity to deeper water or logjam refuges (where big trout often loaf during the day), it may be a logical place to try night fishing. Shallow riffles are also easier to navigate in the dark, and you may sometimes see wakes as trout push through the shallows for food.

A trout that lives in a deeper slot in a riffle won't move around much. If the broken surface offers enough protection from overhead predators, and if the water is deep enough and the slot is long enough so that a trout can maneuver when danger threatens, it may live in a riffle for months. Drifting food is plentiful because most invertebrates live here until they hatch, so a trout in a riffle has everything it needs, as long as food is abundant enough to justify the extra energy needed to hold in the faster current. It might not move around to other deep slots, though, because it might have to negotiate very shallow water, and although trout can move through water that barely covers their backs, they do this primarily when migrating, and usually at night. So if you find a pod of trout in a riffle, as long as the water level or water temperature has not changed much, they'll probably be

in the same place the next time you pitch your flies into the same hotspot.

SEASONAL CHANGES

Riffles offer a glut of food but not much protection or security. When hatches are sparse, in the fall, winter, and early spring, you might find trout feeding here but they'll be more comfortable in deeper pools and runs, where they can loaf at a time of year when most of the food occurs in short bursts in the middle of the afternoon. But once the water warms and hatches begin to burst throughout the day and into the evening, trout will slide up into riffles, sometimes for just an hour when hatches are heavy, sometimes for weeks at a time. Spring and summer are the best times to fish riffles.

Late summer, when water temperatures peak and rivers get very low and clear, riffles may be the best place to find feeding trout. There are a number of reasons you may find most of your trout here. One is that riffles may be the only places with enough current to bring trout food at an adequate rate. In low water, the current running through pools may be so slow that a trout might only see a drifting mayfly once every 10 minutes, but a riffle not only produces hatching insects but also brings them to a feeding trout at a more rapid rate. Riffles also keep the dissolved oxygen content of a river higher because of the mixing of the air with the

Although the deep middle of a pool might look tasty, in late season you'll be more likely to find trout closer to the riffle at the head of a pool than in the depths, even though there is plenty of cover in the deeper water.

water on the broken surface of the riffle, and this higher oxygen content comes out of solution quite rapidly, as the river flows into slower and more stagnant water below. One benefit of riffles in late summer is something I don't think many anglers realize: The broken surface of a riffle hides trout from predators, and in slow, clear flows a riffle may be the only place in a river that provides this cover, other than logjams and rock piles.

Even though you should quit fishing at about 68 degrees because you risk killing fish inadvertently by building up excess stress hormones, trout may still be concentrated in riffles at lower temperatures in late season. It might be early in the day and the water has not warmed to a maximum, or perhaps it's been hot previously but a cold front has dropped the temperature to a fishable range. Trout will still be there.

One August day I decided to explore the lower reaches of a rocky stream that flows through a miniature gorge in upstate New York. It was at the downstream limit of the trout population because the river gets quite warm during the summer, but I knew the river in this stretch held a sparse population of large brown trout, as these marginal stretches often do because of the abundance of crayfish and minnows in the warmer water. It had been cool enough that water temperatures were in the low 60s, but the river was extremely low and clear. It was really the wrong time of year to fish water like this,

but for some reason I just had the itch to fish it, even though my chances of success were slim.

This stretch consists of deep ledge-rock pools sprinkled with shallow riffles that flow over fine gravel and room-sized wedges of slate. Figuring the trout would be in the deeper pools in this low water, I thrashed them hard with nymphs, dry-dropper rigs, and small streamers fished almost dead-drift with an occasional twitch to imitate a crayfish. I didn't even have a suspicion of a strike. I moved up into the head of one of the pools where a riffle dumped into it, and suddenly the stream came to life. I missed one strike on a nymph and then caught a couple other fish. Instead of the big browns I was hoping for, these were fat, wild, foot-long rainbows but they sure saved the day. I was not sure why they would be nose up into the shallower riffles when they could be loafing in deep pools, but then a flock of a dozen mergansers flew over my head. Now the presence of the fish in the riffles made a lot more sense. The pools were deep but the water was clear as glass, and the only place the trout could mask their presence was under the choppy ceiling of the riffle.

Although riffles in early spring and late fall may not be optimum places where trout hold, fish migrating on their spawning run must pass through them, usually in the deeper spots. Brown and brook trout move in preparation for spawning any time from August through November, and rainbows may begin moving on their spawning run February through May, depending on the altitude of a river and water temperatures. Trout that have just pushed through a stretch of fast pocket water or a chute may drop into the deeper slot in a riffle to rest before moving on. Trout prior to actual spawning may loiter in the vicinity of gravel patches suitable for spawning, sometimes a good month before they begin the act of digging redds and laying eggs. Riffles often have the most pea-sized gravel suitable for spawning trout, and the necessary current to keep oxygen flowing around the developing eggs. It's not cool to fish for trout near redds when you begin seeing the oblong spots of clean gravel where they have begun the act, but if you don't see any visible redds, fish may still be in the neighborhood.

I'm not going to tell you that you'll never find trout in a riffle in the middle of winter or early spring. If a riffle dumps into a deep pool, or if the riffle offers enough depth to protect trout in its deeper pockets, you may find trout there even in the coldest weather. And if a warm-spell reprieve or a day with strong sun warms the water even a few degrees, trout can nose into riffles, especially if the warmer water stimulates a hatch of small olive mayflies or those tiny black stoneflies that hatch all winter on warmer days. But in winter, the smart money is on the slower, deeper reaches of pools and runs.

APPROACH

A great aspect of riffles is that you can approach a trout from almost any angle. Whether the broken surface totally hides your presence or the trout know you are there but feel more secure, I'm not totally sure. What I do know is that in any given stream, where you can only get to about 30 feet from a trout in a slow pool, you can almost stand on top of one in most riffles. This helps because you can determine your angle of approach solely by what the current flow will do to your line, leader, and fly without worrying much about whether you'll scare a trout in the process. You can even get away with some pretty sloppy wading in the riffle. Pushing through shallow water does not move as much mass, so you are less likely to push fish-alerting waves ahead of you, and the broken surface dissipates the surface disturbance of your wading. I can't tell you the number of times, when fishing a riffle, I've had to back up because a trout rose right under my rod tip and I couldn't even get a cast to it.

Trout rising in riffles can be tough to spot because they often just poke their noses through the film, especially when the current in the riffle is gentle. You can see the trout rising in the foreground here, which would be difficult to spot unless you were quite close to them.

The great thing about riffles is that you can get closer to trout than in any other kind of water without spooking them. This doesn't mean you can be overly sloppy with your wading, but you don't need to wade on eggshells either. And short casts invariably mean a more accurate presentation.

That doesn't mean you should be sloppy and cavalier when fishing a riffle. Sometimes those little slots and pockets deep enough to hold fish don't appear as slicks on the surface, and you may not be able to see the slots until you get out into the river and wade close enough to see the color change that indicates deeper water. One day fishing the lower Blackfoot in Montana, I was wading a riffle that didn't look very productive, as from the bank I couldn't see any water that might hold a trout. As I was working upstream through the riffle, I noticed a darker spot that I couldn't see from the bank, about the size of a large area rug. That little pocket gave up several nice cutthroats on a big Chubby Chernobyl dry fly, fish I would have passed up if I had been walking the bank instead of immersed in the pool. It's my "secret" hotspot (I'm sure many others have found it), and in subsequent years it's always produced for me.

During hatches or spinner falls, trout may already be there, or they may move up into a riffle from deeper water below. Look carefully. When trout are in shallow riffles they make little disturbance when feeding. Because the water is shallow, they won't need to move up far when taking an insect from the surface, so they seldom exhibit the splashes you see in deeper water, because a trout coming up through 3 feet of water builds up momentum and can't help but create a splash when breaching the surface. Riffles, despite their broken surface, don't have much velocity because the downstream progress of the current is sidetracked in all directions when mild turbulence forms, so this combined with a shallow-lying trout allows the fish to gently tip up and sip an insect with little commotion. In riffles, often you'll only see the snouts and sometimes the backs of trout poking into the surface film, which you can sometimes only see at certain angles, depending on the light. Getting into a position where you get glare on the surface sometimes helps, and this is one time you may want to remove your polarized sunglasses. The fish show up as black bumps momentarily rising above the surface.

I like to fish trout rising in riffles straight upstream, from directly below them if possible. You can get closer to trout in riffles, and by sneaking up behind them you can make short, accurate casts, gently laying just your tippet over their heads. The closer you get to the fish, the better you can see them, and your fly, which is a tactic you can't always use in pools or smooth runs because you can't get as close to the fish.

My favorite way to fish riffles is with a dry-dropper combination, but they are also perfect for Euro nymphing techniques or swinging a wet fly.

TECHNIQUES TO TRY

I'm hesitant to suggest a particular technique for fishing riffles because, well, everything works in riffles. Finding a productive riffle with enough deep water in it to hold trout for most of the season is most of the battle. Then you can try to tempt them with whatever method you most like to fish. Trout are here for one reason—to feed—and because they see different kinds of foods, from baitfish to crayfish to nearly every insect a trout stream produces (because most of the larvae live in riffles), it may not be as difficult to find something that interests them because they see a great variety. And the broken water of a riffle means they don't get as close a look at your fly.

Still, there are some methods that seem to be more productive than others. High on my list is a dry-dropper combination with a relatively short dropper on the nymph, somewhere around a foot between the dry fly and the nymph. Pick a dry fly that floats well and looks vaguely like common flies for that time of year, like a size 14 Parachute Adams for early in the season, a stonefly-like dry like a Stimulator or a Chubby Chernobyl in early summer, and a foam hopper for late summer and early fall. Start with any old nymph you like in about a size 14

and either scale down to a smaller nymph or try different patterns until you find out what interests the trout.

Fish upstream or quartering upstream, and because riffles are often expansive, look for either the soft edges of slower water, deeper pockets in the middle, or around larger rocks that break the current. Don't try to cover it all. Fish the prime spots first and if they all produce fish, go back and cover water that didn't look so great the first time around. The nice thing about prospecting in a riffle is that the broken water hides the splash of your cast and fly line, and in riffles, unlike other kinds of water, you can sometimes drop your fly line right on top of a trout without spooking it.

If you don't have any faith in dry flies and prefer to fish just nymphs, riffles are wonderful for fishing with a pair of nymphs, either with an indicator or with Euro nymphing, tight-line methods. You won't spook fish often with an indicator in a riffle, and you can get closer to fish in the broken water so it's easier to get a tight-line presentation right off your rod tip. Serious tight-line anglers fish a grid pattern, where they start out close, work farther out gradually, and then move upstream a few steps and repeat the process. You can sure cover a lot of water this way, but it's tiring and I'm not sure many people want to reduce trout fishing to a grid pattern. You know more about reading the water now, so you shouldn't need to try to cover all the water. You know where trout should be feeding. The edge of a shelf where it deepens is one of the easiest and most productive places to fish a nymph, and if I want to teach someone how to fish nymphs and make sure they start out with confidence and success, that's the first place I would take them. If you find a riffle just packed with trout, you might want to fish a grid pattern. I'll leave that to you, though. I'm not patient enough.

Riffles, because of their uniform currents and shallower depths, are also some of the best places to swing wet flies, soft hackles, or streamers. You can cover a lot of water this way by making a swing, taking a few steps downstream, and covering slightly different water with the next swing. Because most riffles don't have big swirls or conflicting currents, it's easy to control your drifts with simple mends because the line drifts in a uniform manner instead of being yanked all over the place. And, yes, I know, covering the water this way *is* working in a grid pattern, but each grid covers more water, and the casting is easier and more relaxed than slogging weighted nymphs.

CHAPTER 6

Runs

DESCRIPTION AND HOW THEY ARE FORMED

The way I look at trout streams, a run is not quite a pool but is typically narrower and deeper than a riffle. It's a place where a river is deeper, but without the dramatic decrease in streambed slope and accompanying deep, slow water that would make the river a full-blown pool. Many trout streams don't exhibit classic riffle-pool structure, but consist of interlocking runs, sometimes punctuated by shallow riffles where the river widens, that alternate between faster and slower, deeper, and shallower spots but never quite settle down into full-blown pools. Runs have heads where they are faster and tails where they flatten out before moving on to the next water type, but these are often shorter in length and don't have a slower middle section like you would find in a true pool.

Runs form when the slope of a streambed is steep, and the faster velocity of the water cuts a narrower channel. Sometimes they are pinched between two hills, which prevents them from spreading out as a pool would, or they may just course through erodible gravel and smaller rocks. Because the energy of a river is constricted into a narrower slot, its power is magnified, and runs pick up and deposit volumes of smaller rocks and gravel. When a slight obstruction pushes a run off its straight course, there is a natural eroding on the outside of the arc and a deposition of smaller rocks, gravel, and silt on the inside where the current is slower. This eventually forms a bend or meander in the river. It's a lot more complicated than that, and entire textbooks have been written on this process because it's critical for hydrologists to predict how a river will develop in the future. But we're just interested in what is in front of us in the present moment when looking for trout.

In general, if you look at a piece of water and don't know what to call it, I would probably consider it a run.

WHERE TO LOOK FOR TROUT UNDER NORMAL FLOWS

In a riffle, the main limiting factor in finding trout is to discover places with enough depth to protect them. Runs are typically deeper and faster because the same amount of water that flows through a wider riffle is squeezed down into a narrower channel. Here the challenge

Runs are not quite riffles and not quite pools. They have deeper water than riffles, but don't open up into the slower middle section you see in pools. They're great places to fish, though, and you'll find them on all sizes of trout streams.

This is what I would call a run. It's deeper than a riffle, but without the distinct slower, deeper water you might find in a pool. You may call this a riffle or a pool, and that's fine because there is no official designation for a run. As long as you understand the kind of water I'm referring to, we'll be fine.

in finding trout is not so much depth as it is looking for places where the current is broken enough to give trout relief from the current so they can feed or rest but still not have to expend excessive amounts of energy. One type of run that I call a chute is a steep, fast stretch of water with a uniform bottom that offers no breaks in the current. There might be a narrow seam of slower water right along the banks, but in a chute that water is typically shallow and without any protection for fish. Chutes are usually a waste of time and you can safely pass them up.

Runs can be deepest in the center or might display a deep side and a shallow side. Where trout live depends on the speed of the current. In fast current, trout will be found off to the side of the current because it's difficult for them to hold their position. Look for the seams between fast and slow water. In slow or moderate currents, you'll find trout from the deeper channel out to the side, as long as the water is a couple of feet deep and offers some current to bring them food.

This reference to slow and fast water might be frustrating to you because they're relative terms. What's fast and what's slow? To help you get a visual picture of this, where the central current in a run throws up little plumes or standing waves, with some big swirls mixed in, it's probably too fast and fish will be on the edges.

And you'll probably notice very apparent seams. If the central current in a run is mostly flat with a gentle broken surface, trout may be found right in that central channel. In this water, you may not notice any distinct seams, and if they are present they'll be quite subtle.

As in any kind of trout water, structure holds fish because it not only offers them protection from predators, but also moderates the current in faster water. Rocks are obvious places, and just as I discussed in riffles, they should be about twice as big as a trout. And multiple rocks create more places for trout to hide and more complex currents, so trout can find a current speed that suits them. If you find a spot in a run that has large rocks on the bottom, it will hold more trout than a fine gravel or sand bottom.

In my experience, logs are even better than rocks. Logs are seldom as smooth as rocks, so they break the current and form gentle turbulence where the current runs along their length. Logs also have more linear space, giving a trout more places for protection along their length. I've also learned over the years that a log that lies parallel to the current, whether it's submerged on the bottom or jammed up against a bank, is better cover than a log or tree that juts out from the bank at an angle. The more of a log's length that lies parallel to the

This piece of water is what I would call a chute. These are found in places where the streambed drops rapidly without any large objects or bends in the river to break the flow. Fish just don't get any respite from the current here, and you may occasionally find trout in the slow edges along both banks—but it's not a high-percentage spot. I usually pass these up in favor of better water.

In this run, the standing waves in the central current indicate the current is quite swift. I'd spend more time in the softer, slower edges than I would putting my flies in that fast water in the middle. You need to be careful in this kind of water because trout may be close to the banks.

In a run with slow current, trout may be concentrated around the central channel, but as this run is deeper on the far side and those rocks offer great habitat, you'd also want to pay attention to the opposite bank. Trout could feed almost anywhere here and might even slide into the edge between deep and shallow water in the foreground.

In this run with mostly small rocks and gravel, you'll find trout on the seam between fast and slow water where the color changes in the middle of the river. You'll also find trout in the calm water along the banks. However, you'll probably find fewer trout here than you would if the bottom was covered with larger rocks.

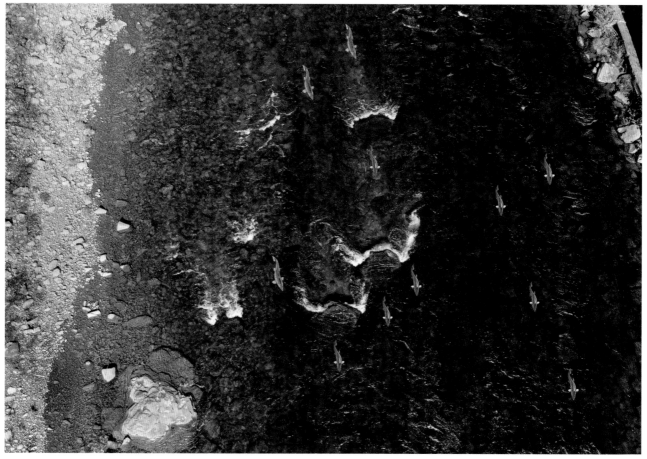

The larger rocks on this cobbled bottom offer many more places for trout to live and feed. Rocks offer protection from predators and a break from the current, and the more large rocks in a given stretch of water, the more potential targets for your casts—and hopefully each one of your casts is more productive.

A log that lies parallel to the current offers more potential fish-holding spots than one that lies nearly perpendicular to it. Nearly every spot along the length of this log, on both sides, could harbor a feeding trout. You'll seldom find this many fish near a single log—the point is that it could hold multiple fish and will be more productive than even a large boulder.

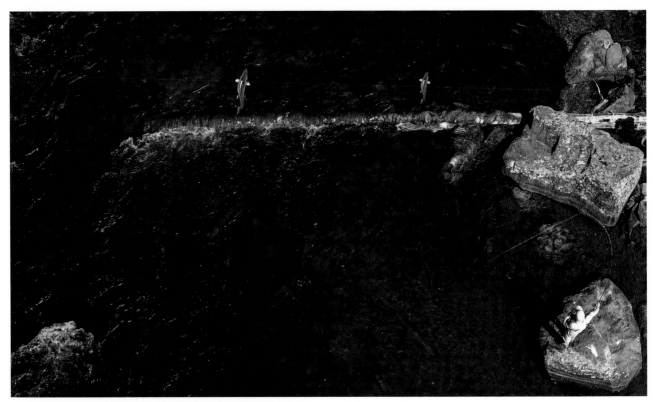

A log like this that lies perpendicular to the current will provide shelter but not so many good places to feed. The water behind the log is too turbulent for a trout's liking, although they may feed in front of the log in the cushion of current it offers and nearby shelter.

current, the more places a trout will find to its liking, where there is a gentle break from the current, a constant supply of food, and a secure place to hide by just darting sideways under the log or right up against it.

Downed trees or logs that are anchored to the bank by roots but lean out into the current, usually at an angle less than 90 degrees (because the current wants to push their outer edges downstream), are called sweepers and they certainly offer protection under their branches. You'll often see anglers fishing downstream of sweepers, in the pocket below them, because it seems like an obvious place to find trout. You may catch fish there, but you'll likely find more and larger trout *feeding* in two places: at the outer end of the sweeper, and in the crotch at the upstream side of where the sweeper is anchored to the bank. In the backwash behind the sweeper, food is sparse because the sweeper strains all the food from the current and either concentrates it in that upstream slot along the bank or at the sweeper's outer edges. Just watch the foam line in a current along a sweeper or where the bugs drift during an insect hatch, and you'll see what I mean.

If the deeper part of a run hugs one bank, look for projections along the bank that break the current and present optimum feeding places for trout. The obvious hotspots are rocks and logs along the bank, but don't ignore small points of shoreline that protrude into the current. Even a tiny point that extends 6 inches into the current will create a productive spot, and you'll often miss these places when you spend your time looking for the obvious rock piles and trees. Trout will be found in the little bays downstream of these points where the current is slower, but don't ignore the slot upstream of them. I've more often found large trout just a bit upstream of these points on the gradual shelf just in front of them, where a trout can lie close to the surface during hatches, barely tipping upward into the drift to feed.

For years I waded, or perhaps a better word is haunted, a half-mile stretch of the West Branch of the Delaware. I became especially fond of one bank along a narrow run that would always produce large wild brown trout for me, and if there was no one around I would walk the bank and fish straight upstream to the fish, as opposed to fishing it from the opposite side, which is easier to wade and the side most people fished it from. There were three little bumps in the 50 yards of bank, and I always approached each one because I could be sure of a trout over 18 inches long in front of each of them. Although I prefer to wade this river, last spring I floated it with a couple of friends and we rowed into this bank just before dark, when it was tough to see all the bank features in the wilting light. But the bumps were still there, and because

This handsome brown trout was caught by dropping a small nymph alongside a submerged log. You won't know exactly where a trout will be in relation to a log, so cover this kind of structure carefully.

I knew their exact location we hooked a decent trout in front of each one of them. When you find these special places, burn them into your synapses.

Runs have heads and tails, although not as pronounced as those in pools. At the head, the river flows from a shallower place, usually a riffle or a piece of flat water, and deepens into a run. Water flowing from a shallower place into a deeper spot dissipates some energy to fill the space, and the current slows, especially below a lip or shelf that drops off into deeper water. A gradual shelf with a smaller slope isn't as valuable as an abrupt one, because the sudden change in depth creates a zone of slower current as the water rolls off the shelf. Trout can suspend in the slower current and dart up into the faster current to feed.

If you watch the surface currents, you should be able to pinpoint where trout are most likely to be. If the current running over the shelf is fast enough to form strong turbulence, betrayed by standing waves or large cells of swirling water, trout will be happier farther down the shelf, where the turbulence settles down into more comfortable, less pushy water. You may also find these gentler spots on the seams on either side of the main flow. However, if the current flowing over the shelf is slower and the surface is just gently riffled, without standing waves, you may find more trout right

in the main flow of current, and closer to the upstream end of the shelf.

A few years ago I explored a section of a trout stream that I hadn't spent much time in because it was a long walk from the nearest parking place, and I had fished it once in the early season during high water and never moved a fish. This time the water was lower, as it was midsummer, and with the more moderate current I was able to see two deep runs that ran along heavily forested rock cliffs. Both runs were fed by gentle riffles without strong turbulence and dropped off abruptly. At a time of year when I expected to catch a few 8-inch fish, the head of each of these runs produced trout almost twice as large as I had expected, one on a nymph and the other on a dry. Both fish were right in the center of the run and took the fly so close to the drop-off, they must have been resting their noses on the lip. Since that day, I have never taken a fish in the tail of the runs, occasionally in the middle, and almost always at the head. It could be that I spook the fish in the slower water below and can only catch the easier fish in the head, but as the trout I catch at the head are about as big as they grow in this stream, I assume it must be the most favored location.

I haven't found the tails of runs quite as valuable as the heads or the middle section, but they are still a viable place to look for trout. Food is concentrated here because

Where the deep part of a run favors one bank, other than the obvious rocks and logs, look for small projections in the bank. You might think trout prefer the little bays behind these points, and you will find them there, but I seem to find the better fish at the upstream edge of the bays, just above the point.

Of course you'd make sure to cover the deep slot in the middle of this run—but don't ignore the place at the head of the run where the fast water drops quickly into deeper, slower water, betrayed by the abrupt change in color.

a river typically narrows and shallows at the tail, before a run widens out into a riffle. The faster current of a run, however, does not offer as many places protected from the current as in a wider pool, where the slower water in the middle of the pool begins to pick up speed from a velocity that is sometimes too slow for efficient trout-feeding into current that is just right. A run, which by definition does not slow down and widen, still carries a lot of current force at the tail. Fish will sometimes be concentrated at the shelf where the bottom begins to shallow, I expect because the current hitting the shallower tail may form a pillow of slower water, as it does when it hits a rock or other object. The more abrupt the transition from deep to shallow, the more likely you'll find trout there. If the run still carries considerable current at its tail and turns into a chute without any breaks in the current, it may not hold many fish—if any at all.

What you often find in the tail of a run is a surface that is frequently described as a glide, which is the perfect description for this kind of water, as it slides along, unbroken by any riffle or white water, sometimes without even a bump on the surface that might indicate a submerged rock. What this tells you is that either the bottom has few projections on it, and is smooth sand, bedrock, or fine gravel, or the water is deep enough

that turbulence formed under the surface is not strong enough to reach the surface. Trout may feed in glides, but look very carefully for the slightest bump or wrinkle that indicates some kind of projection off the bottom that will give relief from the current.

In that same stream I talked about previously, where I found those productive heads in runs, there is another spot that looks, at first glance, to be a worthwhile location. A different run in the same section tails out into a riffle, and it looks worth a cast because it is deep enough to hold fish, deep enough that I can barely see bottom. Yet it quickens so much, without any rocks to break the current, that I can't eyeball a place that might hold a trout. And every time I fish this stream, I work the tail over thoroughly with both nymphs and dries (usually with a dry-dropper so I can try both at once). I have never even seen a trout move for my fly in this tail, nor have I ever spooked one out of it.

Rivers seldom run in straight lines, and you'll often find bends in a river's course in a run. Bends are always productive places to find trout because the faster current that hugs the outside of the bend digs a deeper trench. Don't always assume the deepest part of a bend in a run is the best place for fishing, though. Deeper water is not always more productive for fishing success, but

The outside of this bend, where the fast water meets the cliff, looks so good. Trout might lie under that deep, fast water when spooked, but they'll more likely feed on the inside of the bend, especially where the current drops over the shelf into deeper water.

its adjacency means trout have a secure place to bolt to when threatened. The change in direction of the river's flow also serves up a variety of current speeds. Somewhere in the complex movement in a river bend will be the ideal depth and current speed for feeding trout. Exactly where the sweet spot of Goldilocks water is found depends on the speed of the main flow and the severity of the bend. Trout can be found anywhere in a bend, but sometimes they'll be concentrated in discrete sites.

Watch how the current runs along the outside of the bend, where it will always be faster than on the inside. Where turbulent water kisses the bank is not the best spot, but most people fish this location because they assume it's the deepest. But below and sometimes above the point of impact, you'll find smoother, slightly slower water with a more uniform flow. These seams are more

Notice how the foam line in this run at low water hugs the far bank. Even though the water on the right side of this river is just as deep and has adequate cover in the form of large rocks on the bottom, the money spot will be directly under the foam line. That's where drifting food will be concentrated, and trout know it.

likely to hold feeding trout. If the bank where the current rounds the bend is smooth, it won't be as productive as a bumpy one punctuated by rocks, logs, or other obstructions. These will hold more discrete positions for feeding trout.

Although they don't look as tasty, the insides of most bends are more productive than the outsides. They don't look as good because they don't provide as much cover as a deep, undercut bank, or one festooned with rocks or logs. The inside seams just hang out there in the middle of the river, usually uncluttered by structure, but they're hidden gems because the inside of a bend still offers plenty of drifting food but the reduced current allows trout to feed easily without fighting the heavy flow. In addition, subsurface water hitting the bank flows back under the surface to the inside of the bend, so the fish there have both the smooth surface current for hatching insects and the sideways-directed subsurface current converging at their position. The lack of cover isn't that important because they can quickly dart to the deeper, more turbulent outside of the bend, often with an undercut bank, when danger threatens.

The severity of a bend determines where trout will feed. In a very tight bend, where the change in a river's course is close to 90 degrees, there is a strong but compact burst of turbulence against the bank, which will form lower-energy whirlpools both upstream and downstream of the point of contact. These can both be productive spots if the turbulence in the whirlpools is not too severe. The inside seam of a tight bend is often not as good of a spot because it is small and won't offer as much moderate current coverage. Most bends are not as acute, though, and in general the less severe the change in direction, the more productive places you'll find on the inside of the seam.

WHERE TO LOOK FOR TROUT IN HIGH OR LOW WATER

High Water

Runs, by definition, are narrower than riffles and thus the energy of higher water is constrained into a channel that can greatly increase the current velocity. Trout that were previously happy right in the thalweg, or main thread of current, might find it too fast for their liking and will move toward the edges of the run, where they'll find lower velocity and less turbulence. Look for seams

Note the high standing waves in the middle of this run. During high water, the central current of a run may be too fast for trout to feed efficiently. They'll move into the softer water, closer to the bank, on the edges of fast water. The inside of a bend is an especially good spot at high water.

off to the side where slower water meets fast, and where turbulence changes from swirls the size of watermelons to the size of lemons. Understand that there very well could be trout 5 feet under that heavier surface current, cozy and protected from floodwaters by havens formed by large rocks or shelves. Some will stay there, but it's difficult to get a fly to them without a full sinking line or enough split shot to make a drift boat anchor. Just as many trout will move to the margins, and those are the ones within our reach.

High water makes those inside seams on bends even more attractive. More current will slam up against the bank, making the outside of a bend a tough place to live unless it is pockmarked with large rocks or downed trees. The inside, however, will be the calm within the storm, and an inside bend that was formerly just a shallow gravel bar without enough depth can become the hotspot within the bend. Trout will line up there to feed where they can pluck insects from the drift without working so hard.

Low Water

Because they are deeper than riffles, runs are more likely to hold fish in low water because of the comfort of depth combined with a quicker current that carries more oxygen in warmer water. Runs that you fish in higher water can be interesting—and misleading—in low water. In skinny flows, the way the current moves through a run might be seemingly erratic and even change sides from the way it moved in higher flows, because lower water exposes features that the current ran right over in the spring, but when levels drop these features can direct the flow in different ways. It pays to study a run in low water before you fish it, even if you know it well and have caught trout there before. Treat it as new water.

Along with the normal features you look for—deeper pockets, moderate current, cover nearby—study the foam line that courses through a run, following the thalweg of main current thread. This is the buffet line, carrying not just bubbles and leaves that fall into the river, but also insects that are hatching or small critters that fall into the water. Ants, beetles, and grasshoppers may fall into a river along the banks, but they'll quickly be drawn into that debris line. Feeding trout will be pegged to this line. The line is not as important in high water or even in average flows, and it might not even be that apparent. But in low water it's as reliable as following a trail of breadcrumbs.

Low water can also change the attractiveness of a bend pool. At high or normal water levels, the current at the outside of a bend may be too strong for trout to hold comfortably. But at low water levels, that outside current may be dramatically reduced so that not only is the flow on the outside of the bend comfortable for trout to hold their position, but it may also be the spot where the most food drifts. So the preferred lane of trout-feeding may move from thc inside of a bend to the outside—or in the middle of the river—as the water drops. The foam line can tell you where the food is most abundant, and by looking at the way the current pushes into the outside of the bend you can guess if trout are feeding there. If the current slams against the bank and pushes up against the bank so that its surface is slanted back toward the center of the river, it might be too fast. If the outside current just kisses the bank, it might be a productive place to pitch your fly.

Many tailwaters have extensive weed beds that grow larger with increasing day length, and then get exposed in low water. When water runs over the top of them, trout lie on top of the weed beds, which like any other object in a river constricts the food supply into narrower lanes and, because weed beds offer many small nooks and crannies, slows the current without introducing the strong turbulence a rock or log might offer. When the tops of the weeds get exposed, they can change the character of a run considerably because they channel all of the food, both surface and subsurface, into new places. Trout love to feed just on the edge of heavy surface weed growth because it forms little eddies to slow the current and offers them protection from predators.

Weed growth, if it blocks a clear, un-weeded section of river and isolates it from the main flow, can turn a previous hotspot into a desert. These places can be stagnant and devoid of much drifting food. The Railroad Ranch section of the Henry's Fork in Idaho is really one long run, punctuated by a few riffles but nothing you'd call a pool. I have a few places that always serve up big rainbows feeding close to the bank, where rocks break the current and give trout a place to hide when the abundant ospreys and pelicans soar overhead. But that's in June when the flow is higher. In August and September,

This rainbow was cruising a back eddy eating I-have-no-idea-what off the surface. There was no visible hatch but the eddy must have concentrated whatever food was drifting in the current, and it took a small Parachute Adams—always a good idea when you don't know what the trout are eating.

In the low water of late season, sharp bends in a run may be the only places you find water deep enough to hold trout. Long, straight stretches, unless they offer a deep channel, may be too thin to offer trout protection.

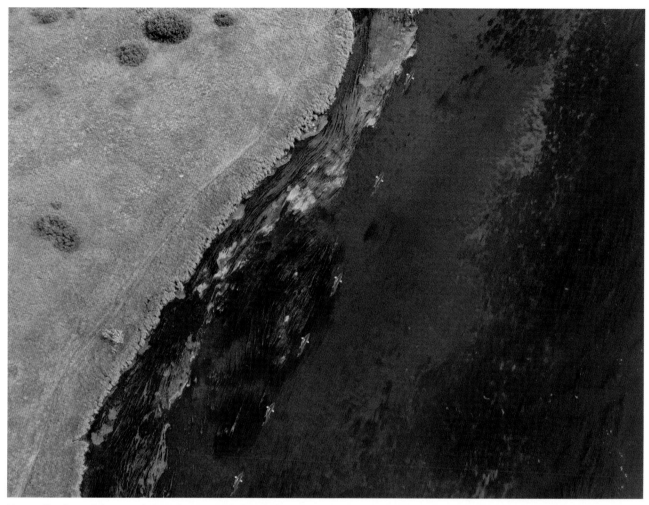

Normally the rainbows of the Henry's Fork feed along the banks, especially the larger fish. In late season, though, when the weed growth builds up, those places along the bank are sometimes blocked from the current by the weeds and become virtual deserts. The trout then feed at the outside edge of the weed beds.

when flows decrease, walls of weeds assemble between the main current and these bank hotspots, blocking the food supply. The spots along the bank aren't choked with weeds and still have enough depth, but large trout can't get enough food there and move out into the main current channel.

WHEN TROUT MOVE IN THIS WATER

Riffles are more-transitory places where you may sometimes find trout or they can be almost empty of any decent-sized fish. Runs, however, provide everything a trout needs, so they'll be less likely to range far on any given day, or even throughout the season.

Where trout in riffles are more likely to move longitudinally, parallel to the flow of the current, trout in runs, with their more powerful and deeper current, are not as likely to move upstream or down. It requires a lot more energy to move upstream in the heavier current of a run,

and although they can slide downstream easily, they might need to swim back against the current to get to the safety of deep water. Their protection lies in the deeper water of the run, and when feeding actively they'll more often slide sideways, into the slower, shallower water on the edges of the main current. They might have been safe under the heavy flow of the main current, close to the bottom, but to feed during an abundance of drifting insects, they'll need to range through the water column, and here they'll be buffeted by heavy current. By sliding into the slower, shallower water along the sides of a run, they'll be in a place where they can easily spear drifting bugs anywhere from the surface to the bottom without getting pushed back in the current and fighting it to get back into position. And when danger threatens, they can quickly slide sideways into deeper water, protected from predators with depth over their backs.

Trout hiding in heavy current on the outside of a bend, in the deeper pocket, might slide to the inside of the bend where feeding is easier. But they might also slide downstream further into the bend on the outside, where the current flattens and slows. This is often a place where a whirlpool spins around and carves backward, in the opposite direction of the main flow. You'll hear these described as back eddies, collectors, or recirculators. I don't know if there is an official technical distinction between these terms; if there is one, I'm not aware of it. But trout that spend non-feeding hours in the protection of the deep water on the inside of a bend will move into these pockets of gentler current, particularly to feed on floating or small subsurface insects. There is even a theory, based on close observation and stomach contents, that some trout wallow in these places just eating insect parts broken up by heavier currents outside of the whirlpool, which then collect into clumps big enough for trout to eat as they rotate again and again in the current. This makes a lot of sense because you can find trout surface-feeding in back eddies even when there is no apparent hatch.

SEASONAL CHANGES

Runs can change quite a bit during the season, because they don't always offer the low-water security a deep pool does. A run that holds nice depth in the spring and early summer will sometimes get quite thin in the low water of late summer and fall. In lower water, you may need to pass up long expanses of water unless the run has a deep pocket, heavy cover along the banks, or large rocks that offer trout protection.

Bends are often great places to find trout in low water because a deeper pocket is almost always formed when a river takes a sharp bend. I have one stretch of a local river that I enjoy fishing in early season because it has nice riffles, a few moderately deep pockets, and good hatches. I can fish the entire half-mile stretch of this river in the spring and hope to connect with a trout or two. However, in late summer, the only place worth fishing is a spot where the river bends almost 90 degrees, forming a deep pocket with fast water at its head. I've learned from unproductive walks through thin water that it's just not worth it to fish the rest of this run in summer, and it's a bit disappointing knowing I'll only have one decent spot in a long stretch of river.

One seasonal shift that bears scrutiny: If you get an early period of dry weather and low water, trout will move out of the shallower places in runs and into pools, or at least to the deeper slots in the runs. When water levels go back up, fish may not move back into places they were earlier in the year—especially if those places

As conditions change in late season in a run, it's better to stay as hidden as you can. Try to keep your profile low, use the bank behind you to break your profile, and stay in the shade if possible.

To get to the nice soft water on the far side of this run, it's important to keep line off the water by using a high rod to keep the line and leader off conflicting currents. Sometimes a better idea is to cross the river if possible to get in the same current lane as the fish.

are separated by long distances from a deep-water refuge. So a period of low water early in the season may set the stage for the rest of the season and trout may not occupy places that look suitable. They'll stay in close proximity to the deeper slots.

APPROACH

How you approach a run depends a lot on where the currents run and where the best feeding lanes and cover are located. In high to moderate flows, you'll typically find a strong central current, or maybe a few threads of current, and one side may look better than the other. If the best water looks to be on your side of the current, it's probably best to work upstream. You'll be closer to the fish, and by working upstream you'll be less visible to them and might be able to get closer. However, if the best water is on the far side of the main current, you might think about working downstream, as a downstream presentation combined with a mend or reach cast will let you fish the slower water on the far side of the current and get a better drift because your fly line and leader will land upstream of the fly, giving you more insurance against drag.

In low summer water, it's best to work upstream because the water is clear and the fish will be spooky. You'll need every edge you can to stay hidden. Try to stay in the shade or up against the bank to give the fish less of an opportunity to spot you. And because you'll need to pass up a lot of unproductive places in low water, try to stay on the bank, or at the very least in shallow riffled water, so you don't push waves up through a run and alert the fish to your presence.

TECHNIQUES TO TRY

Runs are trickier to fish than riffles because you'll find at least three different current speeds, and possibly many more, introducing problems with presentation and drag on your dry fly or nymph. You'll be faced with a main channel with faster current, which could be anywhere from the middle of the run to almost tight to one of the banks. But alongside that faster flow you'll have slower current on each side, and if the central thread of current in the run breaks up into multiple channels, that complicates matters even more. Any technique will work here, but some are better than others.

Trout and currents in a back eddy or whirlpool. Casts are tricky here because of the conflicting currents—remember that the trout on the inside of the back eddy are facing up-current but downstream, so make your casts at the appropriate position so that you get a dead drift coming down to them. It's best to get as close as possible to these spots so your casts are accurate and you don't place your fly over conflicting currents. These fish are often plucking insects from the surface film but will also take a nymph.

If there is no hatch, or if the water is colder than 50 degrees, trout may be tucked under the protection of the central current, in deeper water, especially if the bottom is broken up with rocks that break the flow and offer shelter. At these slower times, your best strategy is to fish a nymph deep, using whatever method you prefer, concentrating on the main current thread and perhaps the inner 10 percent of the slower current on each side of the main flow.

In narrow rivers you may be able to fish the water on the near side of the faster flow, the main flow itself, and the far edge from one position, but for that far edge you'll need to keep most of your fly line off the water or use aggressive mends because the faster flow in the middle of the river will grab your line quickly and pull it downstream in a rush, creating drag and whizzing your fly out of position for the fish on the far side. In wider rivers, where you just can't keep line off the main flow in the center or can't mend aggressively enough to keep your fly from dragging, you may need to try to cross the river somewhere and fish it from the other side. I've learned from painful experience that trying to place my fly on a far seam on the other side of fast water is a losing proposition. I try to keep track of the number of

slow enough and the difference between the main current thread and the seams on either side is not drastic in velocity, you may be able to swing flies effectively.

Prospecting or blind-fishing with a dry-dropper is a great way to fish a run because you know there will always be fish here, so if the fish are at all interested in a fly on the surface or in a drifting nymph, you may be able to tempt them. As with fishing nymphs by themselves, concentrate on the near seam and the central current. The far seam can be tough with a dry-dropper, especially if the central current is swift, but you may be able to fish it effectively by casting at a downstream angle and making as aggressive an upstream reach cast as you can.

During a hatch, fish in runs will often move from under the central current and side seams into the slower, shallower water on each side of the run. If you see bugs on the water, don't wade right in and slap your flies over the deepest water in the center. Work the edges first, even in water that looks too skinny to hold trout. Hatches are also a prime time to find trout on those inside, slow seams where a river bends, so make sure you take time to observe these places and look for rising fish.

Whirlpools with circulating currents are also prime places during a hatch, and will often be the first place you spot rising fish and the last place you'll see them after the hatch is over. Just pay attention to where in a whirlpool a trout is rising, because depending on where they are in its circumference, they might be facing upstream, downstream, left, or right. If you approach a whirlpool from below and a trout happens to be rising in a counter-current that is directed upstream, the trout feeding there might be staring you in the face as you wave your fly rod. Plus you'll need to make a direct down-current presentation to this fish, never a great way to get a drag-free float and a bad hooking angle on a dry fly.

Unless they are spooked, trout may also hold in soft, shallow edges in runs at non-hatch times as well. I got up at first light one morning to fish a fast riffle with nymphs on the Delaware River, and after the sun came up and the nymph fishing there slowed down, I walked back to my car at the edge of a run I typically don't fish unless there is a hatch. I spooked a large trout out of very shallow water so I slowed down, put on my polarized glasses, and soon found a half-dozen fish lying in the shallows that I was able to fish to with an unweighted nymph and no indicator, sight-fishing. I even managed to hook a couple. Because this is typically a busy pool with a well-traveled path along the bank, these trout usually get spooked into the safety of deeper water, and I've seldom had this lucky experience again. But I always look.

times I can catch trout on either a nymph or a dry on the far side of a wide run, and I can tell you my success rate is pitiful. Most times I won't even fish the far side and will try to cross somewhere so I can get to it at a more comfortable and productive angle.

Stripping streamers can solve this problem, because you don't need to worry about drag. You're purposely moving the fly like something that is a strong swimmer, like a baitfish or a crayfish. With this method you can fish all lanes within the run, and you can typically fish the far seam, the center, and the near seam in a single cast. Stripping streamers in most runs is better than swinging them, because the faster current in the center whips your streamer around too quickly. For the same reason, swinging soft hackles and wet flies is not as easy in a run as in more uniform water, but if the run is

Pools take on all shapes and sizes and like fingerprints or spots on trout, no two are exactly the same. Each one has its own mysteries and challenges.

CHAPTER 7

Pools and Flat Water

DESCRIPTION AND HOW THEY ARE FORMED

Just what is a pool and how does it differ from a run? There is no official or scientific definition of a pool; to a scientist who studies river dynamics, anything that isn't a riffle is a pool. Fluvial morphologists study sediment loads and channel formation that depend on physical factors like slope and flow variations and streambed composition. They look at either a wide overview of channel formation or a close view of hydrological events. But we're looking at the intersection of these physical processes and a living creature, which can choose where it lives within the stream channel and may move at will when conditions change. And even within a local trout population, individuals don't behave like ant colonies and may have their own concept of a good place to live. So although we don't get into as much detail on the physical properties of moving water as fluvial morphologists do, we add the complexity of a sentient creature to the equation.

I'm going to make the distinction between a pool and a run because I think treating them separately helps us predict where trout feed. Whether you agree with my definition or not doesn't matter. Just in case, make sure you read the chapters on both pools and runs. Then no matter what type of water you encounter, you'll be able to predict where trout feed. A pool, in my world, has three distinct parts: (1) a strongly defined head composed of faster water, anything from a riffle to a tumbling waterfall; (2) a slower middle section that is often the deepest part of the pool; and (3) a tail where the pool constricts and quickens before it drops off into more fast water. Each of these sections has its own character, places most likely to hold trout, and effects on trout behavior.

The water that flows into a pool could be pocket water, a riffle, or a long stretch of flat water. The slope of the streambed above a pool is more gradual, and suddenly the streambed reaches a plateau or depression where the fast water deepens and flattens. The fast water from above will extend some distance into the pool, depending on its velocity when it enters the pool and the volume of flow. Unless the head of a pool is underlain by solid, slanting bedrock, the force of the

Head

Middle

Tail

Parts of a classic pool. The exact delineations
are arbitrary, but the head is where the fast
current rushes in, the middle is where the pool
deepens and often broadens, and the tail is
where the pool shallows before heading into the
next feature in a river, usually a riffle or run.

turbulence creates a steep drop-off, usually with a shelf above it. The turbulence eventually flattens out and the surface gets smooth, which is the dividing line between the head of a pool and its middle.

The middle of a pool is characterized by mostly flat water, broken by an occasional rock or log, with a surface that is mostly unbroken. Sometimes this flat water can go on for a half mile in larger rivers. Eventually a pool drops into another riffle or run, but before it does, the water quickens as it is drawn into the steeper slope below the pool, and it often narrows as well.

Depending on the composition of bedrock and how the pool was formed, the deepest part of a pool could be at the head or somewhere in the middle. If the water is clear enough, you can often find the deepest part by looking for the darkest water. If the water is discolored, though, it's always a guess unless you've fished there before. But pools typically offer the deepest and slowest water in a stretch of river, which makes them attractive to trout for the protection deep water offers, and for the protection from fast current that slower water provides.

WHERE TO LOOK FOR TROUT UNDER NORMAL FLOWS

The Head of a Pool

The head of a pool is always the first place I'll try. The broken water here lets me get closer to trout without spooking them, and because the head is closest to insect-producing riffles, trout here may feed more often because they see a constant buffet of food.

The head of a pool also has features that are more distinct and easier to parse for fish-holding potential. There is often a shelf where the faster water at the head drops off into deeper water. Trout can lie just below this shelf in the slower water and peruse the current flowing above them for food without wasting energy. If the shelf is gradual, typical of a riffle dumping into a pool, trout may be spread out longitudinally and along the shelf's entire width for quite a distance, because at every part of the slope another slight depression is formed. Trout may be feeding anywhere along the shelf because the current

There is invariably a shelf where the head of a pool enters, and it is always a good place to find trout—and also one of the easiest places to catch trout because the fish are looking up into the shallow water above and the broken water hides our mistakes. And, yes, there will be a trout below that big rock—I couldn't resist putting one in. But the spot immediately behind the rock is not a likely place, as you've learned previously!

is often gentle enough nearly everywhere for them to lie on the streambed and feed in the water column above.

You can determine if the shelf at the head of a pool is gradual by the color of the water—if there is a steady transition from light to dark, it's a gradual shelf. The best place in a shelf like this is usually where, in clear water, the bottom becomes mostly invisible or at least blurry and the rocks or gravel on the streambed can't be distinguished. The shallower places where you can see every stone on the bottom could hold trout during a heavy hatch, or in low light levels like drizzly days or in the evening. But in full daylight trout will favor places where predators have trouble spotting them.

Where faster, more turbulent water from a run or pocket water dumps into a pool, trout will feed in more discreet places. In the center of the main current strong turbulence, with standing waves and lots of bubbles, predominates and trout have trouble holding and feeding in the strong flow. It doesn't mean you won't find trout there. Underneath all the turbulence may be a pocket of quiet water where trout find security because predators can't get to them. But the fish often go there when spooked, not to feed. If you can get a heavy nymph or streamer into the heavy flow, you might catch a trout that has been loafing and not actively feeding, but you'll probably need to get your fly right in their face to interest them—a tough job in heavy current.

However, you'll always find pockets of slower water with more gentle turbulence or flow along the edges of heavy current. And turbulent water flowing into a pool typically forms a more discrete shelf that drops off quickly, which you'll see by a sudden change in color from light to dark. Unlike gradual shelves, trout along abrupt shelves will be more likely to feed right on the edge of the shelf as it dumps into deeper water, because they get respite from the current in the slower water just below the shelf. In the very center of the flow, when the water drops off the shelf, strong vortices create heavy turbulence that can pummel a trout, but at the edges or seams, where the flow is lessened, turbulence is moderate and trout can comfortably hold their position.

The heads of most pools are not symmetrical. The main current may not slam right into the center of a pool, so often one side or the other will hold more opportunities to find feeding trout. One side of the head may be mostly tumbling water with little break from the current, so the opposite side of the main flow will be a better option. Where a pool forms at the bend in a river, under most flows the inside of the bend will hold more trout than the outside.

Look carefully for back eddies or whirlpools just below the head of a pool along the banks. This can be an area of calm right next to violent turbulence because the energy required to recirculate dissipates the flow. Trout

A brook and a cutthroat trout lying at the upper end of a shelf at the head of a pool. These fish are looking up, waiting for food to tumble off the shelf.

This is a more complex head of a pool, with the main flow hitting a rock wall and forming not one but two back eddies with counter-circulating currents, one on each side. There may be trout at the bottom of that very deep water, and you are welcome to try for them, but you'll either need a full-sinking line or about a 10-foot dropper below your indicator to get a nymph down to them. I'd concentrate on the places trout are more likely to be feeding: at the shelf at the head of the pool, and places where the back eddies move onto shallow bars. Note the different orientations of the trout in the current—choose your approach and presentation carefully.

will typically align themselves with the outside edges of the whirlpool, where steady current brings them food. The center of a whirlpool is like the eye of a hurricane—quiet, not much going on, because although insects can get trapped there and whirl around and around, it does not present the same volume of insects as the moving current on the edges. Just remember that trout in these places align themselves with their heads into the current, so the ones on the outside edges will be facing "downstream."

Large rocks often deposit at the heads of pools because the fast current from above pushes them here, and as the current slows down in the pool they're able to settle there during heavy floods. Each rock can produce a miniature pool within the pool and give trout protection from the current, a hiding place, and multiple seams in which to feed. As with rocks in any part of the river, the hotspots will be in front of the rocks, along their sides, and downstream of the rock or rocks where

the seams from each side meet in a V. In most flows the white water just below the rocks won't be a high-percentage target because it's just too turbulent in high flows and dead water in low flows. Rocks are especially valuable where one side of the head of a pool is favored with heavy, turbulent current. In the roiling water the rocks can introduce little refuges in otherwise difficult water for trout to handle.

Rocks often break the heads of pools into different threads. Some of these threads may be shallower and slower, and others may be deeper and faster. Often the threads will be roughly equal. Treat each thread as a separate head, and don't rule out smaller threads that look insignificant. A smaller, secondary thread could hold more feeding trout than the primary one. One of my favorite pools on the Battenkill has a gorgeous piece of water at its head that flows against a rocky bank and sports a deep, tasty-looking bucket. Yet during the May Hendrickson hatch, about the only decent hatch of large mayflies in this river, I catch all my fish in an insignificant little channel, off to one side, much shallower and slower than the main thread. I think most anglers don't even pay attention to it.

Plunge, or waterfall, pools are scenic yet often frustrating places to fish. Some of the most frequent questions I get from fly fishers are about plunge pools: where to find trout in them, how to fish them, and why they don't seem to produce as many trout as people expect. They are difficult to fish because there is often virtually no shelf at the head—water drops off a sheer cliff into deep water, eliminating that gradual shelf that provides so much food and shelter for trout. The vertical drop produces strong turbulence and white water, which as we've learned are not places trout favor when feeding. Intuitively, we know waterfall pools hold nice trout because they often have the deepest water and thus are a great refuge for protecting fish from predators. But they may not hold as many fish as you think, and when trout feed in them, it's often not in those deep pockets that most anglers fish.

Trout do use the deep holes beneath waterfalls and sometimes behind them—for cover. It's almost impossible for a heron or osprey (or for most anglers!) to get at trout in deep, turbulent water below a waterfall, and

The head of this pool has multiple seams, five major ones. Each of these would be a good place to find feeding trout. In high water I'd look at the ones in the foreground, as they are in slower water. In low water I would favor the seam in the more prominent current, which would likely be the seam against the far bank.

Plunge pools are scenic but often frustrating places to fish. Trout prefer to feed at the shallow tail of these pools, but we usually spook them in our enthusiasm to fish the deeper water right under the lip. We see the trout in the deeper water, not realizing we pushed them there, the fish are spooked, and no amount of effort will catch them no matter how many fly changes you try. Next time approach a plunge pool carefully from below and cast into the tail before you move up into deeper water. And don't stand over the falls like this guy. He's already fished the pool and is moving upstream.

getting behind a waterfall is even more difficult. Trout go there to hide, but feeding is difficult because they can't see their prey. While hiding there, if not severely frightened they may grab a nymph or a crayfish, so they can be caught there, but they are not usually actively feeding and you have to almost put a fly in their face.

In a plunge pool, look for trout actively feeding in seams along the edges of the white water. There may also be places at the lip of a waterfall, along the edges of the main current, where the current just barely trickles over the edge with swirly, foamy water, and you may find trout there. Waterfalls typically have back eddies on both sides of the main current that may be more productive than the siren song of the pretty tumbling current in the center of the river. These back eddies can run over rock shelves that give feeding trout a place to rest on the bottom, or the recirculating water can

deposit gravel shelves with a sloping drop-off that provide a break from the current and a profitable location to ambush prey. Always pay attention to both corners when fishing a waterfall pool. In my experience, however, the best places to catch trout in plunge pools are where the current flattens out after the white water ends and in the tails of waterfall pools. We'll cover both of those areas shortly.

Where the disturbance from the fast water at the head of a pool loses its white water and turbulence is the money spot. Look for the place where the plumes or waves from turbulence are less than an inch high. It's one of the best places in a pool because it's still in the main flow of current with its generous food supply, but the flow and turbulence are reduced enough that trout can find a place to feed, especially if the flow is broken by rocks or there are large cobbles on the bottom to

The spot just downstream of where standing waves flatten out in the head of a pool is a prime place to find trout feeding. From that spot downstream, well into the middle of the pool, traces the one place right out in the middle where trout are likely to be found.

break the flow and offer shelter. As always, look for seams at the edge of the main flow. The seams here will be more productive than ones farther up in the pool, closer to the white water at the head of the pool.

Sometimes this area of transition happens suddenly and the turbulence drops off to almost nothing. This is especially common at the base of a long plunge pool or waterfall where all the energy of the current is directed downward. However, where water enters a pool with a more gradual slope, the faster water and areas of turbulence extend much farther into the pool, and the transition section of moderate disturbance extends longer. In one sense this is good because it gives you more available prime habitat. It's also tough because you have more prime water to consider, and you won't know exactly where to find the fish. Sometimes an abundance of riches is not a good thing, especially if you have a large pool to cover.

The Middle of a Pool and Flat Water

In some pools, finding the most likely places for feeding trout can be daunting, especially in large rivers with long, wide pools. In a tiny mountain stream the middle of a pool might only be a couple of feet in length, but in

larger rivers the middle of a pool might stretch over a half mile of streambed. In fact, in many large rivers, especially tailwaters (where the water below a dam may have been cleared of obstacles and straightened to move water more efficiently to downstream irrigation headgates), you may find miles of flat water without much of a break.

A good example is the Henry's Fork of the Snake River in Idaho where it runs through Harriman State Park. The entire river has been moderately straightened and lined with berms. Even though the river offers gentle curves and bends and looks natural enough, looking at it with a critical eye and comparing it to the tumbling rocky stretches above and below the state park, you can see how humans, over the years, have tamed the river and homogenized its flow. You're not going to wade all that water, and even if floating through in a raft or drift boat, you just can't work all of it.

Although the middle of a pool or a long stretch of flat water looks featureless at first, we can peel back some layers to find those spots most likely to hold trout. Don't just look at that flat, boring mirror and lose interest—look around its edges and find the wrinkles. The first feature I look at in flat water is the banks. Not all banks are created equal, so you should first eyeball as much of both banks as you can see, and even beyond what you can see if you carry a pair of miniature binoculars. They're not just valuable for looking at distant stream features—they're also very handy when looking for rising fish beyond what you can see. Of course, that's one more gadget to carry, so decide how much clutter and weight you want in your vest or pack. (Many guides carry binoculars in their drift boats, where it's much easier to safely store extra gear.)

The first thing to look for, even before you decide which bank is deeper, is where the current flow gets close to the bank. Look for that bubble line or other signs of the main flow, like a gentle current, and pay attention to where it kisses the bank. Trout won't be far from this flow. Of course, the main flow could be in the middle of the pool, but right now we're looking at banks, so pay attention to those points of intersection.

One of my favorite pools on the Battenkill has a gravel bar down the center that can be waded even at

high water, and a nice deep pocket with overhanging trees for shelter on its south bank. It's so deep I can't wade through it at normal water levels. The only problem with this deep pocket is that it's on the opposite side of the main flow, and I seldom see trout rising there and have never caught a fish swinging a streamer under the banks. The other side, which is much shallower, probably 2 feet deep in most flows, doesn't have any overhanging trees for cover but it harbors all the feeding fish as best as I can tell, and during a heavy hatch I can concentrate on the shallow north bank and ignore the deep water behind me. I suspect there is one large trout that loafs in the deep water on the south bank and comes out to feed on a sculpin at night twice a week, but it's not a high-percentage spot.

The deeper bank is, however, typically the bank close to the main flow of the current, so you should pay attention to the places where deep pockets form along the bank. In high or dirty water, or when there's a lot of glare

From above you can see the different weed beds and depth changes in the Henry's Fork at Harriman State Park, but at the surface, especially with some glare on the water, the river appears featureless at first glance. Teasing out the better places to fish requires a bit of closer examination. In practice, most anglers fish this water by walking the banks carefully and hunting for rising fish—but you still need to know where to look.

From ground level you can see the darker color indicating deeper water along the far bank, and the subtle ripples made by some large rocks on the left side of this photo.

From overhead it's easier to see the deeper water and the rocks that made the swirls in the previous photo. Trout will likely be found in front of the rocks and in the shelf along the far bank at the edge of deep water. The best places are probably near the overhanging tree and close to the shade, where trout can bolt to when frightened because overhead predators can't see them as well. And, yes, you might also find trout here at the place where deep water meets shallow on the right side of the deep slot.

You can tell the current favors this bank because of the strong bubble line. And the rougher the bank, the better it is for trout habitat. I think the best place in this photo, and probably the place to find the biggest fish, is just upstream of the little projection in the bank. I think it's less likely to find a trout behind the projection because as you can see here, all of the foam (and thus the food) is concentrated above the point and the area downstream of it gets bypassed. Yes, trout could be anywhere along this great bank, but if you're looking for the best one, here is where I'd drop my fly when floating by in a drift boat.

on the water, it's difficult to tell which bank is the deep one because you may not see the color change between deep and shallow water. This is when you need to look beyond the water and into the surrounding terrain. A steep slope or rock cliffs often indicate a deep bank below, because the slope of the land continues underwater. However, a shallow slope to a bank, with a long gravel bar, tells you that bank is the shallow one.

The deeper the water along a bank, the more trout it will hold. But wait, you protest, you told us that trout prefer to feed in water that is 2 to 4 feet deep—why should I look for the deepest water? Here's why: The deep water provides security and cover, but most banks exhibit a shallower shelf along the edge of the water, so trout can lie on that shelf to feed but dart into the deeper water if frightened. And sure enough, when you find a deep slot along a bank with a nice sloping shelf, you'll find more feeding trout. This may be why when you find a sheer rock cliff on a bank that drops off into deep water, you seldom find trout there. At least I don't.

I was floating the canyon stretch of the South Fork of the Snake River in Idaho one day with guide B. J. Gerhardt, and we kept floating by sheer rock cliffs that dropped into who-knows-how-deep water. It just looked so good, and although I tried fishing nymphs as deep as I could and running streamers on a sinking line through this water, I never picked up a fish. I asked B.J. if he thought there were giant trout below those cliffs. "Could be," he said, "but we never catch any." Right after I asked him that, we floated past a place where a 3-foot-square area of rock shelf extended out from the sheer cliff, with 2 feet of water flowing over it. Sure enough, I ran my streamer over that rock and a nice cutthroat jumped on it.

The next layer of the onion is the roughness of the bank. The more nooks and crannies a bank offers, the greater its trout-holding potential. A jumble of rocks along a bank gives trout protection from current on the edge of faster water, yet lets the fish stay close enough to the main current to reap its food-supplying benefits. More roughness, more seams. The rocks themselves, if large enough, can also be places of refuge and trout may not even need to bolt for deeper water if an osprey hovers overhead. Any shelf along a deep bank may be a potential hotspot, but complexity on the bank makes it even more so. You've got a big pool to cover and can't fish it all, so even the odds as much as you can.

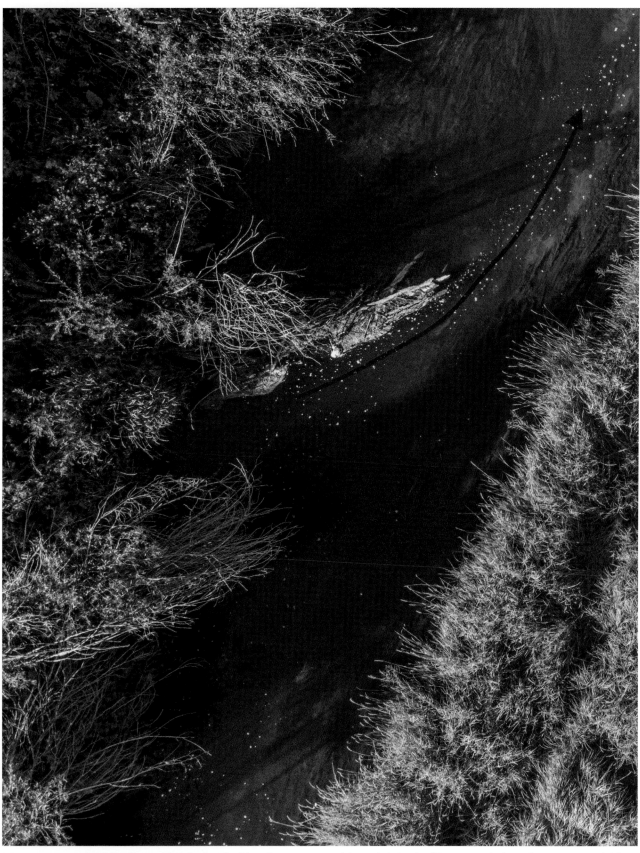

It's easy to see in this photo why the back side of a sweeper, although it looks like a good place for a trout to hide, is not the best place to find a feeding fish. If you trace the bubble line, you can see that all the food drifting in the current gets directed away from the back side—the sweeper acts as a strainer. You are more likely to find feeding fish in front of the sweeper or at its tip.

One feature I always look for, because I often find nice trout feeding there, is a place where erosion from the current creates a tiny bay or divot in the bank. It might be a place where a tree trunk got washed away, or where a boulder used to sit before it was pushed downstream in a flood. Or maybe the soil along the bank there was weaker. This creates a small point that juts into the current with a tiny bay downstream of the point. It may be so small that you hardly notice it, but I've found that even a point that sticks 6 inches into the current with a bay behind it that's only as long as a trout will be the one place that is almost sure to hold a trout in an otherwise smooth bank. Although you'd expect trout to feed in the bay itself, and they often do, I've often found them feeding just upstream of the point, I suspect because the point creates a shelf upstream of where it reaches above the surface, and there is a cushion of slower water formed upstream of the point.

Sometimes these bays are large enough to hold more than one trout. A good one can have a trout just above the point, one in the middle, and another at the little tailout at the end of the bay. I usually find the larger fish either above the point or at the tail end. The middle of a small depression seems like the obvious place, but the food could be more concentrated at the heads and tails of these formations.

Logs, submerged or half submerged, lying parallel to the bank are always prime trout-holding places. If you see one, make sure you give it lots of attention. In my experience trout prefer wood to rock when they can get it, and although you would think a log is only a temporary place that will get washed away or rotted, if it is anchored somehow to the bank by a root wad or between a couple of rocks, water inhibits rot and the log can stay put for many years. If there is some open water between the log and the bank, trout will sometimes feed there if it has a decent current flow, but they're more likely to be on the outside of the log, adjacent to the main flow of the current. And they seem to prefer the upstream end of a log to the downstream part.

I think you can start to see how we can turn a piece of boring flat water into little pockets of potential trout abundance. And we're still looking at the banks, because we have other features to consider. If a bank has enough depth and flow, look for overhead cover like trees or bushes. They don't have to be much, as just one small bush hanging over the water will make a spot more attractive to trout. Yes, sometimes food like ants or beetles or clumsy stoneflies drop off a bush into the water, but overhead cover does a lot more. First, branches over the water block ospreys and eagles from dropping onto a trout and make it difficult for a big heron to sneak close

This bank looks like great habitat, but if I was whizzing past it on a drift boat, I would hold my cast and make sure I got a good one in the vicinity of this overhanging tree—or right under it if I could make the cast.

to a fish exposed in shallow water. But the shade the bush furnishes makes some trout much more difficult to spot, whether by overhead predators or other predators like man, mink, and mergansers. Trout feel more secure when they sense they can't be spotted.

Sweepers, logs or live trees that are anchored to the bank, are always focal points for trout. The branches furnish cover from predators, and the trees generate breaks from the current if they have enough mass. A slender limb might offer some cover but probably not much of a current break, but a larger tree with its trunk anchored to the bank, especially one that extends below the surface a foot or two, will create its own microhabitats. When you encounter a large sweeper, where you can't cover its entire perimeter with a cast or two, pay attention to where trout are most likely to feed. Sweepers are fly-eating monsters, so you should plan your casts with care because every one of them is a potential lost fly, or at the very least a disturbance when you try to dislodge your fly from its greedy appendages.

Although you will see trout feeding in the plume directly behind a sweeper, I see more fish feeding directly above them, especially in the spot just upstream of the crotch where the sweeper meets the bank. Fish underneath the sweeper and behind it won't see as much food as in this spot, because food gets concentrated and funneled into that spot. In slower current, they'll also position themselves at the outside tip of the sweeper, again because it directs drifting food right to them. The area behind a sweeper is mostly a dead zone because food is strained and directed away from it.

Whether trout feed directly under a sweeper depends on how close the tree gets to the bottom. If it only leaves a foot or so of clearance, you're unlikely to find trout there because it's sieving most of the food away from the fish. But if the tree has a few feet of clearance between its branches and the bottom, it offers great security and enough food to keep a trout happy. If there is enough clearance, I always try to drift a nymph or swim a streamer under the branches. And, of course, many times there's that one errant branch sticking down that grabs your fly and ruins the whole thing.

Weed beds in a trout stream, common in tailwaters and spring creeks, offer feeding lanes for trout by

In late season the weed beds on this tailwater block off the drifting food in the shallows. The depth is right in the shallows and the current speed is adequate, but the food isn't there. Thus you can see the trout rising in the deeper water on the outside of the weed beds.

Trout seem to prefer feeding on top of submerged weed beds rather than in the channels between them. Here you can see numerous trout rising close to the gentle undulations on the surface that betray weed beds just under the surface.

concentrating drifting food into discrete highways. Spots between weed beds growing parallel to the current seem to be better than slack water behind large weed beds because the slack water, although comfortable to trout that might have to fight current, doesn't seem to offer enough food. When weed beds are totally submerged and don't reach the surface, trout prefer to feed on top of beds that reach closer to the surface rather than in the deep pockets between clumps of weeds. Again, it's probably because food gets constricted into a narrower vertical band, so trout don't have to swim through the entire water column to catch drifting nymphs. These places are easy to spot in smooth water because the weeds lying closer to the surface will cause minor turbulence that manifests itself as gentle undulations on the surface.

Surprisingly, trout don't use weeds for cover as much as you'd think. Sure, when you hook a trout in weedy water it will go there to try to dislodge the hook, but they don't seem to prefer weeds when predators are around. I've spent some time on the Henry's Fork in Idaho with Jeff Currier, who grew up on that river, and one day I asked him what he looked for when searching

for trout on it, because it's a mostly flat piece of water with lots of weeds but little else in the way of structure. The river also has a dense population of both pelicans and ospreys, so there are plenty of big birds just waiting to pounce on its dense rainbow trout population. Now Jeff has fished there so many decades that he just *knows* where he'll find trout at any water level, but he did tell me that trout seem to key into places where large boulders line the banks, rocks that were placed there many years ago to keep the river in its channel. So even in a stream channel filled with weeds, trout hedge their bets on the extra security big rocks offer.

Sometimes a tributary or even a small spring can pinpoint places to find trout in a big pool. They are not always obvious, and you may need to look hard to spot them. A 10-foot-wide tributary is easy to spot, but smaller ones can sneak into a river unnoticed unless you step over them while walking along the bank. Sometimes a small spring will show up as a tiny depression in the bank, and you may be able to hear one as it gurgles through the brush. In early spring, late fall, and winter, pay attention to little patches of green in an otherwise brown and gray bank. Springs encourage growth of

vegetation year-round, as they provide water and keep the ground from freezing. And in late spring and summer, if you notice a dry streambed entering a bigger river, don't assume it won't have value. Chances are the streambed, although totally dry on the surface, can be funneling groundwater into the river under the surface and could still be cooling the main river, unseen.

Tributaries generally—although not always—have more groundwater than surface water influence, which means they more closely reflect the mean temperature of a region and thus are cooler in the summer and warmer in the winter than the main river. Trout are attracted to these more favorable temperatures unless the water in the main river is in the optimum range of 45 to 65 degrees. In that case the tributary may not offer any benefit, although they sometimes have different hatches than in a bigger river, so trout may be attracted to a tributary for the food supply. One more factor to consider is that trout often spawn in tributaries, so in the late summer or early fall you may find brook or brown trout staging around the inflow. Rainbows and cutthroats are attracted in the same way in late winter and spring.

The beneficial effect of a tributary can extend some distance downstream until it completely mixes with the

Most anglers know that small tributaries coming into a larger river are often refuges of cold water during heat waves, but they are also sources of warmer water during the winter because if fed by springs they reflect the mean annual temperature in a region. So in a flat, otherwise uninteresting pool in midwinter, a tributary can attract trout with its warm water flow.

Although the banks of this pool look good, and they well could be, don't rule out the middle of the pool because the bubble line seems to favor the center of this part of the pool as opposed to the banks.

main flow. I can't give you an exact distance because it depends on the temperature difference between the two waters and the volume of both flows, but the influence of the tributary will hug the bank for a considerable distance, so don't just work your flies right at the confluence. Sometimes you can see a color or clarity difference between the tributary outflow and the main river, so if you can see that pay attention to how far it extends downstream.

In the flat water of a pool, the first place I'll look for trout is along the banks, but in some rivers, and in parts of some big pools, the banks aren't the best place. Both banks could be lined with water that's too shallow, or too slow. In this case you'll invariably see the bubble line stay toward the center of the river. That's where the main flow is, and where the food drifts. It's also a hard place to read the water because in a half mile of flat water, it's sometimes difficult to find any structure, and there may not even be any structure. Trout could be feeding anyplace along the bubble line—or no place.

You at least have the bubble line to narrow your search, but not much else.

But look a little closer. Your first step, if there is enough clarity in the water, is to look for color changes. If most of the pool is over 5 feet deep, look for lighter patches of water where it may be a bit shallower. In shallow, flat water, look for darker patches of deeper water. And then look for the edges. Trout love to feed on the edges of shallow and deep water, where the shallow water squeezes the flow of food and they have the security of deep water to dart into. Avoid areas of "frog water," which are places where the current is not fast enough to hold a trout in position and doesn't bring much food. You find this frog water by looking for places where the bottom is covered with leaves, silt, or other lightweight debris. The current deposits junk there and the water isn't fast enough to remove it, so it settles to the bottom.

Look for wrinkles. Once you look closely, you'll see that the surface is not completely flat if the pool has any

The subtle bumps and swirls where this angler is fishing indicate relatively large subsurface rocks in the middle of the pool, which offer trout protection from predators and from the current.

current at all. You'll see swirls, subtle lines that indicate seams, and subtle bumps in the surface. All of these are caused by some interaction of an object with the current, although that object could just be another seam of current that is running at a different speed, as well as physical objects on the bottom. But any furrow on the surface can indicate a potential trout-holding place, and these are especially useful if the water is discolored or the glare is strong enough to prevent you from seeing color changes or objects on the bottom.

A bump in the surface most likely indicates a rock or pile of rocks on the bottom. Trout won't be found right under the bump, though. The current pushes the turbulence caused by its interaction with a rock downstream before it propagates on the surface. Because trout around rocks are often found in front of them, you may find fish a considerable distance in front of the bump. And because trout don't like to lie immediately behind a rock because of the turbulence formed there, you may also find them well below the surface disturbance. Cast to the bump if you want, but just make sure you cover the water upstream and downstream of it. How far? I can't give you an exact distance, as it depends on how big the rock is, how deep the water is, and the speed of the current.

A longitudinal seam, parallel to the current, shows you where currents of two different speeds meet. It could indicate an underwater shelf, or it could be a place where a slice of faster water meets a slower pocket. When currents of different speeds meet, mild turbulence is formed, which reduces the velocity of the water and gives trout a place to feed in slower water. One of these seams along the length of a bubble line is a good place to start if you don't see anything else of interest.

The Tail of a Pool

The tail of a pool is the most difficult part of a pool to fish but under the right conditions can produce the largest fish in a stretch of water. Why is it so difficult? First, the tail is often shallower and smoother than the rest of the pool, so trout there can spot you easily unless you employ lots of stealth. Smooth water also betrays all the mistakes in our casting and presentation and does not offer the safeguard that broken water does. But probably the most important reason the tail of a pool (you may also hear this place described as a tailout—same thing) is difficult is because the current speed increases dramatically. For a dry-fly or nymph presentation, if you fish upstream the fast water under the tip of your rod yanks the leader and fly abruptly downstream, sometimes

The tail of a pool is one of the most difficult places to fish because of smooth currents and difficulty in avoiding drag. Yet it can also be one of the most productive places, especially during a hatch, because it concentrates all the food flowing through a pool into a narrower vertical band as the water shallows.

almost immediately, and makes the fly drag. And with a downstream presentation, the fly end of things moves faster than the water at your feet, so it gets held up in its drift—again causing drag. You'll need to pull all the casting and line tricks you know to prevent this drag.

The tail is also a prime spot for trout-feeding because it acts as a funnel for all the food drifting through a pool. Usually, the banks narrow as a pool moves into its tail and it shallows, so the water is constricted in two dimensions. Trout know this and position themselves to take advantage of this cone of abundance. The tail of a pool can hold trout all the time, if its physical structure is right, or the trout there can be transitory, as we'll explore in the section on when trout move in a pool.

When the water from the middle of a pool reaches the tail, the most common scenario is a gradual upward sloping of the bottom. At the point where this slope reaches that magic 2- to 4-foot depth, trout position themselves along this line, sometimes from one bank to another. If the current is relatively slow, they'll be almost anywhere, and if the current quickens dramatically before dropping into the riffle or run below, you'll most likely find them on one side or both sides of the main current. It's just such a great place to feed. They can see food coming for

quite a distance because the water is not usually turbulent. The upward slope of the bottom develops a cushion of slightly slower water in front of it. And all those drifting insects coming down through a pool get focused into a narrow band, so a trout does not have to work as hard to forage for its prey.

Structure always increases the desirability of a tail. Rocks on the bottom larger than an orange create even more micro-seams underwater and offer more places for a trout to rest. Boulders furnish protective cover so a trout can live in the tail all day long, even in the bright sunlight of midday when predators can see them best. And bushes, trees, or logs along the bank are also cover that may keep a trout in the tail of a pool—even in very shallow water. I can't tell you the number of times I've found large trout that I almost missed, tucked in along the bank at the tail of a pool, in less than 10 inches of water. I usually spook them before I get to cast to them, as I imagine happens to all but the craftiest of fly fishers, but they'll be there if you're smart enough to look for them.

Tails are often asymmetrical, particularly if the pool bends before moving on to faster water. Pay attention to how the current moves through the tail. If the main current is slow, trout may be on the outside of the bend,

The best place to find trout in the tail of a pool is where the bottom slopes upward and the water goes from deep to shallow, as seen by the color change in the water. Always look for structure as well, either near midstream rocks or close to rocks or other structure along the bank.

Structure in the tail of a pool is always helpful. It offers more places for trout to live but also gives you places to look. As usual, you are likely to find more trout, and bigger trout, in front of rocks like this than behind them.

in the main flow. If it's running more than 2 feet per second, they may be more likely to feed on the inside, or slower, part of the tail.

There is one tailout on the West Branch of the Delaware River I love to fish because no one ever seems to wade it, and when drift boats slide through they never seem to pay much attention to it. Trout line up on the inside, where the current punches against a point of land that extends into the tail, and the fast current slides off to the other side. The inside is always full of rising fish and the opposite, faster side pushes parallel to the smooth far bank, which doesn't provide much protection from the current. I have never seen a trout feed on that far bank. I once had a spectacular day during the Hendrickson hatch on that inside, where the best fish poke their noses up just off the shore where the current runs into it, and the hatch was so heavy that not only did it seem like every fish in the river was feeding on the mayflies, but the abundant geese in this pool also took advantage of the bugs, swimming in place in the current and gobbling the mayflies like they were ears of corn in a field.

Side Channels and Islands

If given the choice between a large pool with a single channel and one with an island or even multiple islands in it, I'll take the one with the islands every time. Islands add so much more complexity and they increase the number of seams and thus places with soft water, so they're a great multiplier of available trout habitat. Especially in high or fast water, side channels may offer more gentle, easily waded current, as when they channel water off the main flow, they slow it down because of friction between their narrower banks and because the redirection of flow takes some energy out of the current.

There are hotspots around islands at both their heads and their tails. At the upstream end, there is usually a shallow flat that extends into both the main flow of the river and the side channel. Just like the tail of a pool, this upward-sloping bottom offers trout a great place to feed in shallower, slower water. If the water is clear, look for the change in color, and if it's dirty, just assume there's a shelf and trout will feed there. At the tail or downstream end of an island, you may be tempted to fish in the slack water immediately downstream of the island, and sometimes it's a great place, especially if the current is fast. But an even better place is along the seams that form in the plume behind the island, on both sides of it. And where those seams eventually come together in a downstream V is the best spot of all. Never pass up this spot.

Here are the places I'd consider the best spots in relation to an island. The heads and tails of islands are always hotspots, especially where deep and shallow water meet. Also, don't overlook side channels, as they are often better places than the main river. This is especially true in high water because side channels usually lessen the velocity of the current. This side channel looks especially good because of the strong bubble line running through it.

You may find trout in the side channels themselves. As long as a channel offers some cover, at least 2 feet of water, and a moderate current, it will probably hold fish, and these may be fish that drift boats pass by or wading anglers don't bother with because the channel looks too shallow. Don't assume side channels are fishless until you walk or float the entire channel, because there may be a hotspot that's not apparent when viewed from the main river. You can find some productive spots on side channels in places that are hidden from view when on the main stem of a river.

WHERE TO LOOK FOR TROUT IN HIGH OR LOW WATER

High Water

When fishing pools in high water, there's an easy part and a hard part. The easy part is to fish the edges, right up against the bank. Trout will even move into places that are dry most of the year, and they'll also migrate to slower water that might have been unproductive frog

water before the water level rose. The hard part is that I suspect not all trout move into the shallows during a flood. Some of them are quite content lying on the bottom in a boulder garden because the velocity close to the bottom does not increase nearly as much as the torrent at the surface. The difficulty is getting to them. Even if you peg enough split shot to your leader to get it deep enough, the fast current between the surface and the bottom will whisk your leader—or even a fast-sinking line—downstream quickly, so you'll often only have your fly in front of the trout briefly. And because the fish are reluctant to move out of the comfortable slower water near the bottom for fear of getting pushed downstream, you need to get the fly right in their face. I won't say you can't catch these fish, but the ones that move into shallow edges are more agreeable.

At the head of a pool in high water, look for the softer edges on one or both sides of the main flow moving into the pool. You'll probably see more turbulence and white water than usual, so look off to the side, in the very corners of the head. Look for lenses of flat water or gentle turbulence. Where the main force of the current

At the head of a pool in high water, if the main current favors one bank, look to the inside seam on the opposite side of the current, where the velocity is lower. Also look farther down from the head, where standing waves settle out.

favors one side, look to the other side. Plunge pools or waterfall pools may offer more-productive water than pools with a gentler slope at their head, because the hydraulic jump over a falls releases a lot of energy in a short distance, so the current and turbulence may ease up closer to the very head of the pool than you think. Look for the line where the bubbles and turbulence settle down to a gentle rippling. It's often closer to the foot of the falls than you would expect.

This is a time when those recirculating whirlpools at the head of a pool may be very productive. All that energy spent whirling back upstream can lessen the flow, and it's a great place for trout to get into a comfortable spot away from heavy turbulence. The force of the current at the outside of the whirlpool could still be too heavy, and if you see standing waves at the edges of a whirlpool, look for trout closer to the center of the circle, in the eye of the whirlpool.

If the entire head of a pool is a roiling mess and you don't see any potential soft spots, trout may have moved farther down into the pool where the current is gentler. Forget about where you caught trout during normal or

low water. Look to those places along the edges, close to the bank, or in the slowest part of the pool. Also look around large rocks, boulders, and logs. These places will give trout shelter from the current. In high water, the hardest place to find trout will be in the main current flow where you don't see any boils that indicate submerged rocks. And if a pool is long and deep enough to slow down the flow, you might even be able to get to those trout that are hugging the bottom. But I'd still put my bets on the banks.

Exactly where along the banks trout will feed in high water has always been a mystery to me, known only to the fish. But they will slide into discrete places, and unless floods change the structure of the bank, they'll use those same high-water spots year after year.

One year I floated the West Branch of the Delaware with a couple of friends, not my favorite way to fish that river because I prefer to wade and stalk individual fish. But the flow was at 2,500 cfs, too much water to wade, so we floated the same stretch three days in a row. All three days we found a pod of six large trout feeding in the same little pocket along the bank, with no fish feeding for 50 yards upstream or downstream of them, even though there appeared to be other pockets that looked just as attractive—at least to us. Because there were three of us in the boat taking turns on these trout, I spent over an hour just watching the fish, looking at the water, trying to figure out what enticement that pocket held for them. After I got home, I studied photos of it. If I were to guess, I think it may have offered just a slightly lower current velocity than the other pockets, but it could also have been some attractive bottom structure we couldn't see. It's riddles like this that keep us interested in chasing trout.

The productivity of the tail of a pool in high water depends on its bank structure and shape. A narrow tail concentrates the flow, and unless the banks are uneven, broken up with jumbles of rocks, or you find large boulders in the center, the tail will be hard to fish and may not even hold many trout at high water. However, if the tail of a pool is wide and bulbous before it necks down, it can be an excellent place to find trout in high water because the current gets spread out over a wider area, and the places where the current pushes up against the banks before the tail narrows can be hotspots. Look for

In high water, in the middle of a pool look along the banks, especially where there is a shallow shelf and good structure on the bank. In some cases you may even want to stay on the bank and not wade, especially if the current is very swift.

During high water, trout may move down right to the very bottom of the tail where it abuts the shore, especially if the tail is wide. The transition between deep and shallow water combined with the cushion of slower water formed by the current bouncing off the shoreline makes this an attractive place for trout to feed.

trout here right off the shoreline, in the cushion formed as the current shoves against the solid shore.

Low Water

If high water spreads trout out to a pool's margins, low water constricts them toward the center. The soft spots with gentle current that you found in the spring may be dry or stagnant. If they're slow enough to collect leaves, twigs, and silt, they're probably too slow—trout have trouble holding their position in slack current and they don't get enough food. So look to the middle, in the main thread of current that's faster and carries all the food. The bubble line is your best friend in low water, and you'll find all the feeding trout anchored to this line from the head right down to the tail.

Low water is usually warmer and holds less oxygen, so many of the fish that held in the middle of the pool or in the tail may move to the head to take advantage of any turbulence and white water. Some of the great spots along the bank in the middle of the pool may be

dry or too shallow, another reason for fish to move to the head. And the fastest water in the pool will be in the head, so trout will find the best supply of insects there. In low water it's to our advantage to fish at the head not only because you may find more trout there, but because the water in the middle and tail may be so flat and clear that you may spook whatever trout are present with your wading or casting.

In low water, pay attention to the way weed beds, if present, channel the flows, because low water will change the character of weedy rivers, moving trout into different places. The Henry's Fork in Idaho is known for its large, wild rainbows, and if you know nothing else about the Henry's Fork, you have heard the biggest trout in the famous Railroad Ranch section, which is flat and shallow without many large rocks, are found up along the banks. Banks are the main protection from predators, and the slower current along the banks makes it easier for the trout to feed on its rich insect supply. That's the case in June and July. However, if you fish

In low water, look for any current at all, especially if it's near some kind of structure like midstream rocks. That bubble line is key here because it is the only part of a current that holds a reliable food supply. Notice that this trout is rising in front of a rock—the area behind these rocks is a dead zone with almost no current.

this river in August and September, as I often do, to avoid the crowds of the early season, you may be disappointed if you concentrate on the banks. In low water years, there is often an open pocket of water along the banks, then a patch or two of weeds, and then the main current flow out in the center. There is enough water along the banks to hold trout, but the floor-to-ceiling weeds between the banks and the main current flow choke off the food supply and much of the current, so in many places those great spots along the bank can be stagnant and fishless. In these places the fish move out into the center of the river, moving into the water along the banks if a hatch is so heavy that mayflies and caddisflies are everywhere, even in the sluggish pockets close to shore.

In low water, in the slow section of pools you may encounters cruisers, or trout that don't stay put and feed and act more like pond fish than stream fish. It's an excellent reason to observe the water before you wade in or drift your boat through a pool, because you may see a trout rise and try to get into position to catch it, only to find that the fish is either out of range when you get into position or gets so close to you that you spook it.

I've watched trout doing this, and it's fascinating how they start. You see a trout rising, and if you can see the fish you watch as it moves to a spot and samples an insect, and then you can almost sense the impatience of the fish as it waits for another insect, so it moves upstream or to one side to find a better spot. If that doesn't satisfy the fish, it starts to move, usually upstream, to try to find a better place to feed, and if it doesn't it will typically keep moving slowly upstream, intercepting food as it comes down, eventually reaching water that's too fast or too shallow. Then the fish will swim slowly downstream, turn around, and arrive back at its starting point, beginning the whole process again. We usually get busted by the fish when we try to wade up behind it, and when it turns around to start a new cycle, it swims right into us and bolts for cover. Game over.

WHEN TROUT MOVE IN THIS WATER

Trout in most pools, especially in the middle and tail sections, are more mobile than fish that live in the faster water of riffles, runs, or pocket water. Because much of a pool is slower, deeper water and they don't have to fight the current as much, it's an easy glide to move from the center to the edges, or the center to the tail. In a pool, the slow current and adjacent deep water also assures trout that cover will be close at hand in an instant, which is not the case in places like riffles because if a fish leaves the security of a deeper pocket and moves, it may need to cross a large expanse of shallow water.

Trout in pools don't just have one feeding spot they stick to all day long. Although they'll often defend a site that they're feeding in at the moment, once they move they carry this territoriality with them and will then defend the new spot—almost always the water upstream of them. They may have one site that is favored, but they'll cycle through a half-dozen spots depending on what prey is available and the presence of larger fish that might push them around. Don't get complacent about fishing in the same spot you caught trout last week. Nobody may be home at the moment.

When few insects are around, trout tend to stay closer to the main flow of current and closer to deep water. These are the opportunistic fish you catch when prospecting with a nymph, streamer, or dry fly. They're not actively feeding and may not be too picky about what they eat because they're in faster water, don't have a chance to look their food over carefully, and may not be seeing a lot of any one food source. However, in times of abundant food, especially during a hatch, trout will slide out of the main current and deep water and move into shallower water, where it's easier to see and feed on everything from insects drifting close to the bottom to hatching insects at the surface. As long as there is a moderate current, you'll be surprised at how shallow even large trout will enter to feed. They might move over to the shallow riffles at the sides of the head of the pool, in front or behind islands, on top of shallow bars, or very close to the banks. This is also a time when you'll see more fish dropping down into the tail of a pool.

During a hatch, you'll often find pods of trout rising together, often so close to each other that their fins seem to touch. These fish don't live in pods all the time, and any member of a pod might come from a completely different part of a pool. Abundant food seems to break down any territorial behavior. I don't know if they gather in these pods because some unseen structure or perfect current combination attracts them, or if they feel more secure in a large group when they are so exposed close to the surface. But they seem to form these same pods year after year in the same place in any given pool, so if you come across one, make a careful note of its position for future trips.

Many tailwater rivers that are used for hydropower have wide swings in water discharge in a single day, depending on electricity usage in the grid, which regulates the amount of water flowing through the dam. Trout adapt to these extremes quickly. One example is the Little Red River in Arkansas, famous for its very large wild brown trout. Jamie Rouse is a longtime guide on this river, where water flows can go from 50 to 2,000 cfs in a matter of hours, which to put it into perspective is like seeing a river go from pond-like pools with trickles running between them to a raging flood that kisses streamside trees. Trout feed throughout these swings, Jamie tells me, and when flows are high it's much easier to find feeding trout because they'll be up against the banks, in the shallow, slower water. It's a narrow band and the trick is to find the places along the bank with that happy 2- to 4-foot-per-second flow and a few feet of water. It's when flows drop to more "normal" levels or extremely low levels that finding trout gets tougher, says Jamie, because now the fish have the entire river channel at their disposal and can be almost anywhere. That's when you need to put all your other stream-reading skills to the test.

SEASONAL CHANGES

Trout that live in pools often don't move very far in a calendar year. Pools offer deep water; protection from predators in other forms like boulders, trees, and brush along the banks; a variety of water types for feeding at all flow levels; and oxygenated water at the head. Although many trout migrate into headwaters and tributaries for spawning, some may not even leave the pool to spawn if the water has the right flow and gravel size for building redds. Riffles, runs, and pocket water don't offer all of these enticements in one neat package, so no matter when you hit the river, you can always count on finding trout in pools.

Trout from other water types will migrate to the sanctuary of pools, and under extreme conditions from one end of the scale to the other, pools may be the *only* place you'll find trout. In extremely low water, riffles and runs can get so skinny that trout aren't able to escape predators, so they migrate to the deeper water pools supply.

My friend Shawn kept telling me about a medium-sized river in upstate New York that he has fished for years and regularly pulls some jaw-dropping trout from it on nymphs, streamers, and dries. I was traveling through that part of the state one summer and decided to try his secret stream for a few hours. He carefully drew me some maps, detailing exactly where the best spots were, and I was especially interested in some of the pocket water he told me about, as I enjoy fishing that kind of water.

When I got to the river, there was a lot of glare on the water and not even polarized sunglasses would cut it, but I began prospecting with a dry-dropper in the pocket water. My nymph kept ticking bottom well before I thought it should, early in the drift. When I waded up into the pocket water, I could see it was not more than ankle-deep throughout, and I was ready to curse Shawn for a disappointing detour. I kept this up through a half mile of what might have been decent water earlier in the year but didn't even spook a trout, and in the pockets that I thought might be deep enough for at least a 6-incher, nothing splashed at my dry.

Ready to call it a day, I walked upstream, as I thought that route would get me closer to my car. I rounded a bend and like something out of a fairy tale a pool so deep that I could barely wade unfolded in front of me. I made a half-hearted cast along the bank, just upstream of the tail, still not convinced there were any trout around. My dry-dropper dipped under. What I thought was another snag turned out to be a large brown trout. Exactly how large I never determined because it broke off after a short battle. But it wouldn't have fit into my net. As I worked up through the pool I caught a half-dozen fish, none as big as the first one but all

A pool like this will hold trout all year long. It has enough oxygenated water at the head for the low water of summer, and the depth and slower water to keep trout safe from ice floes during the winter. The depth also gives trout places of refuge from predators throughout the year.

the bill perfectly. If you do catch a fish in this water during the cold months, continue to work the same area slowly and methodically. Trout will converge on these places and sometimes group up like a bunch of kids hiding under a big umbrella in a downpour. Trout may also move miles upstream or downstream to find these winter refuges, as not all places in a stream offer these havens. Whether trout know how to find them from past experience or they just keep shifting until they find one, I have no idea. But find them they do.

APPROACH

Approaching the head of a pool is usually best done from downstream, on the near side of the fast water at least, because trying to cast over the fast water in the middle of a pool will make your fly drag immediately. Try to fish those edges along the fast water from your side first. If you want to fish the seam on the far side of the head and can't cross the river below and walk up the far bank, you may have to get upstream of the place you want to cast to and use a reach cast, so you at least get a semblance of a drift before the fly drags. As you work up into the head of a pool, be careful of those shallow edges on either side. They may not look deep enough to hold trout, but there is always a possibility . . .

If the head of a pool has a whirlpool or back eddy, take care in your approach. Trout usually prefer the outside edge of a whirlpool, and those fish will be facing "downstream," so the best approach is to get on the bank if you can, walk upstream of the whirlpool well away from the river, and then sneak down from the head of the pool so you are behind those trout facing "backwards." (They're not really facing backwards, but compared to trout in the rest of the pool they're facing in the opposite direction.)

One mistake I'm often guilty of is spotting fish rising in the middle or tail of a pool, in the flat water, and going right to those fish instead of looking first at the head. Trout rising in the head may not show up as well because they'll be in broken water, and unless they're really smashing insects with aggressive rises, you may miss them altogether. And once you get preoccupied with the fish in the middle of the pool, you may be too far away to spot the fish rising in the head. Fish rising in the head are also typically easier to catch, as they

respectable. Once I finished with the pool I was not so eager to get back to the car, but was faced with shallow water like my first half mile. And I never saw another fish after the pool.

At the other end of the scale, if you do any fishing from late fall through early spring, pools are your best bet. You've seen that trout don't eat much in cold water, but they do need some current flow to hold their position and to remove wastes from their system, and also need to stay away from predators if possible, so they migrate to the deepest, slowest water they can find as long as it isn't stagnant. And the center of a deep, slow pool fits

At almost any time of year except in the high water of spring, you need to wade carefully in the flat middle part of a pool. Pushing waves in flat water scares trout even more than a bad cast or wearing a bright red shirt, yet not enough anglers pay attention to this. You may need to spend five minutes or more just getting into position if you don't want to scare the fish. You can see the waves pushed by this angler propagate almost to the far bank, even though he was wading slowly.

don't get a good look at your fly, and who can complain about easy fish?

The flatter water in the middle of the pool makes your approach fiddlier. The worst approach is to push waves ahead of you in flat water because trout see those waves very well, even gentle ones, and know something big is approaching them. Even though otters are fast and herons are crafty, both push waves if they get careless. Instead of wading into a pool and then figuring out where to fish, study the water first. Decide where you think trout are most likely to feed and then either walk the bank or wade in very shallow water until you get closer to your spot. Look for shallow water with a gravel bar, log, or weed bed between you and the main flow so the waves get blocked. If you do have to wade through deeper water, try to wade downstream, as you can creep along with the current and push less water than you would working against the flow.

In low water, be especially careful of fish feeding in shallow water. I teach an advanced dry-fly course on the Henry's Fork every year, and one year we took our students down to a flat stretch of water. As we were standing on the bank talking through how we would approach the water, I had trouble concentrating on what I was saying, as there were thousands of flying ants on the water and big rainbows gobbling them in the shallow water. I couldn't take my eyes off them. When we let our students off the leash to try what they had learned, they immediately waded into the shallows to get to the deeper water beyond, and all those happy trout disappeared. In fact, the trout that were rising all over the pool quit feeding. The students waded out to the edge of the deeper water in the center of the river and soon those trout began feeding again, more comfortable over deeper water. But the fish in the shallows behind the students that had been rising so eagerly when we first arrived never moved back into the thin water.

If the middle of a pool is tricky to approach, the tail can be maddening. It's very risky to cast to fish in the tail from downstream, which is where you typically want to be so that trout aren't alerted to your presence as easily. Drag takes over almost immediately unless the current in the tail is moving slowly, or unless you can drop your line over a rock or log to keep it from getting snatched away. You can cast upstream to fish in the tail but you'll need to make a pile or parachute cast, so your leader lands in a big pile and gives you extra insurance before drag takes hold. Thus, an approach from upstream gives you a better angle for a cast, but try to keep your profile low so trout don't spot you. Unless the water is stained or the light is very low, like evening or early morning or a rainy day, you'll need to make a longer cast so you stay farther away from the fish. It's sometimes best to fish the tail in the middle or on the opposite side of the river from where you're standing or where your boat is anchored, because it's so hard to make a direct downstream presentation.

TECHNIQUES TO TRY

Pools are the places we fish most often, so for me to tell you how to fish one would be silly, because it all depends on water conditions, hatches, and your own desires of how you want to fish. But I can tell you what techniques I would use to fish a pool and some of my thought processes as I go through the water.

The first thing I'll do is stay on the bank and look at the middle and tail of a pool. If I can't see both of them from one vantage point, I'll walk the bank to see the other. I'll look for rising fish, and if I see some I won't need to do anything else about reading the water—I'm

going dry-fly fishing. But typically I won't see any fish rising, so I'll walk up to where the head of the pool starts to flatten out. If nothing else is going on, I will almost always start at the head of a pool because fish there are the easiest and I feel I can get closer to trout and not spook them in the broken water. Again, I'll look for risers, but if there weren't any in the middle or the tail, chances are there won't be any in the head.

I'll start out with something like a dry-dropper rig, some nymphs with an indicator, or Euro nymphing— dry-dropper if it's late spring or summer, nymphs with indicator if I need to fish more than 20 feet away, and maybe Euro nymphing if there is fast water I can get to without needing to make a long cast. I'll gradually work my way upstream, casting directly across, angling upstream, and then straight upstream. I'll work my way all the way up to the head of the pool with one of those rigs. I'll try to stay on the near side of the current, really concentrating on the seam between fast and slow water on my side or any drop-offs I can see. If the water along the bank looks like it could hold fish, I'll wade out a bit into the current so I can fish both the water along the banks and the seams toward the middle of the river. If I have the option, later I'll wade up the far bank and fish the seams on the other side, because casting over the fast water in the middle to hit the seams on the far side seldom works well because of drag problems.

A dry-dropper rig worked up into the head of a pool is my preferred way to fish if I see nothing rising. Sometimes you get a big surprise when a trout takes that big foam indicator fly instead of the nymph hanging below it.

Euro nymphing is a deadly way to fish the faster water in a pool, especially where the shelf at the head of a pool drops off.

If the water is dirty or I get absolutely nothing on nymphs and dries, I might tie on a streamer and fish it at all angles—from almost directly downstream to straight upstream and everything in between. I'll even cast to the far bank if I can reach it, because drag is not a problem when yanking a streamer through the water. I won't always take the time to re-rig my leader for a streamer, but if the pool seems totally dead, a streamer can sometimes be used just to locate trout because even if they don't take it, trout will sometimes chase a streamer and might give away their location.

If the head doesn't produce, or if I've been lucky enough to catch a few, I'll move to the middle of the pool—still looking for rising fish because I'm an optimist. In the slower water in the middle of the pool, I probably won't go to the Euro nymphing technique. I know many great fly fishers have good luck with this technique in slow water, but I'm just not good enough. In this water I'll probably try a dry-dropper or a nymph or two suspended from an indicator. I'll concentrate on the banks, on any seams I see, around midstream rocks, or any place the current gives me an indication that there is some structure on the bottom. If the water

is relatively clear, any time from mid-spring to late fall, I'll try a hopper or beetle or ant pattern, either without any dropper or maybe a small nymph hanging from it.

If there is moderate current in the middle of a pool, another way to cover a lot of water with less effort is to swing a pair of soft hackles or standard wet flies. Where with a nymph or dry you have a short window of effective drift before drag sets in, with soft hackles or wet flies trout may take them when they are dead drifting or after the current takes over and swims them across the pool. It's an efficient way of fishing more water without endless casting. Regardless of which method I'm using, I'll usually work slowly downstream from the middle of the pool to the tail.

You can fish the tail of the pool by working upstream, but as drag is such a problem, I don't fish upstream into the tail unless I see fish rising, because I can pinpoint them and hopefully get my painfully short drift in the right place. If you see fish rising, or if you want to fish the tail of a pool from downstream because of casting obstructions or if you feel you might spook fish in clear water by getting upstream of them, you'll need to use a slack-line cast with anything but a streamer. If you don't know how to make the parachute cast or the pile cast, get a lesson or watch a video. You really can't fish the tail of a pool without them.

If you don't know where the fish are and nothing is showing, I think it's far better to fish the tail of a pool from upstream. You can fish nymphs with an indicator or dry-dropper rig or a single dry fly downstream into the tail, but again drifts will be short and I think there are better ways of covering this water. One is to swing wet flies or soft hackles, using the current to your advantage. I also find that fish in the tail of a pool are real suckers for a fly swung over them. A streamer is also a great way to fish the tail of a pool if you think conditions are right for a streamer. Sunny weather is generally not great streamer weather, but overcast, rainy days or dirty water are good conditions to fish a streamer. Trout seem to hunt the tails of pools for baitfish and crayfish more than any other place in a pool, and the shallow tails of pools without much current are great places to swing a big streamer or wet fly at night.

There is one final method that seems to work better in the tails of pools when nothing else is happening, I think because it works best in smooth but fast water: skating a caddis. In this technique, you use a heavily hackled fly like an Elk Hair Caddis, Stimulator, or any other fly with bushy hackle (parachute patterns don't work well). Apply some paste or gel fly floatant to your entire leader right to the fly. Cast 45 degrees downstream and immediately raise your rod tip and wiggle the fly while stripping in a bit of line, then drop the rod tip and let the fly float naturally. Then repeat. You often get short strikes, but this seems to really excite trout and when they come to the fly it's usually a vicious rise. It doesn't often work, but when it does you'll have some fun.

The one caution about fishing pools I would give you is not to get all excited because someone looking over a bridge once saw a big trout lying on the bottom of a particular pool. First of all, many people mistake suckers, large whitefish, or pikeminnows for trout. And even if it is a trout, chances are if it's really that big, it probably hides in deep water or near a logjam; comes out every few days, often after dark, to eat a 6-inch trout or a large crayfish; and then hangs around and digests its meal for a few days. The chances of you arriving at a pool when that fish is eager to eat something, approaching it without spooking it, and convincing the fish to eat is a low-percentage prospect. Try to catch that fish if you want, but I'd rather hear someone tell me they saw a dozen 12-inch trout rising in a pool. Those fish I can catch.

Rainbow trout are often suckers for soft-hackle flies swung through a pool. The advantage of this method is that you can cover a lot of water if you aren't sure where the fish are located.

Pocket water is tricky wading, and dry rocks are not as slippery as wet ones. Still, you have to balance the risk of spooking trout by elevating your profile so much. Luckily, trout in pocket water, with its broken water, are not as spooky as in flat pools.

CHAPTER 8

Pocket Water

DESCRIPTION AND HOW IT IS FORMED

Usually when river channels run over a fast gradient, rocks in the middle of the river get pushed downstream into slower water or get moved off to the banks. But when rocks are large enough to resist even the heaviest floods, we get what is called pocket water. Another term you'll sometimes hear is boulder garden, which is a more descriptive term. Technically, pocket water is a run filled with boulders. (If we can even look at this technically, since "run" and "pocket water" are angler's terms and not recognized by hydrologists.) It's not a pool because there is usually no head or tail or deep middle to pocket water—it's mostly just water of overall uniform depth with little pockets of deeper and shallower water sprinkled with large rocks. But in terms of finding trout and fishing techniques, we usually approach pocket water differently than in a run.

Many rivers, like the Madison and Gallatin in Montana, the South Platte in Cheesman Canyon in Colorado, and the McCloud in California, are mostly pocket water. Some rivers, like the Ausable in the Adirondacks of New York, the Beaverkill in the Catskill Mountains, or the upper Colorado River, have stretches of pocket water separated by slow pools. Many small mountain streams, unless they have areas of sudden steep changes in slope that cause plunge pools, are mostly pocket water. Regardless, you'll know it when you see it. There will be some rocks that rise above the water, some partially submerged, and others will be totally submerged but will show themselves by telltale turbulence of the surface. Do just a few boulders in a run make it pocket water? That's really up to you and how you want to classify these features, but I'd say it isn't pocket water unless a run is liberally sprinkled with large rocks, has turbulence throughout most of its surface, and has plentiful foamy, white water.

I am drawn to pocket water because it's full of potential. Unlike a pool, where there may be three or four spots with high promise for finding trout, pocket water unfolds with an entire candy store in front of you, each rock a bon-bon to be tasted. Not every rock or jumble of rocks may hold a trout, but each one has potential, and it's the unwrapping of each puzzle that fascinates me. In good pocket water, you can spend hours in a few hundred feet of water if you want to.

I also search out pocket water because it's often harder to reach, harder to wade, and harder to fish than pools or riffles. I'm less likely to find another angler in a spot I want to fish, and even if there is no one fishing it now, it's less likely the fish have been hammered with flies over and over.

Pocket water is often harder to reach because it's common in canyon areas. Those big rocks don't grow up from the bottom; sometimes they get rolled down by floods from upstream reaches, but even more commonly, they roll off steep hillsides or cliffs and are too heavy to be moved downstream by the current. Getting to pocket water can require a steep climb down, and some anglers look at the vertical ascent they'll need at the end of the long day and move on to find water with easier access. I find that most anglers don't like to walk much at all, and even fewer relish walking against gravity.

Once you get to the river, pocket water is much harder to negotiate than the fine gravel of a riffle or the level bottom of a pool. Negotiating each and every rock requires secure footing, good core strength, felt soles or rubber soles with studs, and either superb balance or a wading staff. Currents are tricky as well. One minute you'll be in calm water behind a rock, but when you step around it to move upstream you're suddenly blasted with current two or three times as fast, while you slip on those round rocks under your feet.

Pocket water on the Madison River in Montana. Some people might call this a riffle, but by my definition it has too many large rocks to be a riffle, and I think you'd look for trout in different places and use different techniques than you would in a flat-out riffle. Often you'll have riffles or runs punctuated by pocket water, but in some rivers you may see miles of it.

Pocket water in a Labrador brook trout river. In some of these rivers you'll see miles of pocket water without a single large pool, and in many of them you'll find just stretches of pocket water between lakes. Because these rivers are not as fertile as something like a Rocky Mountain tailwater, trout density is lower and you need to search out the very best places among many trouty-looking locations. Wading is so difficult in most places that rock-hopping is the best way to negotiate them.

If wading requires more care and deliberation, fishing pocket water demands even more. You can't cast in any direction as you might in a pool. The constantly churning, turbulent water grabs your leader and line and moves them off course in a matter of seconds, and unless you plan and pay attention to exactly where everything lands, your presentations won't be effective.

When I was a teenager, I spent a couple of weeks each summer on the West Branch of the Ausable River in the Adirondack Mountains. Much of it is spectacular, rough-and-tumble pocket water with rocks ranging in size from a basketball to half a basketball court. I remember fishing it quite casually, partly because I only had a pair of rubber-soled hip boots and kept falling in, but also because I grew up fishing the flat water of a spring creek and didn't know how to read turbulent

water. I threw my fly everywhere. And didn't catch many. Now, when I come back to this river of my childhood, after learning to fish all kinds of water over the years, I'm much more thoughtful and thorough when fishing the river and it seems I catch more and larger trout. And I now have felt-soled wading shoes and ones with sticky rubber and metal studs. The good old days are not always as good as the present.

WHERE TO LOOK FOR TROUT UNDER NORMAL FLOWS

It's so important to estimate where you think trout might be in pocket water because unlike in pools and riffles and runs, they are often hemmed in by currents and live and feed in discrete places. You won't get long drifts, and here

In pocket water look for places where the slope of the streambed is not so dramatic. If you can't really discern the slope of the land, look for places with less white water and more flat areas between the rocks. The current will be less violent here and you'll find more trout.

it's truly a game of inches, so estimating the best place for trout is critical for success. And given the difficulty in wading pocket water, it's best to plan your approach to those productive spots because it might take some effort to get there. Battling the current and slippery rocks is no fun if you blindly walk into the water, get out from shore, and realize you're not in range of productive water.

Get a Long View First

Pocket water can be intimidating because a stretch of water studded with rocks all looks good. There seems like potential for a trout every few feet because there is so much cover and so many seams between fast and slow water that you might feel like the first time you stood in front of an expansive fly display in a tackle shop. It all looks so good. Given the difficulty in wading pocket water and how precisely you'll need to make your casts, though, it pays to skim the cream off the top first. If the water seems productive, you can return later to cover less-likely spots.

The first aspect to examine is the slope of the piece of pocket water and the variations in that slope. Where the slope is steepest, the current may be too fast for trout except behind the largest rocks and the number of

trout found there could be limited. You can gauge this sometimes by the slope of the banks, and also in places where the river seems to form small plateaus, as the vertical drop in a piece of pocket water is seldom uniform, instead going through a series of ramps and flat spots. You'll find most of the trout in the flatter spots.

You'll notice that in the flatter spots, you'll find lenses of flat water that are neither white water nor swirly turbulence. They indicate water that's slightly deeper or slower, and either one can be a place to hold a feeding trout. White water is the stuff you should avoid. Although you nearly always find abundant white water in pocket water, trout won't hold in it when they feed. Spooked trout might use it for cover, but for the most part it's too unbalanced for trout to hold their position in the current, and too hard for them to see their prey— and their enemies. The edges of white water are often productive—just don't waste efforts by trying to put your fly into it. Remember that every cast you make not only has the potential to catch a fish, but also has the potential to spook one by dropping your line on top of a fish. Casting to white water is just empty calories.

Next look at the banks. Rocks piled along a shoreline, if the water has enough depth to hold trout, are always hotspots, and they have the added advantage of being easier to negotiate because you can often fish them without even getting your feet wet, working along the banks. So before fishing, while examining a stretch of pocket water, check both banks. Sometimes both sides of the river look productive, but you may also notice that one side is shallower than the other or may be out of the main current flow and in stagnant water. Check for that bubble line to make sure it runs close to the bank you intend to fish.

Learn to Read Rocks

Although every rock in a piece of pocket water is like a fingerprint, with unique swirls of current around it, there are general principles that apply to most of them. If you haven't read the chapter on currents in a while, I'd recommend you first go back and refresh your knowledge on how the hydraulics around a rock works. That was theory, and now we'll delve into how to examine the rocks in a piece of pocket water with a more practical bent—finding trout and catching them.

With a submerged rock of average size and shape, let's say a relatively round one that is 2 feet in diameter, and with its top lying a foot below the surface, there are two spots most likely to hold feeding trout. One is in the place where the turbulence flowing down both sides of the rock settles down and doesn't create standing waves above the surface. Another way to look at it is the point where the boiling water behind a rock settles down and begins to resume its downstream progress in a uniform manner. I've heard steelheaders call this "clean flow." Sometimes this area remains wide but often it comes to a point. And the relief it offers from the current might extend well below the rock, even farther than you think. The best spot below a large rock could be 20 feet below the white water in its wake.

I call this region below the rock the focal point for lack of a better term, and you won't find it in hydrology texts or in any other trout-fishing books I'm aware of, and in that focal point below the rock, trout are downstream of the area of high turbulence immediately behind the rock but still in a place where the rock's presence slows down the

With this rock in fast current, about the only reasonable places for a trout to hold and feed are in front of the rock and in the focal point below it. You can gauge the position of the focal point by the smoother, softer water.

The best places to find trout in the vicinity of a rock in fast water: 1 is in the cushion in front of the rock, which often contains the largest fish. 2 is in the focal point below the rock where the current is still broken but turbulence has settled down; there are often several fish in this location. 3 and 4 are lesser places along the side seam of the rock and are better locations when the current of the river slows down.

Here, the current is slower and you may find trout closer to the downstream side of the rock because there is not as much turbulence. Any drifting food will still be pushed off to either side, so the trout will favor the seams along the side. And the spot in front of the rock, as always, is still a great spot.

current to that magic 1- to 2-foot-per-second velocity they love. To a lesser degree, you'll find trout feeding in the two side seams that extend below the rock, and, yes, sometimes they'll lie right behind the rock. But not as often as the focal point, which is often a bit deeper and thus slower than the water just behind the rock. The turbulent flow behind a rock often deposits as much or more sand and gravel than it digs out, but downstream in the focal point the current resumes its downstream progress and digs a bucket into the bottom.

Pay attention to the surface of the rock in question. Like the dimples on a golf ball, which reduce air turbulence, rocks with a rough surface will have a narrower and shorter locus of turbulence behind them, and trout may lie closer to the downstream edge of a rough-surfaced rock than a rock with a smooth, polished surface.

Trout in front of a rock settle into the cushion of slower water found there. The cushion itself often does not extend very far in front of the rock, and you wouldn't think it would be a prime place to find trout. But it is. I keep a mental note of where in the vicinity of a rock I catch trout, and if you're talking about the immediate perimeter, in front of a rock beats out behind a rock

about 10 to 1. I think this spot is so desirable because the force of the current often digs a trench in front of the rock, just enough below the streambed and the main current to give a trout a comfortable place to live and feed. This location may also be desirable because it's easy for a trout to spot its food drifting down in the current above—much easier than in the turbulent water behind the rock.

I was floating a pocket water stretch of the Henry's Fork in Idaho with my friend Norm Schneeberger and guide B.J. Gerhart. In this stretch, running through a remote canyon upstream of Mesa Falls, the river is studded with big rocks and drops precipitously. Before we started BJ gave us the game plan: "OK, in most places I won't be able to drop anchor because it won't hold, so we'll be doing drive-by casting to these fish. You'll only have a cast or two to each spot, so make sure you either drop your flies in front of the rocks or a few feet below them—don't cast right behind the rocks. You'll be wasting your time." It was music to my ears to hear an experienced guide validate exactly what I've been advocating for years.

Other factors come into play when you change the conditions from our hypothetical average-sized rock.

This triangular rock, with its point facing upstream, has a narrow cushion in front that may only hold a single trout. But the wide focal point below it might hold several fish.

First is current velocity. The faster the current, the longer the area of intense turbulence behind a rock, so trout will hold farther downstream of the rock. Luckily, unless the rock is deeply submerged, you'll be able to see on the surface how far the turbulence extends. Conversely, in slower current there will be less-intense turbulence behind the rock and in this instance you might find a trout immediately behind the rock. They'll also be more likely to feed in the side seams that extend downstream from both edges of the rock.

Not all rocks are created equal, and shape matters. With a rock that approaches a sphere in shape, there will be a smaller cushion in front of it because most of the flow slips easily past the rock and won't be presented with enough backward-moving water molecules to develop much of a cushion. The rougher the surface of the rock, the more likely the cushion in front of it will support a trout, and as the front edge of the rock approaches the shape of a flat plane, perpendicular to the current, the larger the cushion in front of it. And because it presents so much resistance to the flow of the current, a bigger trench may be formed in front of it. A triangular rock, with its point facing upstream, will have less of a cushion in front of it but a wider area of slower water behind it, after the turbulence settles down. If the

point of the triangle is facing downstream, the cushion in front of it will be larger but the area of reduced flow behind it is narrower and may not offer as much wiggle room for more than a single trout.

Whether a rock is submerged or not can also determine where trout feed in relation to it. You might think that trout will move closer to the downstream edge of the rock in this case because there is not as much turbulence immediately behind it, since there is no water flowing over its top edge to create that turbulence. True enough, but what happens when a rock sticks its top into the air is that an area of real stagnation appears behind the rock. The rock effectively strains all the food from the current and pushes it off to both sides. It's true that some drifting insects do get caught in the recirculation behind the rock after the water flows along its sides, but the amount of food there is limited because it's only by chance that an insect gets drawn in behind the rock. However, the seams on either side of the rock become even more attractive because all the food is pushed to the sides, where trout wait for the more consistent and constant flow of food. I've also seen that when rocks are not submerged, the slow recirculation behind them deposits sand and other fine particles, and often instead of a deeper pocket that gets hollowed out by turbulence coming over the top of the rock, you'll be faced with a mound of sand that makes the water too shallow.

The larger the rock, the more potential it holds. Where our basketball rock might hold a single fish, a rock three times as large might hold several trout because they are visually isolated from each other. Trout won't defend a feeding spot if they can't see their neighbors, so the mass of a large rock will keep a number of fish happy. In addition, a large rock usually supports a deeper trench in front and along the sides, offering not only some break from the current but also a good place to hide from predators. A larger rock also creates a wider plume below it, so the focal point below the turbulence will sometimes be wide enough to hold more than one fish. You'll find the biggest rocks by looking for the plumes of white water, because the biggest rocks are the ones that reach the surface and create the mixing with the air that forms white water. You'll remember I said not to put your fly in white water—but look for it and place your fly above and below it.

I was fishing the Madison River below Three Dollar Bridge one late summer and had been working up the bank with a dry-dropper, catching rainbows and browns up to about 14 inches in their usual haunts, especially when there was enough of a trench along the bank to hold a decent fish. I kept eyeing a larger rock 100 yards upstream of me, the size of a kitchen table, but took my time and covered all the water in between. Finally, when I got to the rock, instead of fishing behind it I made my first cast so that my dry and nymph landed a few feet in front of it and the nymph drifted into the pocket in front of the rock. Instead of taking the nymph, as all the other fish had, an 18-inch brown trout huffed my dry fly and jumped three or four times in the shallow water before I landed it after a teetering dash downstream to follow it. That nicer fish was exactly where I would have expected it to be. It's heartening when your theories pan out.

Interactions between Rocks

Rocks get lonely and often form aggregations, where smaller rocks get rolled by the current up against a larger, immobile rock. These jumbles are often big enough to form miniature pools, which as you might imagine are great trout-holding spots. Even if all of the rocks are submerged, you'll be able to spot these places by a wider expanse of flat, smooth water below an area of turbulence. Even better is where a clutter of rocks forms a tiny pool with another bunch at the tail end of

A miniature pool formed by two large piles of rocks. You can see how the focal point of the upstream rocks coincides with the front of the downstream rocks—the perfect situation for finding trout.

Don't just look at single rocks. Pay close attention to how the currents around one rock intersect with the currents coming from another. Looking at these two rocks, you can see that both of their plumes intersect in a single focal point that enhances its value. A nice, slow, deeper slot is formed that might hold some nice fish.

the pool, enclosing the bucket with rocks at the head and tail. The preferred feeding place for trout in an assembly like this is at the tail end, as a trout lying there will be in the focal point of the rocks above and in the cushion of the rocks below. And it has all kinds of options if a predator appears, so these fish are more comfortable feeding and less likely to be spooked by your presence. If I scan a stretch of pocket water and see one of these modest pools, it will be the first place I try.

In pocket water rocks, or groups of rocks, will develop currents that make some spots better and others worse by their interactions because the currents around objects extend downstream, sometimes for quite a distance, and intermingle with the currents around other rocks. When you begin to notice these relations, you've arrived in your water-reading skills. Before you even step into the water, and when you approach each section of pocket water, look around for these interfaces.

A single rock, off by itself in the middle of a river, doesn't offer much. Trout seem to like a variety of feeding stations in the course of the day, and a lone rock may only offer one or two spots—and only one place to dart to if a predator is around—at the base of the rock. Multiple rocks, or piles of rocks, are always more desirable to fish for the diversity they offer. Thus when scoping out a piece of pocket water, besides looking for the largest rocks, look for the places where rocks are concentrated.

Next, examine the current flows and try to envision the water below in three dimensions. The best places will be where the focal point of an upstream rock intersects the front of a rock below it. This is just doubling down on features a trout prefers and puts it in the best currents, and with the safest place to bolt to when threatened by predators. Look for places where the outside seam coming off a rock kisses the edge of another rock. Look in the focal point behind a large rock for smaller, submerged rocks in the plume. The current here may not be fast enough for these rocks to develop much turbulence, so a trout has security and some added break from the current without getting buffeted by instability. In all cases, look for prime current plus security.

Logs sometimes get jammed into rock piles in pocket water, and when you find a log mixed among the rocks you'll find trout. Logs impart cover and a break from the current and trout seem to gravitate to them, perhaps because of their softer surface or because when they are parallel to the current they offer a long piece of security and numerous little nooks for trout to hide. A log that has wedged itself perpendicular to the current on some rocks may look intriguing, but they don't seem to shelter as many trout, possibly because they aren't as permanent and may be whirled away by the next flood.

A waterlogged tree trunk lying parallel to the current doesn't present as much resistance and has possibly been there for years.

WHERE TO LOOK FOR TROUT IN HIGH OR LOW WATER

High Water

In high water, feeding trout must deal with faster currents and may not be able to hold their position in much of this water. The first place to look is along the banks. Places that might have been stagnant frog water under normal flows will have a flush of current that creates feeding places in areas that might have been dry or even grassy in lower flows. The banks add extra friction to any streambed structure and slow down the water even more, and the higher flows may add enough depth to regions that were too shallow before the water went up.

Look for places without a lot of turbulence, with uniform flows, and moving less than a couple of feet per second. You might find little pockets that hold a single trout, or you may find larger cutouts along the bank that have the potential for several fish. These bays may have recirculating currents that collect any insects hatching in the higher flows.

You may also be able to catch trout out in the main flow of the river during high water, but you'll need to pick your battles. One consideration is that in high water you may not be able to wade far enough out to get to these spots. Wading that was exacting under normal flows may be dangerous in high water. Those round rocks are still on the bottom, but you might not see them and the force of the current will be magnified.

Your best bet, if you can reach them, are places with large rocks. Smaller rocks that might hold trout in normal or low flows may have so much water rushing over them that there may not be a slower pocket below them. Or it might be slower but still too fast for a trout to position comfortably. Larger rocks are more likely to have some respite from the current, and the ones that extend out of the water, with stagnant places below them in normal flows, might have enough current now to bring sufficient food to a trout. This is one of those circumstances where you may find trout immediately behind a rock.

In the miniature pools created by assemblies of rocks, there may be enough lessening of the current to hold feeding trout. Look for the flat, smooth areas in these pockets. These places indicate slower, less turbulent water. You'll usually find them at the downstream end of the small pools rather than at the head, which will

In high water, or fast water in general, it's probably best to ignore the smaller rocks unless they are aggregated to form a larger pocket. A better bet is to concentrate on the larger rocks, especially in the slower focal point well below them. I'm not even sure there would be a trout in front of the large rock because its face seems to slope forward and may not offer a decent cushion in front of it.

likely be too turbulent. Here and in other places, avoid standing waves. A standing wave indicates strong turbulence from a hydraulic jump that goes all the way to the bottom and then circulates. You can be quite sure trout won't be feeding close to any standing waves. There's no break from the current.

Low Water

In low water, when flows are at late season levels, flow might be reduced to the point where you see no standing waves and little white water. The water level may be so low that most of the area is too shallow to hold trout comfortably. In that case, look for the deeper pockets. Look for dark water, places where you can't see every stone on the bottom. If you can't see the bottom, predators will also have a problem finding trout and they will feel more secure. Pocket water does have the attraction of lots of rocks, but the depth around the rocks needs to be at least a couple of feet.

Reduced flow in pocket water also dictates where trout feed. Unless the main current hugs one bank, the rocks close to the bank may not hold trout because the water there is too stagnant, or too shallow. As with any

low water scenario, look for those bubble lines that indicate the main current flow and an abundance of drifting food. Often in pocket water the main flow separates into multiple threads and there could be more than one bubble line in the same section of river, so look closely for each one. Chances are most of the good rocks will be closer to the middle of the river, as trout will migrate from along the banks to the security and depth of the middle of the river.

Reduced flow will lessen the amount of turbulence found behind rocks, so although trout will always be directly in front of rocks, they may be closer to the downstream side of a rock instead of lolling well downstream as they would in higher water. In this case the size of the rock and whether it sticks above the water matters. If water is running over the top of the rock, trout may be immediately behind it. If a partially submerged rock is basketball-sized, trout may also be found close to the rock. But if the rock is larger, the water behind it could be stagnant and mostly devoid of food, so look for trout back in the focal point or in the seams that extend downstream from either side. They'll have better access to food here.

Trout may also be found in different places in those mini pools formed by piles of rocks. In reduced flow, the turbulence at the head of these pools is reduced and trout may move up closer to the upstream ends, where current is faster and more broken. They'll get more food there, and the broken surface will help them hide from ospreys and herons. As the water warms in low water, these places could also hold more oxygen because of their broken water. In this case, white water can be your friend—trout are unlikely to be directly under it, but they may be closer to it, especially downstream of it, than in higher water levels to take advantage of the increased oxygen supply.

WHEN TROUT MOVE IN THIS WATER

I don't believe trout living in pocket water move around much in the course of a day. They have an ideal place to feed, rest, and bolt to when danger threatens, and it's too much effort to fight the many currents to move to another spot. If they're in a place with a number of rocks in close proximity, they may move from one rock to another, or move from the side of a rock to the pocket in front of it. If you catch a nice trout in front of a rock in pocket water and return the next week, as long as water conditions haven't changed, it will likely be feeding in the same place.

During a hatch, a trout that was resting or hiding in a depression along the side of a larger rock might move in front of it to get better visibility and access to food close to the surface. Trout in those small pools downstream of a scattering of rocks may also move down to the very bottom of the pool, where the water is smoother and a bit slower, and it is easier to spot their prey. There is a long stretch of pocket water on the Madison River that I enjoy fishing because the shoreline is peppered with modest pools formed by jumbles of rocks. The last time I fished it, I had an hour in the evening, when hatches of caddisflies, midges, and mayfly spinners are often denser

Low water in a pocket water stretch. Turbulence is greatly reduced and trout will now be concentrated in the strongest current lanes and may lie much closer to the downstream edge of rocks—as long as the rocks are not big enough to block all the food coming down. The area on the left side might have been great in high water, but now it's a dead zone with slack water and no drifting food.

than during the day and trout lose their caution. All the trout I found rising were in the tails of these modest pools, and I didn't see a single fish feed at their heads. I suspect those trout lived within the pocket throughout the summer, but dropped back into the smoothest and slowest water they could find within those compact pools.

SEASONAL CHANGES

Pocket water is usually not year-round habitat and is mainly spring and summer water. You'll find that most trout abandon this water in colder temperatures when hatches are not active. From what I can tell, as soon as the hatches of spring appear and continuing through summer when both aquatic and terrestrial insects are abundant, trout move from deeper pools and runs into pocket water for the wealth of current seams and cover it offers. In rivers that don't have deeper pools and slower runs, you'll find winter and early spring trout in the areas within pocket water that are deeper and slower and offer some winter refuge. Anchor ice is a real problem in pocket water, because the constant interchange of the colder atmosphere with the sides of rocks and bottom of the river builds up ice that coats them, making it a dangerous place for trout. Only the deepest pockets offer respite from it.

During the spring spawning season for cutthroats and rainbows, and in the fall for brook and brown trout, you may see evidence of spawning. There are sometimes nice patches of gravel below rocks that are just the right depth and current speed for hatching eggs, and trout may migrate to these spots and stage there before spawning. As always, don't target fish that are actively spawning, and during spawning season try not to walk on any large expanses of gravel, because you never know if trout have already spawned there and you don't want to crush their eggs.

APPROACH

One of the great attributes of pocket water is that you can get quite close to trout. The swirling water negates most waves you'll propagate while wading, and the broken surface water makes you less visible. Trout are also more comfortable and less skittish because they live in close proximity to the safety of a rock, and the rocks themselves can actually block you from a trout's view. You can sometimes get almost on top of a trout feeding on the far side of a large rock, and sometimes it seems like you could just dap your fly on top of them without even making a cast.

Wading is difficult, however, so part of your approach should be to look over the entire piece of pocket water

first. Figure out where you think the prime spots will be and walk the bank, if possible, and then get into the water as close as possible to the fish. If the best water is out in the middle of the river, plan a route before you get into the river, from a high vantage point so you can spot the deep holes that might not be visible when you are at water level. Look for patches of gravel, which usually show up a lighter color than piles of rocks. The best way to navigate pocket water is to move from one gravel patch to another.

Another refuge for your wading will be in the pockets behind rocks, which reduce the force of the current greatly. Those spots might be quite turbulent and trout may not like them, but the turbulence lessens the downstream energy of the river and you can usually stand quite comfortably in white water pockets, even though they look difficult to navigate.

Rocks in the middle of the river can be approached from either upstream or downstream, depending on what it takes to get close enough to them to make a cast. But with pocket water along the bank, upstream is really the only way to go. Direct downstream casts are tricky to

If you can't get in the water and have to fish from a rock in pocket water, try to block your profile by using a rock or tree so that you are not silhouetted against the sky.

execute and your presentation won't be great, and working downstream you'll most likely spook trout before you get a chance to place a fly over them.

When working a bank, avoid wading at all if you can. If you watch a savvy angler on a river like the Madison, where much of the good pocket water is inches from the bank, they hardly ever get their feet wet unless a bush prevents them from approaching a likely spot while standing on the bank. Just be aware that while on the bank your profile is higher and more visible to trout, and sometimes crouching or kneeling is the only way to approach them. It's not fun, and often uncomfortable, so choosing the spots where you crouch (like when approaching a patch of smooth water where the surface is unbroken) should be part of your plan. If the water ahead of you is riffled and turbulent, you may be able to stand fully upright and get away with it.

Resist the urge to stand on rocks. Getting on top of a rock gives you a better view and typically their dry surfaces are not slippery. And casting is easier. But creeping around the edge of a rock instead of standing on it will make you stealthier and less visible to fish.

Staying relatively hidden behind a big rock in Labrador allowed me to get close enough to this brook trout—the biggest of my life.

Look over a stretch of pocket water first, before you wade in. Figure out where you want to fish and navigate to the spot either by walking the bank or staying in the shallows. Pocket water is tricky wading, and you don't want to spend all day slipping around if you can help it.

My one trip fishing for the giant brook trout in Labrador happened in an unusually dry summer: The water was low and the trout were spooky, not something you associate with wilderness brook trout. But trout bolt from moving objects above them regardless of how many humans they've seen in their lifetime, because natural predators are always present and they are hardwired to be wary of movement above the water. I was fishing with a young guide who had not been in this stretch of river for a few weeks, so he hadn't experienced the river so low. Every time we approached a new stretch of pocket water, he'd climb on top of the largest boulder to peer into the pockets behind the rocks to look for fish. Although we saw some fish, we couldn't get these normally eager trout to chase a mouse fly or a streamer. I'm reluctant to tell guides what to do, as they usually know more than I do, but in this case I didn't think his approach was wise. At one point I suggested he take a break and eat his lunch, and I waded upstream 50 yards to water we hadn't looked at yet. I stayed low and crept around the boulders instead of mounting them, and sure enough I was able to fool a few fish before he finished his lunch and joined me. It was all downhill after that.

TECHNIQUES TO TRY

Pocket water is not the place for hero casts. No other water type you experience will present as many opportunities for drag as pocket water, and the more line you have on the water, the greater the chance the current will grab your line and leader and move your fly's drift off course or make it drag in an aberrant behavior. Even trout that have never seen a fly will mostly avoid one that is dragging, because their food doesn't act that way. This is another reason to avoid those tempting areas right behind rocks. Even if you place your fly behind a rock with the strategy of letting it drift into the focal point below the rock, the swirling turbulence in that pocket will usually move your fly off course in a way you didn't predict. Instead of drifting nicely downstream, it will often drag to one side or even move upstream instead of downstream.

Along with short casts, you should only expect short drifts. Sooner or later drag will thwart your presentation, and often sooner than you expect. Short upstream casts with a dry-dropper, nymphs with an indicator, a single attractor dry fly, or Euro nymphing techniques are the best approach. It's also helpful to keep your rod tip high and most of your fly line off the water. Even when fishing with a dry fly, take a hint from the notebook of Euro nymphers and try to keep a direct line in the air between your rod tip and your fly. Don't waste a lot of time with each drift. As soon as drag takes hold, get your fly out of the water and make another cast—unless a trout takes your fly when it drags. It won't happen that often, but when it does pay attention. You never know what might work.

Streamers are good in pocket water because you manipulate your fly and can make the fly independent of drag. Insects seldom swim across current lanes, but minnows and crayfish do. Sinking lines or sinking poly leaders might be helpful in high water, but most of the time you'll want to use a heavily weighted streamer with a floating line so you can drop your streamer into those pockets in front of and behind rocks and get them down to the trout's level quickly. This is a place where a direct upstream approach often works well with a streamer, as it will help get the fly deeper into the pockets. Sinking lines often get you hung up on the rocks, but dropping a weighted streamer into pockets with a floating line, or even with a high rod and only the leader on the water, and then manipulating it with strips or short twitches works best. Try to keep your streamer moving but don't move it too fast. Trout in pocket water are reluctant to chase a fly very far, because moving out of the comfortable pocket presents them with tumbling currents that might make it difficult for them to get back into place. Trout in pools will sometimes chase a streamer 30 feet before taking it. Not so in pocket water.

You might even try hanging a streamer or a nymph directly downstream, letting it marinate in the current. The turbulence in pocket water will give your streamer all the action it needs, and sometimes a fly hanging close to a trout will induce a strike from territoriality or just the idea of a tasty morsel within reach. You can also try an occasional twitch, a few short strips, or moving your rod tip from side to side so the streamer moves off and then comes back into position.

Unless you're presented with a relatively uniform piece of current, unusual in pocket water, swinging a streamer or soft hackle is difficult, especially when some of the rocks protrude above the surface. The many varying currents will push and pull on your fly and won't allow it to get that smooth, uniform swing that seems to be attractive to trout. You'll also have trouble manipulating your swing, as your line and leader will get hung up on rocks. If all or most of the rocks are submerged, you may be able to get a decent downstream swing, as long as the turbulence of the submerged rocks don't monkey with the progress of your drift.

A dry-dropper is perhaps the best way to fish pocket water, and this brown trout took the nymph end of a dry-dropper rig in heavy pocket water. Keep your casts short and keep as much fly line as possible off the water, because pocket water introduces tricky currents that can make what appears to be a great presentation wonky because the swirls pull your line in unexpected directions.

CHAPTER 9

Big Rivers and Tiny Streams

DESCRIPTION

Most fly fishers, especially wading anglers, are accustomed to fishing rivers of a comfortable size: intimate enough to wade almost anywhere, but wide enough that casting room is seldom an issue once you wade in a bit. By this I mean rivers the size of the Beaverkill in New York or Gallatin in Montana or the McCloud in California. Let's say between 30 and 150 feet wide for a baseline. If you've done much fishing and have paid attention to the behavior of trout, your brain evokes similar scenarios and you have a decent idea where trout live, just as when you reach the outskirts of any city or town you know what kind of roadside scenery attracts fast-food joints.

When fly fishers who have spent their lives on these "average" trout streams encounter a large river for the first time, one that stretches beyond anyone's longest cast and doesn't look like it could be waded from one bank to the other anywhere, they panic. They don't know where to start. It's all in your head, though—you have the tools to find trout if you've been paying attention to this book, but to make you more comfortable I'll give you some tips on how to lower your stress on spacious water. You do have to approach it differently at first. I find the mystery of large rivers compelling because they hold so much potential. You just know that somewhere in that immense mass of water swims a trout bigger than anything you've ever caught, and often big rivers have multiple species to delight and surprise you. I've caught smallmouth bass, largemouth bass, pike, carp, American shad, and walleye in trout streams where you would never expect one.

By small streams I mean flowing waters less than a two-lane highway wide, all the way down to ones you can jump across without a running start. Tiny streams and brooks aren't daunting; on the contrary, they're intimate. Not daunting but frustrating to some. I've seen great anglers accustomed to fishing wide waters from drift boats totally lose it in the confines of a tiny brook because they kept getting tangled in brush or made casts that were way too long. Small brooks don't scare anglers away, but I think they too often get ignored. It's partly because of that backcast-room issue, but I think that many anglers look at a tiny brook from the road and figure it's not worth fishing. Either they won't

Large rivers are overwhelming at first, and one tactic is to look for islands and side channels that break the river down into more manageable bites.

Large rivers can, at first glance, look intimidating and sometimes featureless. Where do you even begin? Learning to dissect them into manageable pieces is a great skill and it's not that hard once you get an overview of the river and focus on the right places.

hold any trout (often not true) or they won't hold any trout large enough for their egos (mostly true).

Let's take a look at these two extremes in the world of trout fishing and figure out how differently we need to think when hunting for trout.

WHERE TO LOOK FOR TROUT UNDER NORMAL FLOWS

Big Rivers

The worst advice I've ever heard about transitioning from small trout streams to big rivers is to "just divide the big river up into a bunch of smaller rivers." Doesn't work that way most of the time. In a massive river trout will be concentrated in discrete places, and in some of them less than 10 percent of the water holds trout. You can jump into a big river at a random spot, start fishing it like you would a bunch of small rivers, and you might as well be fishing in a parking lot. All the trout could be a half mile upstream or downstream.

The Missouri River tailwater in Montana is a large river where it is almost impossible to find a place that won't hold trout at one time or another. Less fertile rivers with sparser trout populations are much harder to fish because trout will only be found in the very best places.

As in nearly everything in trout fishing, you'll find exceptions to the rule, for instance very rich tailwaters like the Missouri River in Montana below Holter Dam, where you'd be hard-pressed to park your butt in any place along the bank without finding a few trout. But in rivers with a more limited trout population, like the nearby Jefferson River or Clark Fork, or the main stem of the Delaware on the New York–Pennsylvania border, you'll need to do some reconnaissance before you begin slicing up that big water into little creeks.

Your first step might be to do some homework to find out how dense the trout population is. For instance, the Missouri in the famous water around Craig, Montana, boasts about 5,000 trout per mile, but if you go into the next valley over, the Jefferson might hold only 300 per mile in a low water year because the river gets severely dewatered in drought years, which affects both the trout population and the insects they feed on. It's not wise to

Discovering those tiny streams that most people will ignore because they look too small to hold trout is one of fly fishing's greatest pleasures. They are not hard to read if you know what to look for, and are an intimate experience.

In a large river with mostly fast water, like the Madison River in Montana, look for the slower pockets as indicated by a smoother, glassy surface. You're always looking for that 1- to 2-foot-per-second zone.

In rivers with mostly slow water, like the main stem of the Delaware on the New York–Pennsylvania border, search out the riffled areas. At least go to them first because they'll be transporting the most drifting food.

park at any old pull-off along the Jefferson and begin fishing. Even if you don't do your homework, you can get a good idea of the density of a trout population in a large river by looking at the number of drift boat trailers parked along the river. Guides make a living from producing trout for their clients, and the internet has made any river with a dense trout population public knowledge.

Even in a large river with a good population of trout, only some of these places are fishable with a fly rod, even from a drift boat. Tim Linehan, owner of Linehan Outfitters of Libby, Montana, and a guide with many decades of experience, describes his home river, the giant Kootenai, like this: "The Kootenai has low productivity because it runs through granite bedrock [which if you remember from a previous chapter, lowers a river's productivity because of its lack of buffering] and because it runs out of the 100-mile-long, very deep Koocanusa Reservoir, which acts as a nutrient trap. There are about 1,600 trout per mile, and I would estimate that 75 percent of the water can hold trout at some time. But there's so much water, and the river is so deep and cold, that trout could be anywhere. Sure, we row through sections, but for reasons of fishability and not habitat. For instance, we call one area the Dead Sea because the river broadens through a super-deep pool and there's relatively no current along the banks. It's hard to target trout in that kind of water. But roll through the Dead Sea before dark in July and there are noses of rising trout everywhere. But trying to target those trout in a giant pool with no features when trout aren't rising is an exercise in frustration. So I would say that the amount of *fishable* water that holds trout in the Kootenai is more like 25 percent."

Let's say you don't know anything about a large river, but it looks trouty and you don't see many other anglers. Where do you begin? I think the first course of action is to look for places with varying depth and current, which typically means riffles, heads of pools, and tails of pools. Big rivers often have monotonous stretches of flat, almost featureless water, and although there may be trout present, like Tim Linehan's example of the Dead Sea, whether you're wading or floating it's frustrating to try to cover very slow or very deep water without some kind of current structure to target. You need to narrow the odds. There could be trout lying in 10 or 20 feet of water, but they probably aren't actively feeding—and even with a full-sinking line you'll have difficulty getting a fly to them.

In big rivers where most of the water is deep, like the Snake in Idaho, pay the most attention to the shallower places. Those deep-water spots may look tasty, but most feeding trout will be in water that is 2 to 4 feet deep.

In rivers where much of the water is shallower than 2 feet, like the upper Connecticut River on the Vermont–New Hampshire border, look for those deeper slots that are over 2 feet deep.

One of the best pieces of advice I can give you for finding catchable trout in big rivers is this: In rivers that are mostly deep, look for the shallow spots; in rivers that are mostly shallow, look for the deeper pockets. A corollary to this is: In rivers that are mostly fast, look for slower water; in rivers that are mostly slow, look for places with more current. It's all about trying to find that magic 2- to 4-foot-deep water with a current speed of between 1 and 2 feet per second. For instance, in Linehan's Kootenai, where much of the water is quite deep, he looks for trout in the tails of pools where the bottom slopes up into shallower water. In big, flat tailwaters like the Henry's Fork, where much of the water is wadeable from bank to bank, look for the deeper pockets. In the Madison, where 90 percent of the current is faster than 2 feet per second, you look for the slower pockets to find fish, but in the Delaware, with giant pools that look more like ponds, you look for places where the current picks up, like in the heads and tails of pools and in deeper riffles.

I like to divide a big river into zones. You can try this before you get to the river with a satellite image, or you can drive along a river if you can see it from the road or walk the banks. If you're floating a river in a boat for the first time, you'll want to do this anyway. What you'll find on many large rivers is few classic pools with a defined head, tail, and middle. What you usually see is long stretches of the same kind of water—riffles, pocket water, long glides, flat water, and everything in between—punctuated by shorter stretches of a different type of water. Here's how I divide river zones:

RIFFLE ZONE

This is a great place to start in any large river. Insect food is produced here, so you know trout will *want* to be close to a riffle. Whether the habitat supports them depends on the depth of the riffle, as by their very nature, riffles are not often too fast for trout unless you see standing waves on the surface. A gentle riffle, with at least 2 feet of depth, is likely to hold trout. Narrow it down first, though. Some riffles are mostly barren water unless they hold the correct depth and current speed for trout. Look for edges where a riffle deepens, and for trenches and buckets that offer slower water and a bit more depth. Look for seams in a riffle where faster water meets slow, and for those glassy flat lenses on the surface that indicate buckets. In long stretches of riffle water less than a foot deep, look for the places where it eventually drops into deeper water.

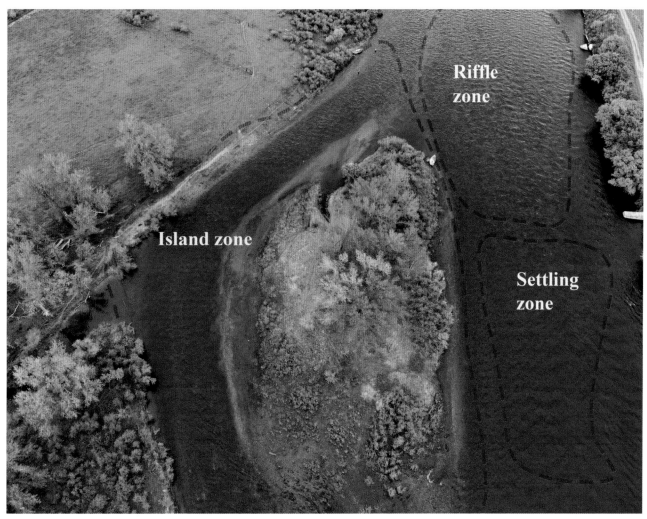

This one piece of water has lots of features to explore and is the type of water I would look for in large riffles. It has an island zone and a side channel, a riffle zone, and a settling zone. You could spend all day in a piece of water like this.

Watch how the riffle interacts with the bank. In large rivers, often riffles are bounded on one or both sides by gradual shallows. Along a shallow bank, trout will be in the transition zone where you just lose sight of individual rocks on the bottom in clear water. If a riffle deepens along one bank, which often happens on the outside of a bend in the river, that should be a hotspot. The bank offers protection and lots of structure to create different water speeds

SETTLING ZONE

I call the settling zone any place where fast water flattens out, loses most of its turbulence and standing waves, and begins to slow down and become more uniform. This zone has the advantage of a fast water conduit above for food and current slow enough to be comfortable for trout. You'll find these zones below riffles, downstream of the heads of pools, or at the lower end of a stretch of pocket water. This is also a great place to fish because it's often a short and narrow piece of water. This gives you a target, and a place to put your fly with the confidence that a trout might be there. I like these transition zones, especially on an unfamiliar river, and this is usually the first area I'll try after scouting the water.

PINCH ZONE

A pinch zone is where a stretch of big water narrows down, typically because the river has cut through bedrock or there are immovable obstructions on both banks that restrict its flow horizontally. Pinch zones aren't always great places to fish because they speed up the flow of the river, and in a river that's already quite fast a pinch zone will limit even more the places with current slow enough to shelter trout. However, in a river that's either very wide and shallow or very slow, a pinch zone speeds up the current and almost always increases the average depth of the water, so trout may find more suitable habitat. Regardless of the depth or speed of a river, the area just below a pinch zone where the river widens is usually a great place to find trout.

Pinch zones are places where a wide river narrows. If most of the river is quite shallow with no features, pinch zones often hold deep slots that give trout refuge when all the other water exposes them to predators.

A view from ground level of the head, middle, and tail zones of a large river. In this case, the middle zone does not slow down much and still retains adequate current, so all areas of this pool hold potential—the head for prospecting with a dry-dropper when nothing is rising, the middle zone for looking for rising fish and also for prospecting with nymphs or a dry-dropper, and the tail for heavy hatches or for fishing a streamer or swung wet fly. (You can reasonably fish any part with any technique you want—those would only be my choices.)

ISLAND ZONE

Places where islands break up the river channel turn it into smaller streams for you, and if you're not comfortable in bigger rivers, side channels along islands may be the place you'd feel at home. Islands are especially attractive in fast, deep rivers that may not offer comfortable wading and fishing in any other place, and luckily you can spot these on a satellite map so you can plan to fish them when you hit the river. Try to determine when the satellite image was taken, by looking at the foliage along the banks or ascertaining the date of the satellite photo. Not all satellite maps show the date the image was taken, but Google Earth does. If you can't find the date, if the foliage along the banks looks like spring, side channels that look full of water on a map could be dry in midsummer, and trout move in and out of side channels based on water conditions. A side channel that holds water in high summer should hold trout any time of year. Look in the side channels themselves, and also on the seams at the heads and tails of islands.

HEAD ZONE

The heads of pools, or places with large hydraulic jumps like waterfalls, are intimidating places in big rivers. They announce themselves like a trumpet fanfare, and you'll have no doubt where they occur. Although these places can be intimidating, especially at high water, they're still great areas in larger rivers to narrow down your decision making, because you'll always find some slower and less turbulent places along their edges, or where a side current is less dramatic and more inviting.

Always look for back eddies downstream of the head of a pool or a hydraulic jump. Tim Linehan targets them on the Kootenai because, he says, "back eddies are traps for insects and other food sources and provide trout with readily and concentrated food sources and easy holding water due to the hydraulics of the currents. Feeding trout can often be seen suspended in back eddies and are readily visible from a slightly higher vantage point above the river or while standing in a drift boat."

TAIL ZONE

The tail of a pool anywhere is a place that concentrates trout, and in big rivers they're even more attractive because they may be the only place you find with water slow enough and shallow enough to target fish. Many tails shallow up gradually, so you will have an easier time wading and you'll always be able to find water of the right depth for feeding trout somewhere along the sloping shelf. Tails are not as easy to fish as other types of water, especially when prospecting with dry flies or nymphs, so it would not be the first place I would go unless I see a hatch, as tails are often the first places trout begin to rise.

SLOW ZONE

This zone is one place I try to avoid unless I see rising fish, or perhaps I've been there before and know exactly where I might find feeding trout. You look at a long, slow stretch of water from the bank or from a satellite image and although you know trout live there, trying to sort out exactly where they'll be is a daunting prospect. These places often look like one long slice of white bread. A long slow zone might be mostly too deep or mostly too shallow or may not even offer enough current to keep a trout happy. But some rivers have miles of seemingly featureless water and if that's all you have, there are ways to distill this water into something worth fishing.

First look at the banks. Tim Linehan looks for banks with a bit of current running along them, and sometimes parts of this water will have places where the current picks up along the bank, even though the water in the rest of the pool looks bland. The water here does not even need to be very deep. Current running along a deep bank always looks fishy, but don't rule out a thread of current along a shallow bank that's only 2 feet deep. Often a gravel bar in a deep pool will push the current to the bank and when it hits a shallower spot, it speeds up enough to attract trout. The more structure along a bank, the better its prospects, but I've also found trout in these little side currents along banks that seemed to offer little protection or structure. If you're moving through one of these dead zones in a drift boat, examine the banks carefully before you commit to one bank or the other and follow the bank that has the most current.

If the banks aren't any good, look for subtle boils on the surface that pinpoint large rocks or other obstructions on the bottom. These won't be apparent from a satellite map or even with a casual glance, but once you examine that piece of white bread, you'll find little nooks and crannies if you watch the surface carefully. I have a favorite stretch on the Delaware that looks so flat and boring, I think most people pass it up. But over the years I have found that trout rise up and down its length in very discrete places, separated by many yards with no fish feeding. I couldn't figure out why the trout were keyed to these particular places, year after year, until I noticed one low water year that each of the spots had a large submerged rock. The boils on the surface that betrayed the rocks were subtle, and I missed them at first because I was blinded by the sight of rising fish. With hindsight, if I had been more observant I would have found those places without the Judas fish betraying them.

The slow zone of a large river is usually one tough nut to crack. It's a good place to look for rising trout if any insects are on the water, but if nothing is showing it's hard to figure out where the fish are. Always look to the banks, or near any swirls that may indicate submerged rocks.

There is one location in large rivers that sometimes holds feeding trout, but it's tough to predict and is also in a place where I've told you to avoid looking for fish—in large boils of turbulence. Sometimes, in large, deep rivers, trout use giant cells of turbulence to surf the currents and hold their position over deep water. I first saw this one year on the lower Merced River, well downstream of Yosemite, where I could see big rainbows suspended over deep water in deep canyon pools. Since then I've seen resident rainbows and steelhead in the same kind of water, and it seems to be behavior specific to these fish. I have never seen browns, brook trout, or cutthroats behaving like this.

The one common aspect of fish holding in these boils is that they seem to do it in cells of turbulence that are fairly static and don't move or change shape often. Apparently rainbows are able to sort out the places in turbulence that will hold them in place using the receptors on their skin that give them feedback on surrounding currents. It's not something you'll often see and most large pockets of turbulence are devoid of trout, but if you're in a deep, fast pool and no place else looks like it could hold trout, it's worth looking at places where turbulence isn't oscillating.

Tiny Streams

In one respect, finding trout in a small stream is straight-forward—you look for all the places with enough depth to hold them. If most of a stream is 6 inches deep and you come upon a plunge pool where you can't see bottom, you don't need to know much about reading water to suspect this may be the place trout live. But trout in small streams don't always follow that 2- to 6-foot-deep rule because sometimes they don't have the luxury of water that deep, but still manage to thrive in water that is so thin few people would suspect to find trout there. Which is good news for you and me. In water a foot deep or even a bit less, you can find trout feeding if you find decent cover close at hand—a pile of rocks, a log, or an overhanging tree.

The trick to finding trout in small streams most of the time is to cover a lot of water. I've explored some tiny streams where as soon as I got out of my car, I started fishing and found a trout in every place you might expect one—in front of every rock and in all the deeper slots. But most of the time it doesn't work out that way.

For years I've been eyeing a tributary of a tributary of a trout stream I often fish, poring over it on topo maps to try to identify the best place to fish it. One day I stopped at the one place a dirt road crossed it, and although the water looked too thin everyplace I could see from the bridge, I walked downstream a half mile, averting my eyes as I walked past the big orange "Posted" signs, and fished it back up to the bridge. I only caught one small rainbow and so wrote it off as a failed experiment, as water conditions looked perfect and if trout were present I should have caught more of them.

A year later I stopped on that bridge again and this time looked upstream. The water still appeared to be too thin, and besides it was a tangle of dogwood and buckthorn and I wasn't sure if I wanted to struggle through the tangle and bow-and-arrow cast all afternoon. But I tried it anyway, and a hundred yards upstream it opened up into a relatively open canopy, and even better, a series of nice, deep ledge rock pools. I caught more trout, and bigger trout, than I deserved that day, and even got a Vermont Grand Slam—a brook trout, a brown, and a rainbow. All wild fish. Don't write off a small stream unless you've walked a mile of its banks.

One way to find the best place on a small stream is by determining elevation change, either on a topo map or by walking the creek yourself. Often these streams, once they reach the flat land below the hills, are mostly shallow and featureless, sometimes compounded by agricultural practices that straighten a stream channel or by livestock overgrazing the banks and flattening them, pushing gravel into the channel. But follow that trickle up into a hillside, where steepness and boulder fields make agriculture difficult, and suddenly the abrupt changes in altitude, as the stream drops from one bedrock shelf to the next, forms plunge pools far deeper than you would suspect given the volume of water. We typically think of rivers as getting deeper as you move downstream, but in small streams like this the opposite is often the case.

On tumbling mountain streams with steep elevation changes the opposite is true, and you look for places a brook settles into a plateau. If a slope is too steep, fish have no protection from the ravages of the current unless a large rock or log puts a brake on its progress. Here, look for places where the slope is not as steep, where the water settles into calmer buckets more conducive to trout. These are not hard to eyeball as you walk along

From a road crossing, small streams often look too thin and devoid of cover to hold decent trout. Don't rule these out. Take a hike and you may find much better water.

In small streams, look for places devoid of white water, with uniform flow, and deep enough that rocks on the bottom begin to look blurry. Some type of cover close at hand is also important—a large rock, log, or overhanging tree.

a stream, or you can predict them before your hike by looking at the contour lines on a map.

Because depth is so often a limiting factor to trout abundance in small streams, always look for bends, which are especially easy to spot on a map before you begin your exploration. When a creek hits a bend and is forced to change direction, either from the natural erosion and deposition processes that form meanders or because the course of the stream hits a rocky bank, you'll find deeper water. In some creeks, bends are the only places that furnish pockets deep enough to hold a trout safely.

This is especially true in low-elevation, slow-moving meadow streams where bends may be the only place the creek gets deep enough, and trout in this smoother water need a bit more depth for protection than they do in tumbling mountain streams. When I'm plotting to explore a small stream I have never fished, I'll always check a map and look for the place with the most bends. Conversely, if I see a tract of creek that runs in a straight line for a long distance, I'll often rule it out—at least in my first exploration. If I find a stream hosts a dense population of trout, I might explore these places, but only after I've checked out the more plausible bends.

Warm water temperature is less likely to be a problem on small streams because they are often closer to the sources of cool groundwater and are usually more shaded because of their narrower channel. But it's always best to check first. There is a stream I like to fish in the Green Mountain National Forest that holds a moderate population of trout, and after it leaves the national forest it runs through open meadows with hay fields, but with some attractive deep pools. The first time I fished the meadow stretch in late June, I didn't catch a single trout and didn't even see one. I finally took a water temperature and it was a surprising 75 degrees, which I attribute not only to the open hay fields, but to a wide, shallow beaver pond a half mile upstream that warms the creek by exposing all the water to a dark, open bottom.

This is something you need to check in late spring or early summer. In spring, it won't be a problem with cooler temperatures and snowmelt, and you might find perfect water temperatures then. But check the same stream in midsummer. If it runs close to 70 degrees not only should you not fish it, but the stream will probably not hold any wild trout at any time of year because the uncomfortable and possibly lethal temperatures will

After a short hike, water that looks too thin to support trout may offer up plunge pools formed by rocks or logs that may hold enough depth and cover to support trout.

Bends in small streams, especially when they encounter a steep bank or other immovable object, usually form deeper pools, so I always look for places where a small stream has numerous bends.

push all the trout farther upstream where water temperatures are cooler.

Weeds in small meadow streams can often indicate the presence of a spring creek, and these usually stay cold all summer long because of their heavy groundwater influence. Ranunculus, often known as water buttercup or water crowfoot, grows well in cold, clear water and is a good sign. So is watercress, which has similar ecological needs. Streams with plants more common to ponds like arrowroot or duckweed or introduced milfoil are not as good an indicator of a spring creek, though, and may indicate a stream that although it looks like a spring creek, could be too warm to hold trout.

Once you've found a stretch of creek that holds potential, it's time to look closer at features. Even though you can cover most of a small creek with casts, you should avoid this because throwing your fly everywhere could spook trout that you might have caught with a pinpoint cast to just the right spot. Again, depth is key. I find that

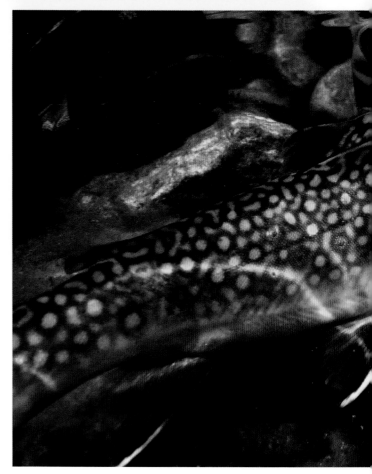

Small-stream trout may not be giants, but they are usually wild fish with brilliant colors. Well worth the effort.

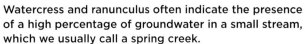

Watercress and ranunculus often indicate the presence of a high percentage of groundwater in a small stream, which we usually call a spring creek.

I catch nearly all of my trout in small streams where the water, if it's clear, is deep enough so that individual stones on the bottom become blurry. It's a handy clue to finding the right depth.

Along with the right depth, as in streams of all sizes, avoid white water and overly turbulent water and place your fly on the edges of these places. Where turbulence starts to settle down and flow in a general downstream direction without a lot of side detours is where you'll most often find trout. And as with rocks in larger rivers, you're more likely to catch a trout in front of rocks or in the focal point below them than right behind the rocks. Cover is also important because trout in small streams may not have as many avian predators such as ospreys and herons, which have a tough time hunting in tight quarters, but an exposed trout is just a swipe away from a mink or raccoon.

Undercut banks, where the stream flows under a slight overhang of the bank above, also offer shelter, especially in meadow streams where rocks and logs might be absent or uncommon. These are most often

In small mountain streams, look for plateaus instead of places with a steep drop. There might be a trout here, but I'd pass by water like this to find something a bit more inviting.

found on the outside of a bend but can also form where the exposed roots of a streamside tree touch the water. I have one undercut in a small stream I often fish that is so good, and always produces at least one nice fish, that I don't fish the water downstream of it thoroughly enough, and I'm probably missing good fish because I'm in a hurry to get to the undercut. Someday I'll fish this stretch with the express idea that I won't fish that undercut and maybe find some good fish in other places. Someday.

When you come across tiny pockets or plunge pools, make sure you try a few casts at their lip, just before they drop over into faster water. Trout are inclined to back down into these miniature tails when feeding, and often in our hurry to get to the tasty water at the head of a plunge pool we dump our fly line on top of this lip, or we wade into it to get a better shot at the waterfall above. This does nothing except spook the trout that were under your rod tip into the safety of the white water upstream, where they'll hide but are unlikely to feed.

One thing I've noticed in small streams is that if you have a much larger and deeper pool than anyplace else in the creek, the water immediately upstream and downstream of it, despite having enough depth and some cover, will often be devoid of trout. Places that somewhere else, in a long stretch of water that's too shallow, would be logical places to find trout just don't cut it here. I suspect that the proximity of such great water lures any trout nearby up into it, leaving the margins bare. It could be that I'm just in a hurry to fish the better water I see close at hand, but even on those occasions I've steeled myself to hold back and fish a pocket just below a really intriguing one, I've noticed no fish or just small fish on the fringes.

WHERE TO LOOK FOR TROUT IN HIGH OR LOW WATER

Big Rivers

In large rivers, unless you're fishing from a boat or raft, you probably won't be able to fish much of the water. And even if you could reach those deep holes in the middle of the river, chances are you wouldn't be able to get your fly down to any trout living there. You have to know when to limit your casts to the places you can fish effectively. Luckily, in large rivers many trout will move into the margins, just as they do in any river. And I suspect some of the fish just stay tucked into the bottom in deep pools. But those just aren't fish to bother with.

In high water, banks are nearly always the best place to check first. Whether you're in a riffle, run, pool, or pocket water, not only will you be able to negotiate the currents better, by staying on the bank if possible, but those will be the places with the slowest current, places trout migrate into so they can feed without fighting heavy current and turbulence. Hatches often come off in high water, much to our disappointment, but if you can find the right bank, you could be in for a treat.

One May I traveled to the Delaware River and found myself faced with water way up onto the banks and the color of milk chocolate. I stopped at a pool to contemplate my misery and noticed a large number of March Brown mayflies on the water—a big mayfly that seldom hatches in large numbers but seems to dribble off the water all day long. I thought I saw a rise out of the corner of my eye, up against a bank that was dry a week ago. I caught that fish and by carefully wading up the bank I caught several more, never casting more than a few inches from the bank. The trout were, I suspect, in water slow and shallow enough that they could see the mayfly duns on the water, in conditions that would send most of us home to do yard work or other meaningless tasks.

Look for the slowest water you can find in a big river in flood. Spots in pools that are normally stagnant might hold trout. Pools that narrow and quicken in their tails aren't as good, because trout have little respite from the current. But if the tail of a pool is wide, water bumping up against the shallow bar slows down and is another place to look. Whirlpools, because the energy of the current is directed away from the main flow, will be calmer and are generally close to the bank, so you can get at them without drowning.

Riffles in big rivers can also be surprisingly good because all that bumpy water is small cells of turbulence that again slow the downstream progress of the current. They don't look as slow as smoother parts of a river, but if you stop and watch how bubbles or insects float through riffles, you'll see they're moving slower than you suspect. Conversely, places with smooth, fast current are areas to avoid in high water. Any trout there are glued to the bottom and probably won't fight the current to rise for an insect, and even with lots of split shot or a sinking line you'll be hard-pressed to get a reasonable presentation to them.

Side channels are some of the best places to investigate in high water. Siphoning off a section of river slows it down, as it decreases the energy of the main flow by making it take a detour. These are sometimes the only places you can find a reasonable flow, and get your fly down to a trout, when the main river is cranking. Whenever I am faced with a large river in flood or near flood, I'll look at Google Earth or do a drive-by on the river to

In high water on big rivers, sometimes your only option is to look for trout that have moved into the slower, shallower margins along the banks. There may be trout out in the middle of the river somewhere, but chances are you won't be able to get a fly to them.

find these side channels. It's surprising how far trout will move to get into them to feed, and I have some special side channels on many large rivers that I fish that don't get much pressure because at normal levels they are too thin to hold trout, and anglers used to fishing these rivers often pass up the side channels just because they're not accustomed to looking at them.

Low water in big rivers presents a different set of challenges relating to flows and water temperatures. Side channels may be dry or may not be able to funnel off enough flow from the main river to be viable. Big pools may be too slow to hold drift-feeding trout in a place where they can get enough food (although they may cruise pond-like water during a hatch as they would in a lake). Riffles may be too shallow. And because wide rivers offer more surface area to bake in the sun, and don't have as much shaded surface as smaller streams, water temperatures can reach uncomfortable or lethal limits, forcing trout to migrate upstream or into the mouths of colder tributaries to obtain enough oxygen to survive.

In low flows you'll look for the opposite kind of water you did during high water. Look for the deepest, quickest water, which will most often be in the heads of pools, in deeper riffles, and especially in runs where

the river narrows and squeezes all the flow into a tighter package. You should still avoid areas of high turbulence and white water, but look for fish on the edges of these features. The faster water will deliver more oxygen and food, so the places on the edges, where the turbulence settles down and gets more uniform, will be the places you'll find trout.

Trout in low water are more visible to predators, and of course they'll be closer to cover—rocks, logs, and overhanging trees—in the main current flow. But broken water gives them almost as much protection, so they'll move into riffles not only for the greater supply of oxygen and food, but also for the overhead protection the broken surface gives them. Just look for places in riffles that are more than a couple of feet deep. The color of the water will be your guide to this—the darker the color, the deeper the water.

Water temperatures on some large rivers are problematic when they get into the high 60s. You shouldn't be fishing in these water temperatures, at least for trout. You may want to chase smallmouth bass or carp when the water gets close to 70, but trout will move when temperatures are not to their liking, and they are more mobile in large rivers so may travel long distances, usually upstream, to find cooler water.

In low water in large rivers, look for the opposite features you do in high water. Search out those places with the most depth and current. Luckily, you should be able to reach them at this time of year.

You may want to look at the mouths of tributaries, which are typically cooler, but make sure they have a good amount of flow. If a tributary or spring attracts trout with its cooler inflow, they can get quite concentrated and vulnerable when they pack into the cooler water and are best left alone. The Housatonic River in northwestern Connecticut gets quite warm in the summer, and the mouths of some small tributaries are posted with "No Fishing" signs to protect trout ganged up in their outflow. But if a tributary is larger and its cool-water influence extends for 100 yards downstream, it's probably within reason to fish below it. Use your stream thermometer to check how far the influence carries in the main river.

Another way to bypass warmer water temperatures is to move upstream. In tailwaters, moving closer to cold-water releases below dams is one way to find suitable water temperatures, as many of these releases will measure in the 50s or even high 40s during hot weather and the safe temperature regime can extend miles downstream, depending on the volume of flow coming out of the dam. Sometimes these sections are quite short. The Connecticut River, on the border between Vermont and New Hampshire, is a giant river that becomes mostly bass and walleye habitat south of the Northeast

Kingdom of Vermont. Yet a series of dams on the river, although they don't stratify the water and cool it much, offers stretches of highly oxygenated water for a short distance downstream that are home to small populations of large brown and rainbow trout. They are not easy to target, but local anglers have found ways to locate them. Just don't ask for any GPS coordinates. These are tight-lipped New England Yankees.

Tiny Streams

High water is difficult in any trout stream, and I've found fishing to be just as frustrating when tiny brooks are over their banks. I think that trout that live and feed happily in deeper pockets in small streams get pushed out of these places, because due to their shallow nature an entire little bowl in the streambed can be overrun with fast current. I think trout move out of their normal places in high water and look for slower water. You'll want to look for the slowest pockets you can find, and unlike in larger rivers where the banks offer this slower current, the banks along small streams are often just as inhospitable as the middle of the creek.

It's best to explore until you find a deep plunge pool, where the deeper water and hydraulic jump absorb some

When you encounter small streams in high water, search out the deepest plunge pools with a hydraulic jump. This will dissipate the force of the current, and you'll find trout feeding there in the slower current.

of the energy of the water and slow down the current. Trout gather in these spots at high water and then disburse back into the shallower pockets as the water drops and conditions are more favorable. You'll often be dealing with high water in early spring when the water is cold, and trout naturally use these slower, deeper places as winter refuges anyway.

If a small stream floods in the middle of the season when water temperatures are closer to the optimum range for feeding, trout will still seek out slower water, but it might not necessarily be deep plunge pools. Any place the slope of the streambed flattens out, either where a creek runs down into the valley floor or where the slope flattens out a bit in a plateau, will be better than trying to find trout in steeper, more turbulent water where the slope is steeper.

The one advantage of small streams in high water periods is that they drop and clear quicker than larger rivers because brooks have a very short floodplain with fewer tributaries coming into them. So where a larger trout stream might take several days to drop to levels that are easy to fish, a small stream might be clear and negotiable the day following a rainstorm. When I arrive at a small stream and it looks too high or dirty, I always move upstream as far as I can, and can often find better conditions by moving up a mile or so higher in the watershed.

In low water you seldom have problems in small streams; in fact, these waters often fish well when most other trout streams are too warm, or too low and clear for easy fishing. Small streams are usually heavily shaded and closer to sources of cool groundwater, and except for some of the mountain streams in the Southeast, where summer temperatures are warmer than in most other regions of trout streams, you should be able to find water below the high 60s. If you don't, move up in altitude by going upstream. You can even find water cold enough in northern Georgia in the middle of the summer if you push into the headwaters.

Low flows in small streams can be a problem, and trout will migrate quickly if the water gets too low to offer them protection. They may move upstream to find a deeper pool, or they could move downstream. And whether they know where to go from memory or just keep moving until they happen on suitable water, I'm not sure. But they don't hang around in places with lots of shallows, and may be ganged up into the few deep pockets. In creeks that seem to have a trout in every likely place under normal flows, you often hook a fish in one of the deeper pockets and then see a half-dozen others spook in the pool as you play the one you hooked. In small streams, though, it's rare to catch more than one fish from an isolated deep pocket because they aren't

that large and all the trout in the pool sense the danger when one of them is hooked.

And there will be times when you can't find them. One summer we had a choking drought in Vermont, the lowest I'd seen in almost a half century of fishing small streams. My fishing buddy Shawn and I were in a big depressive slump because of the lousy fishing and decided we'd fish one of our favorite small streams, one of those places where all the trout will be small but at least you get a bit of your ego back. We fished up through a mile of water, in thick cover well into the headwaters of a Battenkill tributary of a tributary where I don't think anyone fishes. We never rose a trout and never even saw one, and the water was so thin that you would have at least seen a trout as it spooked. We finally gave up and stumbled back through the woods instead of walking the creek back because we were so disgusted with it. Not ready to give up, we drove to a section of another creek that is one of those "never fail" spots. But it failed that day. I have no idea where those trout went—way up even farther into the headwaters or downstream into the Battenkill to find deeper pools—but they sure moved somewhere.

WHEN TROUT MOVE IN THIS WATER

Big Rivers

Trout in big rivers are more mobile on a daily cycle than in smaller waters because they can be. For a trout in a smaller stream to move to another pool might expose it to shallow water where a predator might attack, but a trout in a large river will invariably be able to find a deeper channel to move upstream or down at will. Tim Linehan, on the Kootenai, tells me, "We know Kootenai trout move great distances. For instance, there are some riffles 500 yards or more above pools that fish move in and out of sometimes daily." And pools in larger rivers are big enough and often have enough slow water that's easy to swim through, and a trout can pick and choose where it feeds, depending on water conditions or the availability of hatches. Large brown trout with radio frequency tags embedded in them have been observed moving miles in a single day, typically sliding out from cover after dark and foraging for bigger food like minnows, frogs, mice, or crayfish, moving until they find what they're looking for. They'll return to their hiding place, usually a logjam or undercut bank, around sunrise.

Hatches are the most common reason trout roam on a daily schedule. Some species of aquatic insects hatch or return to lay eggs more frequently in certain kinds of water: Midges are slow-water dwellers as larvae, and hatches of these tiny but important insects are most common in the slower parts of a river. Burrowing mayflies like the giant Hex and Eastern Green Drake live in silt, and are thus more likely to hatch out of slower water where silt accumulates. Most other mayflies hatch in riffles, and caddisflies hatch in all kinds of water, depending on the species. And when mayflies or caddisflies return to the water to lay their eggs, they most often choose riffles because depositing their eggs in faster water ensures the eggs hatch in the most suitable habitat. So trout that use the protection of a deep pool most of the time may stay close by to feed, but often they begin to move when food doesn't come to them fast enough, and they frequently move into riffles.

Insects don't hatch as much in the tails of pools, but trout will often drop down into the tails because they concentrate food in a narrower band. Thus, in a large river where trout are mobile, look for them closer to deep water if you don't see any insects hatching, but if you begin to see quantities of aquatic insects on the water, look for them in riffles and tails of pools as well, even if the water looks too shallow.

Tiny Streams

Trout in small creeks don't move as often on a daily basis. The deeper pockets they inhabit are often separated by long expanses of shallow water that make them uncomfortable and expose them to danger. They stay put, even during a hatch, which I suspect is one reason trout in small streams are easier to catch: They can't move to other kinds of water when insect food is abundant, so they have to stay put and take what drifts by. This makes them a lot more opportunistic and agreeable to any fly that looks remotely like food. In a larger plunge pool or in the rare large pool in small streams, trout will move from the deep belly of the pool to the head or tail to feed during hatches, but they are still reluctant to leave the immediate vicinity and navigate the uncertainties of different water.

SEASONAL CHANGES

Big Rivers

Trout in large rivers may move many miles in the course of the season, depending on their needs and the conditions at a given point in the course of a river. In winter, trout in large rivers tend to move downstream in search of deeper, slower water. Studies of preferred overwintering habitat of brown trout suggest they need some current, but around 1½ feet per second instead of their preferred feeding velocity of around 2 feet per second. Trout in cold weather may migrate downstream into waters that are too warm and oxygen-depleted for them to survive during the summer. Long stretches of slack, deep water that we think of as habitat for bass, pike, and walleye may hold trout during the winter months, because in cold weather nearly any river is cold enough to hold sufficient oxygen for trout to survive, and these waters supply larger quantities of baitfish that trout can prey on all winter long. Trout in very cold regions may move out of shallower upper reaches to get away from anchor ice, which coats the bottom of shallow water reaches with a thick layer of ice and pushes fish out of their normal haunts.

The largest trout I have ever seen caught on a fly was taken in December by my friend Tyler Atkins, fishing for pike in a warmwater river. The big brown took a 6-inch streamer on straight 60-pound shock tippet. It had most likely been born and raised in a small coldwater tributary but was spending the winter in the trout equivalent of Florida.

When waters warm up in spring and insects begin hatching, trout leave these deep-water sanctuaries to get closer to the source of their food and to leave the warmer water before it becomes oxygen-deprived in the heat of spring and summer. From spring through early summer, trout may be found in almost any region of a large river because there is enough depth and cold water to keep them happy. It makes them difficult to find, and this is the time to look for the very best habitat—places with moderate current, good insect hatches, and sufficient cover to protect them.

In midsummer, many large rivers get too warm and too stagnant to hold that 4-parts-per-million oxygen content trout need as a minimum to survive, and there can be a large-scale migration of fish into colder water, usually upstream or in the vicinity of colder tributaries. The Delaware system is a good example of this seasonal migration. The East and West Branches of the Delaware form the main stem of the Delaware in Hancock, New York. The main stem and the lower East Branch are terrific fisheries spring through early summer, but the lower East Branch has a wide, exposed streambed and a much lower flow (averaging about 300 cfs during the summer) from its cold tailwater source at the base of Pepacton Reservoir. As it warms, it also warms the main stem, but the West Branch, with a higher flow of cold water from Cannonsville Reservoir (averaging closer to 1,000 cfs during the summer), stays much colder. As you'd expect, trout from the main stem migrate up into the colder West Branch, but counterintuitively, trout from the lower East Branch drop *downstream* to the junction of the two branches and then migrate back upstream into the West Branch. How trout know enough to figure this out is a mystery.

Spawning season may also stimulate large-scale movements of trout, although some trout, particularly brown trout, may spawn very close to the places they spend the summer season in, especially if the bottom has expanses of pea-sized gravel and there is some groundwater influence nearby, such as springs or small tributaries entering a larger river, which keeps the gravel clean and ensures a constant flow of clear water. But trout will also migrate for miles during spawning season. Trout, like salmon, will return to spawn where they were hatched, and because many of the larger trout in big rivers were spawned in smaller tributaries or in the headwaters, they'll move back to these places when the urge to procreate overcomes them.

It's usually an upstream migration or a movement into tributaries because successful spawning requires cold, clean water without a lot of silt or other fine material that can choke off the oxygen supply of hatching eggs. Big rivers may collect too much silt for successful spawning. This upstream movement appears to begin up to two months before the act of spawning, which occurs over the course of a week or two. After spawning,

trout quickly move back downstream into slower, deeper winter habitat if they are fall spawners like brook and brown trout, or into food-rich riffles if they are spring-spawning cutthroats and rainbows.

Tiny Streams

Although trout in small streams don't exhibit much daily movement, they can and will migrate in seasonal patterns and you may need to move up and down in their domain to find fish. In winter, most trout will drop down into larger pools lower in the watershed, or if they live in tributaries to larger rivers, most of the fish that occupied a small stream in summer may move into the larger river to find shelter and slower current. Winter water levels can also be lower than summer levels, when precipitation that falls is locked up in snow and ice. And the lower levels make the shallow water more susceptible to anchor ice.

As water levels in the small streams increase with spring runoff, trout will move higher in the watershed to take advantage of increased depth and availability of more habitat. As water temperatures warm in late spring and summer, trout may continue to move upstream to find cooler water, although most small streams don't have the same critically high temperature problems as

Larger trout will be on the move during spawning season and you can find them in unexpected places. This large brown trout was caught in a small brook trout stream in October and probably moved into the stream to spawn. Since it ate a dry fly, it was not actively spawning and was still eating insects.

large rivers because they have more shade and are closer to groundwater. Restrictive depth is what moves them in the height of summer. Pockets that might be wholly acceptable in June can get too shallow in a July drought, so fish shuffle around to find the increasingly rare deep pockets. In midsummer, you may have to walk a hundred yards between spots to find suitable habitat.

Spawning season is when you may find surprisingly large trout in small streams. I don't mean right at spawning season, though, as I have seen trout begin their migration months before spawning. Brown trout in Vermont that spawn in mid-November begin to move into spawning tributaries as early as late August, and I have no doubt they do the same thing in most other

Fishing a large river from a drift boat requires careful planning. Good communication between the anglers and the rower, plus a constant eye on the water ahead, will make sure you hit the best spots.

APPROACH

Big Rivers

In one respect, approaching trout in large rivers gives you an advantage. Because of the breadth of the water, you can get upstream or directly across-stream from the fish without spooking them, because you can stay farther away from them and still usually have backcast room. In addition, when trout are feeding in deeper water they appear to feel more secure and are more tolerant of wading or casting. This is especially true when you have a wall of fast water or turbulence between you and them. For some reason they think predators can't get to them when protected by this barrier.

However, you have a disadvantage because trout won't be everywhere and you'll often need to cover long distances between fish. When wading, get in the habit of looking over a piece of water, deciding which area looks best, and then walk the bank until you find a place to safely wade to the spot you want to fish without excess walking in the water. Wading all over the place in a big river not only increases your chances of taking a bath, but may also spook fish from places you don't expect them, and these fish may bolt to the spot you intended to fish, spooking their buddies.

From a boat, you may want to prospect the in-between water with whatever fly you choose, but pay close attention to the water ahead. Plan your approach to a juicy riffle or pile of big rocks well ahead of time so that you have a place to anchor or park the boat so you can get out to wade the better water. There is nothing worse than floating through some boring flat water that doesn't produce and then drifting right over the best water because you didn't plan the twists of the current beforehand. The next time you fish with a guide, watch how they angle their approach to a good piece of water 100 yards ahead of time.

Tiny Streams

Working upstream is invariably the best way to approach small streams. You'll be approaching the fish from behind, where they are less likely to notice you, and dry flies or dry-dropper combinations are usually the best fishing method, and this is not easy to accomplish with a downstream cast because without a tricky slack-line presentation, you'll get drag on every drift. If you want to work downstream in a small stream, you'll most likely be swinging a wet fly or a streamer, and for these methods you need some width to swing across. You may not have the luxury of a wide enough area to get a

regions. This gives you over a month to target these larger fish before you need to even think about the ethics of fishing over spawning fish. In wild rainbow streams, I've watched rainbow trout that spawn in April gather in what appear to be pre-spawning aggregations in small streams in February.

You can work a small creek either upstream or downstream if you want. I'd always work upstream in a small creek like this because trout are much more likely to spot you and bolt for cover (and not feed) when you work downstream.

swing, and trying to cast across-stream in a tiny brook is tough unless you use a roll cast.

One of the biggest reasons for not moving downstream, however, is that you'll need to stay farther away from the fish to prevent spooking them, and making long casts in a small stream only gets you into trouble, both with your backcast and because lots of line on the water in a small stream means you'll often be dropping your line over several rocks or a log between you and the trout. Either that or you'll need to spend your entire day crawling on your belly. Not my idea of fun.

There are times when fishing downstream is the only way, though. One is when you have a tangle of trees that goes all the way across the creek and you want to try for a fish that could be in front of the logjam. Here you'll need to get out of the water, creep carefully along the bank to a point upstream, and then drop your flies in front of the tangle.

No matter what direction you approach them from, trout in flat-water pools or runs in small streams are tricky to approach. Here you will need to crouch or belly-crawl into position and use big rocks or streamside brush as cover. Although trout are not as likely to notice you when you approach from a downstream direction, there is always a potential for them to spot you because they won't always be directly upstream of you, and when they move from side to side to feed they might turn enough to see you. Try to move as slowly as you can, keep your false casts to a minimum, and cast horizontally when possible instead of vertically to keep your line lower on the horizon, where it is less likely to be noticed.

I honestly don't think clothing color makes that much of a difference, but it does help to blend in. Dull-colored shirts and hats are better than white or bright colors. They blend in better with the background. I don't think camouflage clothing is worth the effort. The minute you move your arm to cast, you've defeated the whole purpose of wearing camo.

In pocket water you can get surprisingly close to trout in small streams because of the broken water, and because many of them will be on the far side of a rock and have no way of seeing your approach. I have a small stream close to my house that is very shallow, clear, and full of wild brook and brown trout. Over the years I've noticed I spook a lot of trout, which doesn't bother me because the stream has such a dense population of fish that there is always another one in front of the next big rock. But I have noticed that I always spook fish that have been hiding on my side of a rock, and the ones I catch are invariably on the far side of a rock or in front of a rock where they are blinded to my

approach. If I were smarter I'd spend more time on my knees when approaching a pool so I could also catch the ones on the near side. But this stream is where I go for a casual afternoon of fishing, and I'm content to catch the other half.

You can be smarter than me, though, and use this lesson to increase your success. Before you get close to a tiny pool, try to determine where the best place for a trout to live and feed will be, and then move right or left so you approach the fish so that it's blinded by the rock or log in question. You might not catch all the fish in a miniature pool, but you may have a chance at catching the largest one, which will usually be in the prime position.

One final suggestion in small-stream trout fishing is: Don't belabor a pool or pocket. Within a few casts, you'll either hook or spook any trout present. Move on to the next pocket. Don't rush, but don't dally either. You'll also want to pass up some water as well because it's way too shallow or just too brushy—and there's no shame in passing up some pockets because they are too difficult to fish. In small streams you'll have plenty of opportunities, and if a section just looks too gnarly, unless you're certain a nice trout lives there, move on and come back and fish it on a day when you have more energy.

TECHNIQUES TO TRY

Big Rivers

Most times in large rivers you need to cover a lot of water to find trout, so the first thing I do is look for rising fish. Not only do you have an opportunity to fish dry flies, but you'll at least know where some fish live, and if they stop rising you can work them over with a subsurface fly, or if you come back another time you'll have an idea of their village, if not their street address. Trout do sometimes move from other places when feeding on the surface, but you'll at least be in the right neighborhood. I'll often walk the bank or float for an hour or so on a big river before I fish, just looking for rises. With the wide variety of water in a large river, it's common to find some feeding fish somewhere, especially in the slow water along deep banks, back eddies, or tails of pools.

But unfortunately you don't always find rising fish and it's necessary to cover some water. Anything you can swing, as opposed to methods where it's critical to precisely place a fly like dry fly or nymph, is helpful in covering water because your fly is in a fishable place throughout the swing and even when it just hangs below you. Trout aren't always interested in chasing a swinging fly, but you may at least get a bump or a swirl that helps you locate them.

In higher water a streamer is probably best, and sometimes even two streamers fished in tandem—a big one and a little one, or a dark one and a light one. Double streamers are not fun to cast, but they can increase your chances of locating a fish. Rig them any way you want—most people just tie them in-line with the second fly tied to the bend of the hook of the first one, but a separate dropper will also work. Experiment with retrieves and also with dead-drifting a streamer in at least part of the drift.

If the water is lower or if it is very low and clear, try swinging a couple wet flies or soft hackles—and in this case I do mean a couple. The sight of two flies swinging in the current seems to far outshine the appeal of just a single fly, and unless I know exactly what fly will work (and do we ever know that?), I'll always start with two. In this case you do want your second fly on a separate dropper. It's much more effective than just a single fly, and effective beyond just getting to try two different patterns at the same time. You're trying to cover unknown water, big water, and you need every edge you can get. It's also a relaxing and satisfying way to fish and you typically work downstream as you go, so you don't need to fight the current.

Don't rule out a nymph-streamer combo, with the nymph or soft hackle tied in-line with the streamer on a separate piece of tippet. I think that often trout are attracted to the streamer and at least inspect it, and if it's too much for them to handle they'll often inhale the trailing nymph because they're less suspicious of it.

If you prefer to fish nymphs with an indicator, a dry-dropper, or just a dry fly or two, narrow down your water first. These methods are not great for covering a lot of water, because you need to place your cast precisely and your effective drifts are typically short, requiring that you pick up and cast again. Pinpoint where you think trout will be first. Start out in the very best places with these methods and only move on to less likely spots if you find them effective.

Tiny Streams

The most effective way of locating trout in small streams is a dry-dropper combination. Trout in small streams are invariably close to the surface and will see a dry fly in all but the highest and dirtiest waters, and if they don't feel like rising to a dry fly, they can see one from farther

In big rivers, if conditions are right (usually slightly elevated water levels and cloud cover), you can cover a lot of water with a streamer and perhaps interest the biggest brown trout of your life.

Working upstream with a dry-dropper combination is one of the best ways to fish a small creek. You can get away with large, high-floating flies in size 10 or 12 and a medium-sized nymph, around size 14, in most of these streams. Keep the dropper on your nymph short—you don't need to scratch bottom in small streams because the trout are usually looking up for their food and might miss your nymph if it is too deep.

away than a sunken nymph, will be alerted, and might take the nymph as it drifts past them. My friend Phil Monahan is a small-stream aficionado, as am I, and we often fish together or compare notes. He's always been a strict dry-fly guy and feels he can interest any fish that's remotely interested in feeding to come up for a dry. Or at least he used to be. He started seeing me catch way too many more fish than he did because I always fish a dry with a nymph hanging off the end. He still starts out with just a dry fly, but if he doesn't get a rise in the first good pocket, he'll hang a nymph on the end.

Just pick a dry fly that's relatively large and easy to see, something with a foam body and light-colored wing like a Chubby Chernobyl or a Stimulator. Small-stream trout are seldom choosy. Then pick a nymph in size 12 through 16 that isn't too heavy, because you don't want it to hang bottom and you don't want it to drown your

dry-fly indicator. And use a short dropper. You don't seem to need to scrape bottom in small streams, as you might need to in larger rivers. Trout need to grab and go in small streams, and the higher a nymph is in the water column, the easier it is for them to spot.

It's not that indicator nymphing or Euro nymphing won't work in small streams. But I've had too many trout try to eat my indicator, even in March and April when all the experts tell you the water is too cold for dry-fly fishing. I've seen trout take a dry fly on early spring days when I doubt there has been a hatch in months. And why work so hard with Euro nymphing when you can just make a quick forward cast or roll cast and also have the opportunity to maybe catch a trout on a dry fly and see the eat? Trout fishing is supposed to be fun, and when the best method, a dry-dropper, is also the most effective, why do anything else?

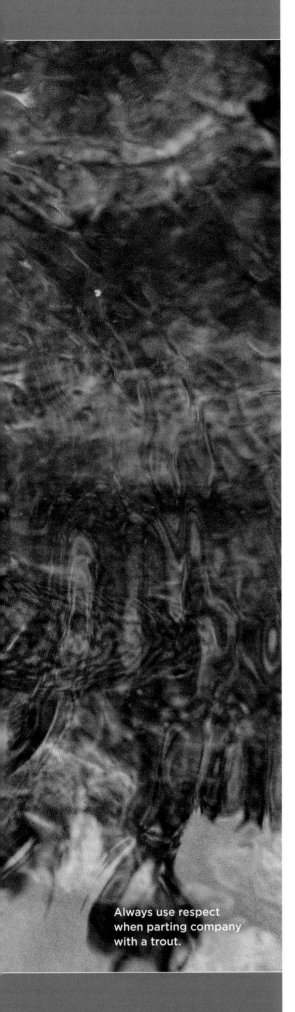

Always use respect when parting company with a trout.

CHAPTER 10

Parting Thoughts

I'd be remiss in attempting to give you ways to find more trout if I didn't also suggest some ways of caring for this precious resource. Much of this may be well known by the experienced anglers who read this book, but in case you're new to the sport and haven't been fully immersed in its mores, here are some ways you can make the experience better for other anglers.

BE AN ADVOCATE

Joining an organization that fights to preserve clean water and wild trout is a force multiplier. There is little we can do as individuals, but organizations like Trout Unlimited, California Trout, and the Wild Steelhead Coalition hire scientists and people experienced in lobbying with politicians to provide the data and convince lawmakers to protect and enhance what we have. That's all these organizations do, and they are powerful and effective. The more members they have, the more voices they can claim, and with bigger budgets supplied by your donations they can increase their power. Note that there are other organizations, especially at the local level, that also do effective work, but I have had personal experiences with the three I have mentioned above so I can vouch for them.

Much of our great fishing is on public land. Our country has vast public resources that *you* own, and to make sure these lands are not threatened with development or other degradation I can't think of a better organization than Backcountry Hunters and Anglers. They are on the front line throughout the country in the battle to protect access to public lands, both at the local level and in Washington. There are other, more local organizations like the Public Land Water Access Association in Montana, and in Utah, the Utah Stream Access Coalition.

Be vigilant. If you see something on a trout stream that doesn't look right, like an open sewer entering a river, road work that does not adequately protect against siltation, or logging that encroaches too close to a river, my advice is to contact the nearest Trout Unlimited chapter and also the appropriate state agency. In some states it could be the Fish and Game Department, in others it can be called the Division of Environmental Protection, or something with similar wording. But find out who handles these kinds of violations first, even before you notice a problem. That way you'll have the appropriate agency to call at your fingertips. This can be frustrating, and you may get bounced around from one department to another if you do see a problem, but keep at it.

Chris Wood, president and CEO of Trout Unlimited, shows his passion for small wild fish in a Vermont brook trout stream. Chris has devoted his life to the protection of habitat for wild trout, salmon, and steelhead. You don't need to devote your life to the cause, but you should still become an advocate and give back to the resource.

Don't try to challenge a landowner or business owner on your own. These kinds of confrontations never go well and are often counterproductive.

Expend your energy on habitat issues instead of promoting catch-and-release. It's far more important. Catch-and-release fishing merely stockpiles trout for a few years so that you or someone else can catch them again. It does make fishing better for the near term, but it's all about the habitat. Trout are tough survivors and can come back if the habitat is intact. Streams are often totally poisoned to remove undesirable species and then restocked and do just fine if the habitat is healthy.

DON'T CROWD

Some trout streams today, especially the larger, more popular ones, have become overcrowded, resulting in a diminished experience for everyone. If you don't like

Don't drive someone else off the water by crowding them. Even in heavily fished waters, a bit of a walk will find you solitude and other anglers will appreciate your courtesy.

crowded rivers, don't go there. This country has many thousands of smaller rivers and creeks with very light fishing pressure because they aren't close to a major road and might require a short—or long—hike. You may not catch as many fish, or they might not be trophy-sized, but you'll be trout fishing in a place where you don't have to dodge river traffic. Do your homework. One of my purposes in writing this book is so that you can find trout streams on your own, without trolling the internet for the most popular hotspots.

If you do encounter other anglers on the river, just use common sense. The best course of action is to hike the bank well away from other people, and it's best to ask first if they plan on working upstream or downstream. That way you can hopefully find your own piece of water where you won't ruin your experience or theirs. There is also a pragmatic reason for staying away from other anglers: Trout get spooked when waded over or fished over and may not feed again for hours. It's always better to find a place where they have not been disturbed for the day, even if it isn't the place you had your heart set on fishing.

If a river is crowded to the point where you can't find a place to fish out of sight of other anglers, perhaps because you don't have the physical ability to hike away from a popular access point, again just use common sense. The Golden Rule works here. Try to put as much space as possible between you and other anglers, and never get in the river within a long cast of another fly fisher. Getting that close to another angler should only be used in extreme circumstances, and honestly I wouldn't get that close to someone else, ever. I'd walk until I had solitude or drive to another river.

If you're fishing in a boat, give a wide berth to wading anglers. They have the right-of-way, and you have a whole river to float. Don't cast through their water,

but float quietly past them and don't begin fishing again until you are well below them. Obviously the same logic applies to other boats. If a boat is drifting down a bank you want to fish, don't row fast and cut ahead of them. Pick a spot to stop and wade fish, drink coffee, or eat lunch. Let the fish settle down before you follow their path. Of course, in a very crowded river you take the chance of having another boat run down the bank ahead of you. In that case you'll need to either follow that boat down and hope they didn't hit all the prime spots or pick another lane and fish the middle or the opposite bank.

CATCH-AND-RELEASE

Catch-and-release fishing is not a conservation tool and it won't save trout fishing for future generations. It does, however, allow someone else—or you—to enjoy catching that fish another day. It also is a show of your respect for the fish by trying to release it unharmed. I don't feel

there is anything wrong with keeping an occasional fish or two for dinner where it's legal and the population is robust, but most of us today release our fish. To do this properly you need to take some precautions.

Play fish quickly. Get a trout to the net as quickly as your tackle allows. Granted this takes experience to determine how much pressure you can put on a fish with a particular rod and tippet, but one of the reasons fishing excites us is that we don't always know if we will land a fish. Trout develop stress hormones when fighting against you that can exhaust them and reduce their fitness, and the quicker you get a fish to hand, the better.

Use the heaviest tippet you can. This may result in not catching quite as many fish in some situations because lighter tippets are often better at fooling fish, but it will help you play a fish quicker.

Use a net with a soft rubber bag. Nets can allow you to remove the hook and take a quick photo easier and can trap a fish so that it doesn't bash itself on the rocks. The rubber bag is easier on a trout's skin, as hard

If you plan on releasing your catch, show the fish some respect. Play them quickly, use a net with a rubber bag to prevent abrasion to their fins and skin, and keep them wet as you handle them quickly. And decide when you've caught enough for the day. Counting fish is a rookie move.

synthetic bags in a net can scrape off a trout's protective slime layer that protects them from infection.

Wet your hands before touching a fish. This also helps prevent removal of that protective slime layer.

Don't use a tailing glove or fish lipping device. Both of these can injure trout—the lipping tool can dislocate their jaws or even their spine, and tailing gloves can remove the slime layer from their skin.

Reduce handling time. Fumbling around with a trout increases the stress on them, and studies have shown that too much handling time is one of the biggest causes of trout mortality in released fish.

Keep water flowing over their gills. Trout can't breathe out of the water. I heard a clever saying that you should hold your breath while holding a fish out of water, but I can hold my breath easily for 40 seconds and that's too long. Keep it under 15 seconds.

Try not to take so many pictures of trout. Most of them look the same. If you do take a photo of a special fish, get your camera ready while you are playing the fish if you are alone, or have a buddy get the camera ready if you are with a group. Keep the fish in the water, in the net, or hold it briefly above the net, especially in a boat so that if you drop the fish it won't bang on the bottom of the boat. Snap a couple quick pictures and get the fish back in the water.

Use barbless hooks. Sure, you may lose a few fish now and then, but if you keep a tight line on the fish it's rare for a barbless hook to slip out. Barbless hooks slip out easily, often in the net without you even touching the fish. And if you manage to hook yourself or a buddy, you will be glad you pinched that barb. If the fish is hooked deeply, use a pair of forceps or one of these clever hook removal tools to reach the fly, rather than forcing your hand into a trout's mouth.

Don't fish above 68 degrees. Full stop. If you don't know why I'm saying this, go back and reread the chapter on water temperature.

To release a trout, just hold the fish in clear water with a light current until it bolts. Don't move it back and forth, because gills are only designed to work in one direction. If a fish takes off as soon as you get it out of the net, you've done everything right. If you have to revive a fish by holding it in the water for minute or so, either the water temperature is too warm or you played it too long. Try to do better next time.

Even if you're conscientious and follow all the tips above, some trout may die after being released. Just seeing it swim away does not mean it will survive. One of the reasons is that on today's crowded rivers, a trout may be caught two or three days in a row. Unfortunately, those stress hormones that build up in a trout's tissues can take days to return to normal, so if a trout is caught and released on consecutive days, stress can pile up and it may not survive.

In the old days, the Trout Unlimited motto was "Limit your kill, don't kill your limit." In today's heavily fished rivers, we may want to revise that motto to say something about limiting our *catch*. You hear stories about fly fishers catching and releasing forty or even fifty trout a day. You even hear about people using clickers to keep track of how many fish they catch. If I may be allowed to preach, my advice is not to count fish and stop fishing when you felt you've had a respectable day. Spend the rest of the day taking pictures of something other than fish, look for bugs under the rocks, or look for exquisite stones in streamside gravel. Be a kid again.

Do we really need to catch-and-release that many fish to have a fun and successful day?

INDEX